Anonymous

The Works of the Rev. John Wesley, M.A.

Late fellow of Lincoln-College, Oxford

Anonymous

The Works of the Rev. John Wesley, M.A.
Late fellow of Lincoln-College, Oxford

ISBN/EAN: 9783743348615

Manufactured in Europe, USA, Canada, Australia, Japa

Cover: Foto ©Lupo / pixelio.de

Manufactured and distributed by brebook publishing software (www.brebook.com)

Anonymous

The Works of the Rev. John Wesley, M.A.

THE
WORKS

OF THE

Rev. JOHN WESLEY, M.A.

Late Fellow of *Lincoln-College*, OXFORD.

VOLUME VI.

BRISTOL:

Printed by WILLIAM PINE, in *Wine-Street*.
MDCCLXXII.

An Extract from Mr. LAW's

SERIOUS CALL
TO A HOLY LIFE.

CHAP. XVIII.

Recommending devotion at three o'clock, called in scripture the ninth hour of the day. The subject of prayer at this hour may be resignation *to the divine pleasure. The nature and duty of conformity to the will of God in all our actions and designs.*

1. * THERE is nothing *wise*, or *holy*, or *just*, but the *great will* of God. This is as strictly true as that nothing is infinite and eternal but God.

* No beings therefore, whether in heaven or on earth, can be wise, or holy, or just, but so far as they conform to *this will* of God. It is conformity to this will, that gives virtue and perfection to the highest services of angels in heaven; and it is conformity to the same will, that makes the

ordinary

ordinary actions of men on earth become an acceptable service to God.

* The whole nature of virtue consists in conforming, and the whole nature of vice in declining from the will of God. All God's creatures are created to fulfil his will; the *sun* and *moon* obey his will, by the necessity of their nature; *angels* conform to his will, by the perfection of their nature: if therefore you would shew yourself not to be a *rebel* and *apostate* from the order of the creation, you must act like beings both above and below you; it must be the great desire of your soul, that God's will may be done by you on earth, as it is done in heaven. It must be the settled purpose of your heart, to *will* nothing, *design* nothing, *do* nothing, but so far as you have reason to believe, it is the will of God.

2. 'Tis as necessary to think thus of God and yourself, as to think that you have any dependance upon him. And it is as great a rebellion against God, to think that your will may ever differ from his, as to think that you have not received the power of *willing* from him.

You are therefore to consider yourself as a being, that has no other business in the world, but to be that which God requires you to be; to have no tempers, no rules, no designs of your own, but to fill some *place*, and act some *part* in strict conformity, and thankful resignation to the divine pleasure.

To

To think that you are your own, or at your own disposal, is as absurd as to think that you created yourself. It is as plain that you are thus God's, that you thus belong to him, and are to act and suffer all in thankful resignation to his pleasure, as that in him you *live, and move, and have your being.*

3. * *Resignation* to the divine will, signifies a chearful approbation, and thankful acceptance of every thing that comes from God. It is not enough patiently to submit, but we must thankfully receive, and fully approve of every thing, that by the order of God's providence, happens to us.

* For there is no reason why we should be patient, but what is as strong a reason why we should be thankful. If we were under the hands of a wise and good *physician* that could not mistake, or do any thing to us, but what tended to our benefit; it would not be enough to be patient, and abstain from murmuring against such a physician; it would be as much a breach of gratitude, not to be thankful for what he did, as it would be to murmur at him.

* Now this is our true state with relation to God; we cannot be said so much as to *believe* in him, unless we believe him to be of *infinite wisdom.* Every argument therefore for patience under his disposal of us, is as strong an argument for thankfulness. And there needs no more to dispose us to this gratitude towards God, than a

A 3 full

full belief in him, that he is this being of infinite wisdom, love and goodness.

Do but fully assent to this truth, and then you will chearfully approve of every thing that God has already approved for you.

When you are satisfied that God does not only do that which is wise, and good, but which is the effect of infinite wisdom, and love in the care of you; it will be as necessary to be pleased with every thing which God chuses for you, as to wish your own happiness.

4. Whenever therefore you find yourself disposed to *murmuring*, at any thing that is the effect of God's providence over you, you must look upon yourself as *denying* either the wisdom or goodness of God. For every complaint supposes this. You would never complain of your *neighbour*, but that you suppose you can shew either his *unwise*, *unjust*, or *unkind* behaviour towards you.

Now every impatient reflection under the providence of God, is the same accusation of God. A complaint always supposes *ill usage*.

Hence you may see the great necessity of this thankful state of heart, because the want of it implies an accusation of God's want either of wisdom, or goodness in his disposal of us. It is not therefore any high degree of perfection, founded in any uncommon *nicety* of thinking, but a plain principle, founded in this plain belief,

lief, that God is a being of infinite wisdom and goodness.

5. This resignation to the divine will, may be considered in two respects: *first*, As it signifies a thankful approbation of God's *general* providence over the world: *secondly*, As it signifies a thankful acceptance of his *particular* providence over us.

* *First*, Every man is, by the first article of his creed, obliged to acknowledge the wisdom and goodness of God, in his *general providence* over the world. He is to believe that it is the effect of God's great wisdom and goodness, that the world itself was formed at such a particular time, and in such a manner: that the general order of nature, the whole frame of things, is contrived and formed in the best manner. He is to believe that God's providence over states and kingdoms, times and seasons, is all for the best: that the revolutions of state, and changes of empire, the rise and fall of monarchies, persecutions, wars, famines and plagues, are all permitted, and conducted by God's providence, to the general good of man in this state of trial.

A good man is to believe all this, with the same fullness of assent, as he believes that God is in every place, tho' he neither sees, nor can comprehend the manner of his presence.

* This is a noble magnificence of thought, a true greatness of mind, to be thus affected with

God's general providence, admiring and magnifying his wisdom in all things; never murmuring at the course of the world, or the state of things, but looking upon all around, at heaven and earth, as a pleased spectator; and adoring that invisible hand, which gives laws to all motions, and over-rules all events to ends suitable to the highest wisdom and goodness.

6. It is very common for people to allow themselves great liberty in finding fault with such things, as have only God for their cause.

* Every one thinks he may justly say, what a *wretched, abominable climate* he lives in. This man is frequently telling you, what a *dismal, cursed* day it is, and what intolerable *seasons* we have. Another thinks it is hardly worth his while to live in a world so full of changes and revolutions. But these are tempers of great impiety, and shew that religion has not yet its seat in the heart.

It sounds indeed much better to murmur at the course of the world, than to murmur at providence; to complain of the seasons and weather, than to complain of God; but if these have no other cause but God, it is a poor excuse to say, that you are only angry at the things, but not at the cause and director of them.

How *sacred* the whole frame of the world is, how all things are to be considered as God's, and referred to him, is fully taught by our blessed Lord in the case of *oaths: But I say unto you, swear,*

swear not at all; neither by heaven, for it is God's throne; nor by the earth, for it is his footstool; neither by Jerusalem, for it is the city of the great king; neither shalt thou swear by thy head, because thou canst not make one hair white or black, Matt. v. 37. That is, because the whiteness or blackness of thy hair is not thine, but God's.

* Here you see all things in the whole order of nature, from the highest heavens to the smallest hair, are to be considered, not separately as they are in themselves, but as in some relation to God. And if this be good reasoning, thou shalt not swear by the *earth*, a *city*, or thy *hair*, because these things are God's, and in a certain manner belong to him; is it not the same reasoning to say, Thou shalt not murmur at the *seasons* of the earth, the *states* of cities, and the change of *times*, because all these things are in the hands of God, have him for their author, are directed and governed by him to such ends as are most suitable to his wise providence?

* For whoso murmurs at the course of the world, murmurs at God that governs the course of the world. Whoso repines at *seasons* and *weather*, and speaketh impatiently of times and events, repines and speaks impatiently of God, who is the sole Lord and Governor of *times, seasons*, and *events*.

7. * As therefore when we think of God himself, we are to have no sentiments but of praise

and thanksgiving; so when we look at those things which are under the direction of God, we are to receive them with the same tempers.

* And tho' we are not to think all things right, and just, and lawful, which the providence of God permits; for then nothing could be unjust, because nothing is without his permission; yet we must adore God in the greatest public calamities, the most grievous persecutions, as things that are suffered by God, like *plagues* and *famines*, for ends suitable to his wisdom and glory in the government of the world.

* There is nothing more suitable to the piety of a reasonable creature, or the spirit of a Christian, than thus to approve, admire, and glorify God in all the acts of his general providence; considering the whole world as his particular family, and all events as directed by his wisdom.

* Every one seems to consent to this, as an undeniable truth, *That all things must be as God pleases.* And is not this enough to make every man pleased with them himself? And how can a man be a peevish complainer of any thing that is the effect of providence, but by shewing that his own *will* and *wisdom* are of more weight with him, than the will and wisdom of God? And what can religion be said to have done for a man, whose heart is in this state?

For

For if he cannot thank and praise God as well in calamities and sufferings, as in prosperity and happiness, he is as far from the piety of a Christian, as he that only loves them that love him, is from the charity of a Christian. For to thank God only for such things as you like, is no more a proper act of piety, than to believe only what you see, is an act of faith.

8. Thus much concerning resignation to the divine will, as it signifies a thankful approbation of God's *general providence:* it is now to be considered, as it signifies a *thankful* acceptance of God's *particular providence* over us.

* Every man is to consider himself as a particular object of God's providence, under the same care and protection of God, as if the world had been made for him alone. It is not by chance that any man is born at such a *time*, of such *parents*, and in such *place* and *condition*. It is as certain, that every *soul* comes into the body at such a time, and in such circumstances, by the express *designment* of God, according to *some purposes* of his will, and for some *particular ends;* this is as certain, as that it is by the express designment of God, that some beings are *angels*, and others are *men*.

9. The scriptures assure us, it was by divine appointment, that our blessed Saviour was born at *Bethlehem*, and at such a time. Now altho' it was owing to the dignity of his person, and the great importance of his birth, that thus much of

the divine counfel was declared to the world concerning the time and manner of it; yet we are as fure from the fame fcriptures, that the *time* and *manner* of every man's coming into the world, is according to the *direction* of divine providence, and in *fuch time*, and *place*, and *circumftances*, as are directed and governed by God for *particular ends* of his wifdom and goodnefs.

This we are as certain of from plain revelation, as we can be of any thing. * For if we are told, that not a *fparrow falleth to the ground without our heavenly Father*, Can any thing more ftrongly teach us, that much greater beings, fuch as human fouls, come not into the world without the care and direction of our heavenly Father? If it is faid, *The very hairs of your head are all numbered*, Is it not to teach us, that nothing, not the *fmalleft* things imaginable, happen to us by *chance?* But if the fmalleft things we can conceive, are declared to be under the divine direction, need we, or can we be more plainly taught, that the greateft things of life, fuch as the *manner* of our coming into the world, our *parents*, the *time*, and other *circumftances* of our birth, and condition, are all according to the *direction*, and *appointment* of divine providence.

10. When the difciples put this queftion to our bleffed Lord concerning the blind man, *Mafter, Who did fin, this man, or his parents, that he was born blind?* He made this anfwer, *Neither hath this man finned, nor his parents; but that*

the

the works of God should be made manifest in him, John ix. 2, 3. plainly declaring, that the particular circumstances of every man's birth, the body that he receives, and the state of life into which he is born, are appointed by a secret providence, which directs all things to their particular *times*, and *seasons*, and *manner* of existence, that the wisdom and works of God may be made manifest in them all.

As therefore it is certain, that all that is particular in our state, is the effect of God's particular providence over us, and intended for some particular ends, both of his glory and our own happiness, we are, by the greatest obligations, called upon to resign our will to the will of God in all these respects; thankfully approving and accepting every thing that is particular in our state; praising and glorifying his name for our birth of such *parents*, and in such *circumstances*; being fully assured, that it was for some reasons of infinite wisdom and goodness, that we were so born into such particular states of life.

11. If the man above-mentioned was born blind, that the *works of God might be manifested in him*, had he not great reason to praise God, for appointing him in such a particular manner to be the instrument of his glory? And if one person is born *here*, and another *there*; if one falls amongst *riches*, and another into *poverty*; if one receives his flesh and blood from these *parents*, and another from those, for as particular ends as

the

the man was born blind; have not all people the greatest reason to bless **God**, and to be thankful for their particular state and condition, because all that is particular in it, is as directly intended for the glory of God, and their own good, as the *particular blindness* of that man, who was so born, that the *works of God might be manifested in him?*

* How noble an idea does this give us of the divine omniscience, presiding over the whole world, and governing such a long chain and combination of seeming accidents, to the common and particular advantage of all beings? So that all persons, in such a wonderful variety of causes and events, should fall into such particular states, as were foreseen and fore-ordained to their best advantage, and so as to be most serviceable to the wise and glorious ends of God's government of all the world!

12. * Had you been any thing else than what you are, you had, all things considered, been less wisely provided for than you are now; you had wanted some circumstances that are best fitted to make you happy yourself, and serviceable to the glory of God.

* Could you see all that which God sees, all that happy chain of causes and motives which are to move and invite you to a right course of life, you would see something to make you like that state you are in, as fitter for you than any other.

*But as you cannot see this, so it is here that your *trust* in God is to exercise itself, and render
you

you as thankful for the happiness of your state, as if you saw every thing that contributes to it with your own eyes.

* But now, if this is the case of every man in the world, thus blessed with some particular state that is most convenient for him, how reasonable is it for every man to will that which God has already willed for him? And by a trust in the divine goodness, thankfully adore that wise providence, which he is sure has made the best choice for him of those things which he could not chuse for himself.

13. Every uneasiness at our own state, is founded upon comparing it with that of other people; which is full as unreasonable, as if a man in a *dropsy* should be angry at those that prescribe different things to him, from those which are prescribed to people in *health*. For all the different states of *life* are like the different states of *diseases;* and what is a remedy to one man, may be poison to another.

* So that to murmur because you are not as some others are, is as if a man in one disease should murmur that he is not treated like him that is in another; whereas, if he was to have his will, he would be killed by that which will prove the cure of another.

* It is just thus in the various conditions of life; if you complain at any thing in your state, you may, for ought you know, be so ungrateful to God, as to murmur at that very thing which is to prove the cause of your salvation.

Had you it in your power to get that which you think it so grievous to want, it might perhaps be that very thing which would expose you to eternal damnation.

* So that, whether we consider the infinite goodness of God, that cannot chuse amiss for us, or our own great ignorance of what is most adtageous to us, there can be nothing so reasonable, as to have no will but that of God's, and desire nothing for ourselves, in our *persons*, our *state*, and *condition*, but that which the good providence of God appoints us.

14. * Farther, as the good providence of God introduces us into the world, into such states and conditions as are most convenient for us; so the same unerring wisdom orders all events and changes in the whole course of our lives, in such a manner, as to render them the fittest means to exercise and improve our virtue.

Nothing hurts us, nothing destroys us, but the ill use of that liberty with which God has entrusted us.

* We are as sure that nothing happens to us by chance, as that the world itself was not made by chance; we are as certain that all things happen, and work together for our good, as that God is goodness itself. So that a man has as much reason to *will* every thing that happens to him, because

cause God wills it, as to think that is wisest which is directed by infinite wisdom.

The providence of God is not more concerned in the government of *night* and *day*, and the variety of *seasons*, than in the common course of events, that seem most to depend upon the meer wills of men. So that it is as strictly right, to look upon all worldly changes, all the various turns in your own life, to be the effects of divine providence, as the rising and setting of the sun, or the alterations of the seasons of the year. As you are therefore always to adore the wisdom of God in the direction of these things; so it is the same reasonable duty, always to magnify God, as an equal director of every thing that happens to you in the course of your own life.

15. There is nothing that so powerfully governs the heart, as a true sense of God's *presence*; and nothing so constantly keeps us under a lively sense of the presence of God, as this holy resignation, which attributes every thing to him, and receives every thing as from him.

Could we see a *miracle* from God, how would our thoughts be affected with an holy awe and veneration of his presence! But if we consider every thing as God's doing, either by order or permission, we shall then be affected with *common things*, as they would be who saw a *miracle*.

For as there is nothing to affect you in a miracle, but as it is the *action* of God, and bespeaks his presence; so when you consider God, as acting

ing in all things, and all events, then all things will become venerable to you, like *miracles*, and fill you with the fame awful fentiments of the divine prefence.

16. Now you muft not referve the exercife of this pious temper to any particular times or occafions, or fancy how *refigned* you will be to God, if fuch or fuch trials fhould happen: for this is amufing yourfelf with the *notion* of refignation inftead of the virtue itfelf.

Don't therefore pleafe yourfelf with thinking, how piously you would act and fubmit to God in a *plague*, a *famine*, or *perfecution*; but be intent upon the perfection of the prefent day; and be affured, that the beft way of fhewing a *true zeal*, is to make *little things* the occafions of *great piety*.

* Begin therefore in the fmalleft matters, and moft ordinary occafions, and accuftom your mind to the daily exercife of this pious temper, in the loweft occurrences of life. And when a *contempt*, an *affront*, a little *injury*, *lofs*, or *difappointment*, or the fmalleft events of every day, continually raife your mind to God in proper acts of refignation, then you may juftly hope, that you fhall be numbered amongft thofe that are refigned, and thankful to God in the greateft trials and afflictions.

CHAP.

C H A P. XIX.

Of the excellency and greatness of a devout spirit.

1. I HAVE now finished what I intended in this treatise. I have explained the nature of devotion, both as it signifies a life devoted to God, and as it signifies a regular method of prayer. I have now only to add a word or two in recommendation of a life governed by this Spirit.

And because in this *polite* age, we have so *lived away* the spirit of devotion, that many seem afraid even to be suspected of it, imagining *great devotion* to be great *bigotry*; that it is founded in *ignorance* and *poorness* of spirit; and that *little*, *weak*, and *dejected* minds, are generally the greatest proficients in it.

It shall here be shewn, that great devotion is the *noblest* temper of the *greatest* and *noblest* souls; and that they who think it receives any advantage from *ignorance*, are themselves entirely ignorant of the nature of devotion, the nature of God, and the nature of themselves.

People of *fine* parts and *learning*, or of great knowledge in *worldly matters*, may perhaps think it hard to have their *want* of devotion charged upon their *ignorance*. But if they will be content to be tried by reason and scripture, it may soon be made appear, that a *want* of devotion, wherever it is, either amongst the learned or unlearned, is founded in *gross ignorance*, and the *greatest blindness* and *insensibility* that can happen to a rational creature.

And that devotion is so far from being the effect of a *little* and *dejected* mind, that it must and will be always *highest* in the most *perfect* natures.

2. And *first*, Who reckons it a sign of a *poor, little* mind, for a man to be full of *reverence* and *duty* to his parents, to have the truest *love* and *honour* for his *friend*, or to excel in the *highest instances* of gratitude to his benefactor?

Are not these tempers, in the *highest* degree, in the most exalted and perfect minds?

And yet what is *high devotion*, but the highest exercise of these tempers, of *duty, reverence, love, honour*, and *gratitude* to the amiable, glorious *parent, friend*, and *benefactor* of all mankind?

Is it a true greatness of mind, to reverence the authority of your parents, to fear the displeasure of your friend, to dread the reproaches of your benefactor; and must not this *fear*, and *dread*, and *reverence*, be much more just, and reasonable, and honourable, when they are in the *highest degree* towards God?

So that as long as *duty* to parents, *love* to friends, and *gratitude* to benefactors, are thought great and honourable tempers, devotion, which is nothing else but duty, love, and gratitude to God,

God, muſt have the higheſt place amongſt our higheſt virtues.

If a *prince*, out of his *mere goodneſs*, ſhould ſend you a pardon by one of his *ſlaves*, would you think it a part of your duty to receive the *ſlave* with marks of *love*, *eſteem*, and *gratitude*, for his kindneſs of bringing you ſo great a gift, and at the ſame time think it a *meanneſs* and *poorneſs* of ſpirit, to ſhew *love*, *eſteem*, and *gratitude* to the prince, who of his own goodneſs freely ſent you the pardon?

And yet this would be as reaſonable, as to ſuppoſe that love, eſteem, honour, and gratitude, are *noble tempers*, and inſtances of a *great ſoul*, when they are paid to our fellow-creatures; but the effects of a poor, ignorant mind, when they are paid to God.

3. Even that part of devotion which expreſſes itſelf in *ſorrowful* confeſſions, and *penitential* tears of a broken and contrite heart, is very far from being any ſign of a *little* and *ignorant* mind.

For who does not acknowledge it an inſtance of an *ingenuous*, *generous*, and *brave* mind, to acknowledge a fault, and aſk pardon for any offence? And are not the *fineſt* and *moſt improved* minds, the moſt remarkable for this excellent temper?

Is it not alſo allowed, that the *ingenuouſneſs* and *excellence* of a man's ſpirit is much ſhewn, when his ſorrow and indignation at himſelf riſes in proportion to the folly of his crime, and the

goodneſs

goodness and *greatness* of the person he has offended?

Now if things are thus, then the *greater* any man's mind is, the more he *knows* of God and himself, the more will he be disposed to prostrate himself before God in all the *humblest acts* and expressions of repentance.

And the greater the *generosity* and *penetration* of his mind is, the more will he indulge a *passionate, tender* sense of God's just displeasure; and the more he knows of the greatness, the goodness, and perfection of the divine nature, the fuller of shame and confusion will he be at his own sins and ingratitude.

And on the other hand, the more *dull* and *ignorant* any soul is, the more *base* and *ungenerous*, the more *senseless* it is of the goodness of God, the more averse to *humble confession* and *repentance*.

Devotion therefore is so far from being best suited to *little, ignorant* minds, that a *true elevation* of soul, a *lively sense* of honour, and *great knowledge* of God and ourselves, are the greatest *helps* that our devotion hath.

4. On the other hand, it shall be made appear, that *indevotion* is founded in the most excessive ignorance.

And, *first*, Our blessed Lord and his apostles were eminent instances of great devotion. Now if we will grant, (as all Christians must grant) that their great devotion was founded in a true knowledge of the nature of devotion, the nature

of

of God, and the nature of man, then it is plain, that all thofe that are infenfible of devotion, are in this exceffive ftate of ignorance; they neither know God, nor themfelves, nor devotion.

Again, how comes it that moft people have recourfe to devotion, when they are in ficknefs, diftrefs, or fear of death? Is it not becaufe this ftate fhews them *more* of the want of God, and their own weaknefs, than they perceive at other times? Is it not becaufe their approaching end, *convinces* them of fomething which they did not *half perceive* before?

Now if devotion, at thefe feafons, is the effect of a *better knowledge* of God and ourfelves, then the neglect of devotion at other times is owing to ignorance of God and ourfelves.

5. Farther, as indevotion is ignorance, fo it is the moft *fhameful* ignorance, and fuch as is to be charged with the *greateft folly*.

This will fully appear to any one that confiders by what rules we are to judge of the excellency of any knowledge, or the fhamefulnefs of any ignorance.

Now *knowledge* itfelf would be no *excellence*, nor ignorance any *reproach* to us, but that we are *rational* creatures.

It follows plainly, that knowledge which is moft *fuitable* to our rational nature, and which moft concerns us, as fuch, to know, is our *higheft*, *fineft* knowledge; and that ignorance which relates to things that are moft *effential* to us, as
rational

rational creatures, and which we are most concerned to know, is, of all others, the most *gross* and *shameful* ignorance.

6. If a *gentleman* should fancy that the *moon* is no bigger than it appears to the *eye*, that it shines with its *own light*, that all the *stars* are only so many spots of light; if after reading books of *astronomy*, he should still continue in the same opinion, most people would think he had but a poor apprehension.

But if the same person should think it better to provide for a *short life* here, than to prepare for a *glorious eternity* hereafter; that it was better to be *rich*, than to be *eminent* in piety, his *ignorance* and *dulness* would be too great to be compared to any thing else.

That is the most clear and improved understanding, which *judges* best of the *value* and *worth* of things; all the rest is but the capacity of an *animal*; it is but meer *seeing* and *hearing*.

If a man had *eyes* that could see beyond the *stars*, or pierce into the heart of the earth, but could not see the things that were before him, or discern any thing that was serviceable to him, we should reckon that he had but a very *bad sight*.

If another had *ears* that received sounds from the world in the *moon*, but could hear nothing that was said or done upon earth, we should look upon him to be as *bad* as *deaf*.

In like manner, if a man has a *memory* that can retain a great many things, if he has a *wit*
that

that is *sharp* and *acute* in arts and sciences, but has a *dull, poor* apprehension of his *duty* and *relation* to God, of the *value* of piety, or the *worth* of moral virtue, he may very justly be reckoned to have a *bad understanding*. He is but like the man that can only *see* and *hear* such things as are of no benefit to him.

7. To proceed: We know how our blessed Lord acted in an human body; it was *his meat and drink to do the will of his Father which is in heaven.*

And if any number of heavenly spirits were to leave their habitations in the light of God, and be for awhile united to human bodies, they would certainly tend towards God in all their actions, and be as heavenly as they could, in a state of flesh and blood.

They would certainly act in this manner, because they would know that God was the *only good* of all spirits; and that whether they were *in* the body, or *out* of the body, in *heaven* or on *earth*, they must have every degree of their greatness and happiness from God alone.

All human spirits therefore, the *more exalted* they are, the more they *know* their divine original, the *nearer* they come to heavenly spirits, the more will they live to God in all their actions, making their whole life a *state of devotion*.

Devotion therefore is the greatest sign of a great and noble *genius*; it supposes a soul in its *highest state* of knowledge; and none but *little* and *blinded* minds, that are sunk into *ignorance* and *vanity*, are destitute of it.

8. If a human spirit should imagine some *mighty prince* to be greater than God, we should take it for a poor ignorant creature; all people would acknowledge such an imagination to be the height of stupidity.

But if this same *human spirit* should think it better to be devoted to some mighty *prince*, than to be devoted to God, would not this still be a greater proof of a poor, ignorant, and blinded nature?

Yet this is what all people do, who think any thing *better, greater*, or *wiser* than a devout life.

So that which way soever we consider this matter, it plainly appears, that devotion is an instance of *great judgment*, of an *elevated nature*; and the want of *devotion* is a certain proof of the want of *understanding*.

The greatest spirits of the Heathen world, such as *Pythagoras, Socrates, Plato, Epictetus, Marcus Antoninus*, owed all their greatness to the spirit of devotion.

They were full of God; their wisdom and deep contemplations tended only to deliver men from the vanity of the world, the slavery of bodily passions, that they might act as *spirits* that came from God, and were soon to return to him.

9. Let

9. Let *libertines* but grant that there is a God, and a providence, and then they have granted enough to juftify the wifdom, and fupport the honour of devotion.

For if there is an infinitely wife and good Creator, in whom we live, move, and have our being, whofe providence governs all things in all places, furely it muft be the higheft act of our *underftanding* to conceive rightly of him; it muft be the nobleft inftance of *judgment*, the moft exalted temper of our nature, to worfhip and adore this univerfal providence, to conform to its laws, to ftudy its wifdom, and to live and act every where, as in the prefence of this infinitely good and wife Creator.

Now he that lives thus, lives in the fpirit of devotion.

And what can fhew fuch great parts, and fo fine an underftanding, as to live in this temper?

For if God is *wifdom*, furely he muft be the wifeft man in the world, who *moft* conforms to the wifdom of God, who *beft* obeys his providence, who enters *fartheft* into his defigns, and does all he can, that God's will may be done on earth, as it is done in heaven.

A devout man makes a true ufe of his reafon; he fees through the *vanity* of the world, difcovers the *corruption* of his nature, and the *blindnefs* of his paffions. He lives by a *law* which is not vifible to *vulgar eyes*; he enters into the world of *fpirits*; he compares the greateft things, fets *eternity* againft time; and chufes rather to be for ever great in the prefence of God when he dies, than to have the greateſt ſhare of worldly pleaſures whilſt he lives.

11. *Laſtly*, *Courage* and *bravery* are words of a great ſound, and ſeem to ſignify an *heroic* ſpirit; but yet *humility*, which ſeems to be the *loweſt, meaneſt* part of devotion, is a more certain argument of a *noble* mind.

For humility contends with greater enemies, is more conſtantly engaged, more violently aſſaulted, ſuffers more, and requires greater courage to ſupport itſelf, than any inſtances of worldly bravery.

A man that dares be poor and contemptible in the eyes of the world, to approve himſelf to God; that reſiſts and rejects all human glory; that oppoſes the clamour of his paſſions, that meekly puts up all injuries, and dares ſtay for his reward till the inviſible hand of God gives to every one their proper places, endures a much *greater trial*, and exerts a *nobler fortitude*, than he that is bold and daring in the fire of battle.

For the boldneſs of a ſoldier, if he is a ſtranger to the ſpirit of devotion, is rather *weakneſs* than fortitude; it is at beſt but *mad paſſion*, and heated ſpirits, and has no more true valour in it than the fury of a *tyger*.

Reaſon is our *univerſal law*, that obliges us in all places, and all times; and no actions have any honour, but ſo far as they are inſtances of our obedience to reaſon.

And

And it is as *base* to be bold and daring against the principle of reason and justice, as to be bold and daring in *lying* and *perjury*.

Would we therefore exercise a *true fortitude*, we must do all in the spirit of *devotion*, be valiant against the corruptions of the *world*, and the lusts of the *flesh*, and the temptations of the *devil*: for to be daring and courageous against these enemies, is the noblest bravery that an human mind is capable of.

I have made this digression for the sake of those, who think great devotion to be *bigotry* and *poorness* of *spirit*; that by these considerations they may see, how *poor* and *mean* all other *tempers* are, if compared to it: that they may see all worldly attainments, whether of greatness, wisdom, or bravery, are but *empty sounds*; and there is nothing *wise*, or *great*, or *noble*, in an *human spirit*, but rightly to *know*, and heartily *worship* and *adore* the great God, that is the *support* and *life* of all spirits, whether in *heaven*, or on *earth*.

An extract from the Rev. Mr. LAW's

LATER WORKS.

An extract from the Case of Reason, or Natural Religion, fairly and fully stated. In answer to a book, entitled *Christianity as Old as the Creation.*

The Introduction, shewing the state of the Controversy.

THE infidelity which is now openly declared for, pretends to support itself upon the *sufficiency, excellency,* and *absolute perfection* of reason, or natural religion.

The author with whom I am engaged, makes no attempt to invalidate the *historical evidence* on which Christianity is founded; but by arguments drawn from the nature of God, and natural religion, pretends to prove that no religion can come from God, which teaches any thing more than that, which is fully manifest to all mankind by the *mere light* of nature.

His chief principles may be reduced to these following propositions.

1. That

1. That human reason, or natural light, is the *only means* of knowing all that God requires of us.

2. That reason, or natural light, is so full, sufficient, plain, and certain a rule in all religious duties, that no external divine revelation can add any thing to it, or require us to believe or practise any thing, that was not as fully known before. A revelation, if ever made, can only declare those very *same* things *externally*, which were before equally declared by the *internal* light of nature.

3. That this must be the case of natural and revealed religion, unless God be an arbitrary being. For if God be not an arbitrary being, but acts according to the reason and nature of things; then he can require nothing of us by revelation, but what is already required by the nature and reason of things. And therefore, as he expresses it, *reason and revelation must exactly answer one another like two tallies* †.

4. That whatever is at any time admitted as matter of religion, that is not manifest from the reason of the thing, and plainly required by the light of nature, is gross superstition.

5. That it is inconsistent with the divine perfections, to suppose, that God can by an external revelation give any religious knowledge, at *any time*, to *any people*, which was not equally given at *all* times, and to *all* people.

† Page 60.

This is the state of the controversy. As to the railing accusations, which this author pours out, at all adventures, upon the clergy, I shall wholly pass them over; my intention being only to appeal to the reason of the reader, and to add nothing to it, but the safe, unerring light of divine revelation.

CHAP. I.

Enquiring, whether there be any thing in the nature *and* condition *of man, to* oblige *him to think, that he is not to admit of any doctrines or institutions, as revealed from God, but such as his own reason can prove to be necessary from the nature of things.*

I Begin with enquiring what there is to *oblige* a man to hold this opinion, because if there is not some strong and plain proof arising from the *nature* and *condition* of man, to *oblige* him thus to abide by the sole light of his own reason; it may be so far from being a duty, which he owes to God, that it may be reckoned amongst his most criminal presumptions. And the pleading for this authority of his own reason; may have the guilt of pleading for his greatest vanity. And if, as this writer observes, *spiritual pride be the worst sort of pride,* † a confident reliance upon our own reason, as having a right to determine all matters between God and man, if it should

† Page 150.

should prove to be a *groundless pretension*, bids fair to be reckoned the highest instance of the *worst* kind of the worst of sins.

Every other instance of vanity, every degree of personal pride, and self-esteem, may be a pardonable weakness in comparison of this. For how small is that pride which only makes us prefer our own personal beauty or merit to that of our fellow-creatures, when compared with a self-confiding reason, which is too haughty to adore any thing in the divine counsels, which it cannot fully comprehend; or to submit to any directions from God, but such as its own wisdom could prescribe? Thus much is certain, that there can be no *medium* in this matter. The claiming this authority to our own reason, must either be a very great duty, or among the greatest of sins.

If it be a *sin* to admit of any *secrets* in divine providence, if it be a *crime* to ascribe wisdom and goodness to God in things we cannot comprehend: if it be a *baseness* and *meanness* of spirit to believe that God can teach us *better* or *more* than we can teach ourselves: if it be a *shameful apostacy* from the dignity of our nature, to submit to any *mysterious providence* over us, to comply with any other methods of *homage* and *adoration*, than such as we could of ourselves contrive and justify; then it is certainly a great duty to assert and maintain this authority of our own reason.

On the other hand; if the profoundest humility towards God, be the highest instance of piety: if every thing within us and without us, if every thing we know of God, every thing we know of ourselves preaches up humility to us, as the foundation of every virtue, as the life and soul of all holiness: if *sin* had its beginning from *pride,* and *hell* be the effect of it, if *devils* are what they are through spiritual pride and self-conceit, then we have great reason to believe, that the claiming this authority to our reason, in opposition to the revealed wisdom of God, is not a frailty of *flesh* and *blood,* but that same spiritual pride which turned *angels* into *apostate* spirits.

Since therefore this appealing to our own reason, as the absolutely *perfect rule* of all that ought to pass between God and man, has an *appearance* of a pride of the *worst* kind, and such as unites us both in temper and conduct with the fallen spirits of darkness, it highly concerns every pleader on that side, to consider what grounds he proceeds upon, and to ask himself, what there is in the *state* and *condition* of human nature, to oblige him to think, that nothing can be *divine* or *holy*, or *necessary*, in religion, but what *human* reason dictates?

I hope the reader will think this a fair state of the case, and that all the light we can have in this matter, must arise from a thorough consideration of the *state* and *condition* of man in this world. If

without

without revelation he is free from mysteries as a *moral* and *religious* agent, then he has some plea from his state and condition to reject *revealed* mysteries.

But if in a state of natural religion, he can't acknowledge a divine providence or worship God, without *as much* implicit faith, and submission of his reason, as any revealed mysteries require; then his *state* and *condition* in the world, condemns his refusal of any revelation sufficiently attested to come from God. This enquiry therefore into the state and condition of man, being so plainly the true point of the controversy, I hope to obtain the reader's impartial attention to it.

Had mankind continued in a state of *perfect innocence*, without ever failing in their duty either to God or man, yet even in such a state, they could never have known what God would or would not reveal to them, but by some express revelation from him. And as God might intend to raise them to some higher, and unknown state of perfection; so he might raise them to it by the revelation of such things as their own reason, though uncorrupt, yet could not have discovered.

But if man, in a state of *innocence*, could have no pretence to set himself against divine revelation, and make his own reason the *final judge* of what God could, or could not reveal to him; much less has he any pretence for so doing in his present state of *sin, ignorance,* and *misery*. His

nature

nature and *condition* is so far from furnishing him with reasons against revelation, against any *supernatural* help from God; that it seems to be inconsolable without it; and every circumstance of his life prepares him to hope for terms of *mercy* and deliverance from his present guilt and misery, not according to *schemes* of his *own* contrivance, not from his *own knowledge* of the *nature*, and *reason*, and *fitness* of things, but from some *incomprehensible depth* of divine goodness.

For if sin, and misery, and ignorance, cannot convince us of our own weakness, cannot prepare us to accept of any *methods* of *atoning* for our guilt, but such as our own disordered reason can suggest, we are not far from the hardened state of those miserable spirits, that make war against God.

For to insist upon the *prerogative* of our own nature, as qualifying us to make our own peace with God, and to reject the *atonement* which he has provided for us, because we esteem it more fit and reasonable, that our *own repentance* should be sufficient without it, is the same height of *pride* and *impiety*, as to affirm, that we have no need of any repentance at all.

For as mankind, if they had continued in a state of *innocence*, could not have known how their innocence was to be rewarded, or what changes of state God intended them for, but as revelation had discovered these things unto them: so after they were *fallen* into a state of guilt and sin, they
could

could never know what *misery* it would expose them to, or *when*, or *how*, or whether they were ever to be delivered from it, and made as happy as if they had *never* sinned; these are things that nothing but a revelation from God could teach them.

So that for a sinner to pretend to appoint the *atonement* for his own sins, or to think himself able to tell what it *ought* to be, is as foolish and vain a presumption, as if man in *innocence* should have pretended to appoint his own method of being changed into a *cherub*.

The writers against revelation appeal to the *reason* and *nature* of things, as *infallibly* discovering every thing that a revelation from God can teach us.

Thus our author; *If the relations between things, and the fitness resulting from thence, be not the sole rule of God's actions, must not God be an arbitrary being? But if God only commands what the nature of things shew to be fit, it is scarce possible that men should mistake their duty; since a mind that is attentive can as easily distinguish fit from unfit, as the eye can beauty from deformity* †.

It is granted, that there is a fitness and unfitness of actions founded in the nature of things, and resulting from the relations that persons and things bear to one another. It is also granted, that the reasonableness of most of the duties of children to their parents, of parents to their children,

† Page 30.

dren, and of men to men, is very apparent, from the relations they bear to one another; and that several of the duties which we owe to God, plainly appear to us, as soon as we acknowledge the relation that is between God and us.

But then, this *whole argument* proves directly the contrary to that which this author intended to prove by it.

I here therefore join with this author; I readily grant, that the nature, reason and relations of things and persons, and the fitness of actions resulting from thence, is the *sole rule* of God's actions. And I appeal to this one common principle, as a sufficient proof that a man cannot thus abide by the *sole light* of his own reason, without contradicting the nature and reason of things, and denying this to be the *sole rule* of God's actions.

* For if the *fitness* of actions is founded in the *nature* of things and persons, and this fitness be the *sole rule* of God's actions, it is certain that the rule by which he acts, must in many instances be *entirely* inconceivable by us, so as not to be known *at all*, and in no instances *fully* known, or *perfectly* comprehended.

* For if God is to act according to a *fitness founded* in the *nature* of things, and nothing can be fit for him to do, but what has its fitness founded in his own *incomprehensible* nature, must he not necessarily act by a rule *above* all human comprehension?

comprehenfion? If he muſt govern his actions by his own nature, he muſt act by a *rule* that is juſt as *incomprehenſible* to us as his own nature.

* And we can be no farther *competent judges* of the *fitneſs* of the conduct of God, than we are competent judges of the divine nature; and can no more tell what is, or is not *infinitely wiſe* in God, than we can raiſe ourſelves to a *ſtate* of infinite wiſdom.

So that if the *fitneſs* of actions is founded in the *particular nature* of things and perſons, and the fitneſs of God's actions muſt ariſe from that which is *particular* to his nature, then we have from this argument, the *utmoſt certainty* that the *rule* or *reaſons* of God's actions muſt in many caſes be entirely inconceivable by us, and in no caſes perfectly apprehended; and for this very reaſon, becauſe he is not an *arbitrary being*, that acts by *mere will*, but is governed in every thing he does, by the reaſon and nature of things.

How miſtaken therefore is this author, when he argues after this manner. *If God requires things of us, whoſe fitneſs our reaſon can't prove from the nature of things, muſt he not be an arbitrary being?* For how can that prove God to be an arbitrary agent, which is the neceſſary conſequence of his not being arbitrary?

Suppoſing God not to be an *arbitrary being*, but to act conſtantly, as the perfections of his own nature make it *fit* and *reaſonable* for him to act, then there is an utter impoſſibility of our comprehending

prehending the reasonableness and fitness of many of his actions.

* For instance; look at the *reason* of things, and the *fitness* of actions, and tell me how they moved God to create mankind in the state and condition they are in. Nothing is more above the reason of men, than to explain the reasonableness of God's providence in creating man of such a *form* and *condition*, to go through *such* a state of things as human life is. No revealed mysteries can more exceed the comprehension of man, than the state of human life itself.

Shew me according to what *fitness*, founded in the *nature* of things, God's infinite wisdom was determined to form you in such a manner, bring you into such a world, and suffer and preserve *such a state* of things, as human life is, and then you may have some pretence to believe no revealed doctrines, but such as your own reason can deduce from the nature of things.

But whilst your own *form*, whilst *creation* and *providence* are depths which you cannot thus look into, 'tis strangely absurd to pretend, that God cannot reveal any thing to you as a matter of religion, except your own reason can shew its foundation in the nature and reason of things.

Revelation, you say, is on your account, and therefore you ought to see the *reasonableness* and *fitness* of it. And don't you also say, that God has made you for your *own sake*; ought you not therefore to know the reasonableness and fitness
of

of God's forming you as you are? Don't you say, that providence is for the *fake* of man? Is it not therefore fit and reasonable, in the nature of things, that there should be no *mysteries*, or *secrets*, in providence, but that man should so see its methods, as to be able to prove all its steps to be constantly fit and reasonable?

Don't you say, that the *world* is for the *fake* of man; is it not therefore fit and reasonable that man should see, that the *past* and *present* state of the world has been such as the reason and fitness of things required it should be?

* Now if the *imperfect* state of human nature, the *calamities* of this life, the *diseases* and mortality of human bodies, the *methods* of God's continual providence in governing human affairs, are things that as much concern us, as any methods of revealed religion; and if these are things that we cannot explain, according to any *fitness* or *unfitness* founded in the *nature* of things, but must believe a great deal more of the infinite wisdom of God, than we can so explain; have we any reason to think, that God cannot, or ought not to raise us out of this unhappy state of things, help us to an higher order of life, and exalt us to a nearer enjoyment of himself, by any means, but such as our own poor reason can grope out of the nature and fitness of things?

Now what is the reason, that all is thus mysterious and unmeasurable by human reason, in these matters so nearly concerning human nature? 'Tis because God is not an *arbitrary being*,

but

but does that which the *incomprehensible perfections* of his own nature, make it *fit* and *reasonable* for him to do. Do but grant that nothing can be *fit* for God to do, but what is *according* to his own *infinite perfections:* let but this be the *rule* of his actions, and then you have the *fullest* proof, that the fitness of his actions must be above our comprehension, who can only judge of a *fitness* according to our *own perfections*; and then we must be surrounded with mystery for this very reason, because God acts according to a *certain rule*, his own nature.

Again: What is the nature of a human soul, upon what *terms*, and in what manner it is *united* to the body, how far it is *different* from it, how far it is *subject* to it, what powers and faculties it *derives* from it; are things wherein the *wisdom* and *goodness* of God, and the *happiness* of man are deeply concerned. Is it not necessary that these things should have their foundation in the *reason* and *fitness* of things? And yet what natural reason, uninspired from above, can shew that this *state* of soul and body is founded therein?

* *Again:* The origin of *sin* and *evil*, or how it entered into the world consistently with the infinite wisdom of God, is a mystery of *natural religion*, which reason cannot unfold. For can we shew from the *reason* and *nature* of things, that it was *fit* and *reasonable*, for the providence of God to suffer sin to enter, and continue in the world? Here therefore the man of natural religion must drop his method of reasoning from the

the fitnefs of things, and that in an article of the higheft concern to the moral world, and be as mere a believer, as he that believes the moft incomprehenfible myftery of revealed religion.

Now as there have been in the feveral ages of the world, fome *impatient, reftlefs* and *prefuming* fpirits, who, becaufe they could not in thefe points explain the juftice of God's providence, have taken refuge in horrid *atheifm*, fo they made juft the fame *fober ufe* of their reafon, as our *modern unbelievers*, who becaufe they can't comprehend the *fitnefs* and *neceffity* of certain Chriftian doctrines, refign themfelves up to an hardened *infidelity*. For it is juft as reafonable to allow of no myfteries in *revelation*, as to allow of no myfteries in *creation* and *providence*.

And whenever this writer fhall think it proper to attack *natural* religion with as much freedom as he has *revealed*, he need not enter upon any *new* hypothefis, or *different* way of reafoning. For the fame turn of thought, may foon find materials in the natural ftate of man, for as large a bill of complaints againft natural religion, and the myfteries of providence, as is here brought againft revealed doctrines.

To proceed: If the *fitnefs of actions is founded in the nature and relation of beings*, then nothing can be fit for God to do, but fo far as it is fit for the *Governor of all created beings*, whether on earth, or in any other part of the univerfe;

and

and he cannot act fitly towards mankind, but by acting as is fit for the Governor of all beings.

* Now what is fit for the *Governor of all created* nature to do in this or that particular part of his creation, is as much above our reason to *tell*, as it is above our power to *govern* all beings. And how mankind ought to be governed, with relation to the whole creation, of which they are so small a part, is a matter equally above our knowledge; because we know not how they are a part of the whole, or what relation they bear to any other part, or how their state affects the whole, or any other part, than we know what beings the whole consists of.

Now there is nothing that we know with more certainty than that God is governor of the *whole*, and that mankind are a *part* of the whole; and that the uniformity and harmony of divine providence, must arise from his infinite wise government of the *whole*; and therefore we have the utmost certainty, that we are *vastly incompetent* judges of the fitness or unfitness of any methods that God uses in the government of so small a part of the universe, as mankind are.

Again: If the *fitness of actions is founded in the relations of beings to one another*, then the fitness of the actions of God's providence over mankind, must be in many instances altogether incomprehensible to us.

For the relation which God bears to mankind, as their *all-perfect Creator* and continual *Preserver*, is a relation that our reason conceives as imperfectly

fectly, and knows as little of, as it does of any of the divine attributes. When it compares it to that of a *father* and his children, a *prince* and his subjects, a *proprietor* and his property, it has explained it in the best manner it can, but still has left it as much a *secret*, as we do the divine nature when we only say, it is *infinitely* superior to every thing that is *finite*.

By the natural light of our reason we may know with certainty, several *effects* of this relation, as that it puts us under the care and protection of a wise, and just, and merciful providence, and demands from us the highest instances of humility, adoration and thanksgiving. But what it is in its own nature, what kind of state, it is to exist in and by God, what it is to see by a *light* that is his, to act by a power from him, to live by a *life* in him; are things as incomprehensible to reason, *left to itself*, as what it is to be in the *third heavens*, or to hear words that cannot be uttered.

But if this relation consists in these *inconceivable* things, in a communication of *life*, *light* and *power*, if these are enjoyed in God, and in ourselves, in a manner not to be explained by any thing that we ever heard, or saw; then we must necessarily be poor judges of what is fit for God to require of us, because of this *relation*. It teaches us nothing but the superficialness of our own knowledge, and the unfathomable depths of the divine perfections.

How

How little this writer has considered the nature of this *relation* between God and man, may be seen by the following paragraphs. *The Holy Ghost*, says he, *cannot deal with men as rational creatures, but by proposing arguments to convince their understandings; and influence their wills, in the same manner as if proposed by other agents.* As absurd, as to say, God cannot *create* us as rational beings, unless he creates us in the same *manner*, as if we were created by other agents. For to suppose that other agents can possibly act upon our understanding, and will, in the *same manner* that God does; is as gross an absurdity, as to suppose that other agents can create us in the same manner that God creates us.

And to *confine* the manner of the Holy Ghost's acting upon us, to the manner of our acting upon one another by *arguments* and *syllogisms*, is as great a weakness, as to *confine* the manner of God's creating us, to the manner of our making a *statue* with *tools* and *instruments*.

But he proceeds and says, *For to go beyond this, would be making impressions on men, as a seal does on wax; to the confounding of their reason, and their liberty in chusing; and the man would then be mearly passive, and the action would be the action of another being acting upon him, for which he could be no way accountable* †.

Here you see the Holy Spirit has but these two possible ways of acting upon men, it must either

† Page 199.

either only propose an argument, just as a man may propose one, or it must act like a *seal upon wax,*

I only ask this writer, whether God communicates *life,* and *strength,* and *understanding,* and *liberty of will* to us, only as men may communicate any thing to one another? or as a seal acts upon wax? If so, it may be granted, that the Holy Ghost cannot act upon us any other way.

But it must be affirmed, that we do, by a continual influx from God, enjoy all these powers, and receive the continuance of all these faculties from him, not as men receive things from one another, nor as *wax* receives the *impression* of the *seal,* but in a way as much above our conception, as creation is above our power; if we have all our *power* of acting, by a *continual communication* from him, and yet as free agents, have all our *light* from him, and yet are *accountable intelligent* beings; then it must be great weakness to affirm, that the Holy Ghost cannot act upon us in the same manner: for it would be saying, God cannot act upon us as he does act upon us.

The short of the matter is this. Either this *writer* must affirm, that our *rational nature,* our *understanding faculties,* our *power* of action, our *liberty* of will, must *necessarily* subsist without the *continual action* of God upon them, or else he must

must grant, that God can *act* upon our *understandings* and *wills* without making us as *merely passive* as the wax under the seal.

This writer says, *Though the relation we stand in to God, is not artificial, as most are amongst men —yet this does not hinder, but that we may know the end he had in being related to us as Creator and Governor, and what he requires of his creatures and subjects.* But how are we to know this? *This,* says he, *the divine nature, which contains in it all perfection and happiness, plainly points out to us* †.

If he had said, since God must act over us as Creator and Governor, according to his own infinite *perfection and happiness,* therefore his conduct over us may be *very mysterious,* he had drawn a *plain* conclusion. But he proves all to be plain, because God is to govern us according to something that is not plain, according to his own *incomprehensible nature.*

His argument therefore proceeds thus. God must govern us according to his own *infinite perfection and happiness*; but we *do not know* what his infinite perfections and happiness are:

Therefore we *plainly know* how he is to govern us.

Now if this writer is capable of taking such an argument as this to be demonstrative, it is no

wonder

† Page 29.

wonder that all his principles of religion are founded upon demonstration.

But if he knows no more of what arises from the *relation* between God and his creatures, than he has here demonstrated, he might be very well content with some farther knowledge from divine revelation.

It is because of this incomprehensible relation between God and his creatures, that we are unavoidably ignorant of what God may justly require of us either in a state of *innocence* or *sin*. For as the fitness of actions between beings *related*, must result from their respective natures, so the incomprehensibility of the divine nature, on which the relation between God and man is founded, makes it utterly impossible for mere natural reason to say, what *kind* of *homage*, or *worship*, he may *fitly* require of man in a state of *innocence*; or what *different* worship and homage he may, or must require of men, as *sinners*.

And to appeal to the infinite perfections of God, as *plainly pointing this out*, is the same extravagance, as to appeal to the *incomprehensibility* of God as a plain proof of our comprehending what God is.

As to the obligations of moral or social duties, which have their foundation in the several relations we bear to one another, these are the same in the state of *innocence* or *sin*, and we know that we truly act according to the divine will, when

Vol. VI.   C   we

we act according to what these relations require of us.

But the question is, What distinct kind of *homage*, or *service*, or *worship*, God may require us to render to him, either in a state of *innocence* or *sin*, on account of that relation he bears to us as an all-perfect Creator and Governor?

But this is a question that God alone can resolve.

Human reason cannot enter into it, it has no principle to proceed upon in it. For as the *necessity* of divine worship, so the *particular manner* of it, must have its reason in the divine nature.

Sacrifice, if considered only as an *human invention*, could not be proved to be a reasonable service. Yet considered as a *divine institution*, it would be the greatest folly not to receive it as a reasonable service. For as we could see no reason for it, if it was of human invention, so we should have the greatest reason to comply with it because it was of divine appointment. Not as if the divine appointment altered the *nature* and *fitness* of things; but because nothing has the *nature* and *fitness* of divine worship, but as it is of divine appointment.

Man therefore, had he continued in a state of innocence, and without revelation, might have lived in an awful fear, and pious regard of God, and observed every duty both of moral and civil life,

life, as an act of obedience to him. But he could have no foundation either to invent any particular *manner* of divine worship himself, or to reject any that was appointed by God, as *unnecessary*. It would have been ridiculous to have pleaded his innocence, as having no need of a divine worship. For who can have greater reason, or be fitter to worship God, than innocent beings? It would have been more absurd, to have objected the sufficiency of their reason; for why should men reject a *revealed manner* of divine worship, because God had given them reason of their own, sufficient for the duties of social and civil life?

And as reason in a state of innocence and perfection, could not have any pretence to appoint the manner of divine worship, so when the state of innocence was changed for that of sin, it became more difficult for bare reason to know what kind of worship could be acceptable to God from sinners.

For what the *relation* betwixt God and sinners makes it fit for God to require or accept of them, cannot be determined by human reason.

This is a *new state*, and the foundation of a *new relation*, and nothing can be fit for God to do in it, but what has its *fitness* arising from it. We have nothing to help our conceptions of the fore-mentioned *relative characters* of God, as our *Governor* and *Preserver*, but what we derive from our idea of human *fathers* and *governors*:

which

which idea only helps us to comprehend these *relations*, just as our idea of human power helps us to comprehend the *omnipotence* of God. For a father or governor, no more represents the *state* of God as our *Governor* and *Preserver*, than our living in our father's *family*, represents the *manner* of our living in God.

These relations are both very plain, and very mysterious; they are very plain, as to the *reality* of their existence; and highly mysterious and inconceivable, as to the *manner* of their existence.

That which is *plain*, in these relative characters of God, plainly shews our obligations to every instance of *duty, homage, love*, and *gratitude*.

And that which is *inconceivable* in them, is a solid foundation of that *profound humility, awful reverence, internal piety* and *tremendous sense* of the divine Majesty, with which devout persons think of God, and assist at the *offices* of religion. Which excites in them a higher zeal for doctrines and institutions of divine revelation, than for all things human; that fills them with reverence for all *things*, places, and offices, that are either by divine or human authority, appointed to assist their desired intercourse with God.

And if some people, by a *long* and *strict* attention to *reason*, and the *fitness* and *unfitness* of things, have at last arrived at a demonstrative certainty,

certainty, that all thefe fentiments of piety and devotion, are mere *bigotry*, *fuperftition*, and *enthufiafm*; I fhall only now obferve, that *youthful extravagance*, *paffion*, and *debauchery*, by their own *natural tendency*, without the affiftance of any other guide, feldom fail of making the fame difcovery. And though it is not reckoned any reflection upon *great wits*, when they hit upon the fame thought, yet it may feem fome difparagement of that *reafon* and *philofophy*, which teaches *old men* to think the fame of religion, that *paffion* and *extravagance* teach the young.

To return: As there is no ftate in human life, that can give us a true idea of any of the forementioned relative characters of God, fo this relative ftate of God towards finners is ftill lefs capable of being comprehended by any thing obfervable in the relations, betwixt a judge and criminals, a *creditor* and his debtors, a *phyfician* and his patients, a father or prince, and their difobedient children and fubjects.

For none of thefe ftates feparately, nor all of them jointly confidered, give us any full idea, either of the *nature* and *guilt* of fin or how God is to deal with finners, on the account of the relation he bears to them.

To afk, whether *fin* hath folely the *nature* of an offence, againft a prince or a father, and fo is pardonable by mere goodnefs; whether it is like an *error* in a *road* or *path*, and fo is entirely at an end, when the right path is taken;

whether its guilt hath the nature of a debt, and so is capable of being discharged, just as a debt is; whether it affects the soul, as a *wound* or *disease* affects the body, and so ought only to move God to act as a good physician? All these questions are as vain, as to ask, whether knowledge in God is really *thinking*, or his nature a real *substance*. For as his knowledge and nature cannot be strictly defined, but are capable of being signified by the terms *thinking* and *substance*, so the nature of sin is not *strictly represented* under any of these characters, but is capable of receiving *some representation* from every one of them.

When sin is said to be an offence against God, it is to teach us, that we have infinitely more reason to dread it on *God's account*, than to dread any offence against our parents, or governors.

When it is compared to a *debt*, it is to signify, that our sins make us accountable to God, not in the *same manner*, but with the same certainty, as a debtor is answerable to his creditor; and because it has some likeness to a debt, that of ourselves we are not able to pay.

When it is compared to a *wound*, or disease, it is not to teach us, that it may as justly and easily be healed as bodily wounds, but to help us to conceive the greatness of its evil; that, as diseases bring death to the body,

so

so sin brings a worse kind of death upon the soul.

Since therefore the *nature* and *guilt* of sin can only so far be known, as to make it highly to be *dreaded*, but not so known as to be *fully* understood, by any thing we can compare to it:

Since the *relation* which God bears to *sinners*, can only be so known, as to make it highly reasonable to prostrate ourselves before him, in every instance of humility and penitence; but not so fully known as to teach us, in what manner, God must deal with us: it plainly follows, that if God is not an *arbitrary* being, but acts according to a *fitness resulting* from this relation, he must, in this respect, act by a *rule* known only to himself, and such as we cannot *possibly* state from the *reason* and *nature* of things.

For if the nature of things, and the fitness of actions resulting from their relations, is to be the rule of our reason, then *reason* must be here at a full stop, and can have no more knowledge to proceed upon, in stating the *nature*, the *guilt*, or proper *atonement* of sin in men, than of sin in *angels*.

For *reason* can no more tell us what the *guilt* of sin is, what *hurt* it does us, how far it *enters* into, and *alters* our very nature, what *contrariety to*, and *separation* from God, it necessarily brings upon us, or what *supernatural* means are, or are not, necessary to abolish it; our *reason* can no more tell this, than our *senses* can tell us, what is the *inward*, and what is the *outward* light of angels.

Ask reason what *effect* sin has upon the soul, and it can tell you no more, than if you had asked, what effect the *omnipresence* of God has upon the soul.

Ask reason, and the nature of things, what is, or ought to be, the *true nature* of an atonement for sin, how far it is like *paying* a *debt*, or *healing* a *wound*, or how far it is different from them? And it can tell you no more, than if you had asked, what is the *true degree* of power that *preserves* us in existence, how far it is *like* that which at first created us, and how far it is *different* from it.

All these enquiries are, by the nature of things, made impossible to us, so long as we have no light but from our own natural capacities, and we cannot take upon us to be *philosophers* in these matters, but by deserting our reason, and giving ourselves up to *vision* and *imagination*.

And we have as much authority from the nature of things, to appeal to *hunger* and *thirst*, and *sensual pleasure*, to tell us *how* our souls shall live in the beatific presence of God, as to appeal to our *reason* and *logic*, to demonstrate how sin is to be *atoned*, or the soul *prepared*, and *purified*, for future happiness.

For God has no more given us our reason to *settle* the nature of an atonement for sin; or to find

find out what can, or cannot, take away its guilt, than he has given us *senses* and *appetites* to state the nature, or discover the ingredients of future happiness.

And he who rejects the *atonement* for sins made by the Son of God, as *needless*, because he cannot prove it to be *necessary*, is as extravagant, as he that should deny that God created him by his *only Son*, because he did not remember it. For our memory is as proper a faculty to tell us, whether God at first created us, by his only Son, as our *reason* is to tell us, whether we ought to be restored to God, with, or without the mediation of Jesus Christ.

When therefore this writer says, *Can any thing be more evident, than that if doing evil be the only cause of God's displeasure, the ceasing to do evil, must take away that displeasure?* †

* Just as if he had said, if conversing with a *leper* has been the only cause of a man's getting a *leprosy*, must not departing from him, be the removal of the *leprosy*? For if any one, guessing at the *guilt* of sin, and its *effects* on the soul, should compare it to a *leprosy* in the body, he can no more say, that he has reached its *real, internal* evil, than he, that comparing the happiness of heaven to a crown of glory, can be said to have described its real happiness.

This *writer* has no occasion to appeal to the nature of things, if he can be thus certain about

C 5 things,

† Page 4.

things, whose nature is not only obscure, but *impossible* to be known. For it is as impossible for him to know the *guilt* and *effects* of sin, as to know the shape of an angel. It is as impossible to know by the mere light of reason, what God's *displeasure* at sin is, what *separation* from sinners it implies, or how it *obliges* God to deal with them; as to know what the internal essence of God is. Our author therefore has here found the utmost degree of evidence, where it was *impossible* for him to have the *smallest degree* of knowledge.

If a man, having *murdered* twenty of his fellow-creatures, should afterward be sorry for it, and wish that he had a power to bring them to life again, or to create others in their stead, would his ceasing to kill, and wishing he had a power to create others in their stead, put him just in the *same state* with God, as if he had never murdered a man in his life? But unless this can be said, it cannot be said that repentance is sufficient to put a man in the *same state*, as if he never had sinned.

The writer has two more objections against the atonement for sin, made by Jesus Christ. *First*, as it is an *human sacrifice, which nature itself abhors*: and which was looked upon as the great abomination of idolatrous *Pagan* worship.

The *cruelty*, *injustice*, and *impiety*, of shedding human blood in the sacrifices of the *Pagans*

is

is fully granted; but *reason* cannot thence bring the smallest objections against the sacrifice of Christ.

For how can reason be more disregarded, than in such an argument as this? The *Pagans* were unjust, cruel, and impious, in offering human blood to their false gods; therefore the true God cannot receive any *human* sacrifice, or allow any persons to die, as a punishment for sin.

For, if no human sacrifice can be fit for God to receive, because human sacrifices, as parts of *Pagan* worship, were unjust and impious; then it would follow, that the *mortality*, to which all mankind are appointed by God, must have the *same cruelty* and *injustice* in it. Now that *death* is a punishment for sin, and that all mankind are by death offered as a *sacrifice* for sin, is not only a doctrine of revealed religion, but the plain dictate of reason. But if reason must acknowledge the death of all mankind, as a sacrifice for sin, then it can have no just objection against the sacrifice of Christ, *because* it was *human*.

I need not take upon me to prove the *reasonableness* of God's procedure in the *mortality* of mankind; revelation is not under any necessity of proving this; because it is no difficulty that arises from revelation, but equally belongs to natural religion; and both of them must acknowledge it to be reasonable; not because it can be proved to be so from the nature of things,

things, but is to be believed to be fo, by faith and piety.

But if natural religion, will not fuffer us to think it *inconfiftent* with the juftice and goodnefs of God, to appoint all mankind victims to death on the account of fin, then *natural* religion, can have no objection againft the facrifice of Chrift, as it is an *human facrifice.*

And all that *revelation* adds to *natural* religion, on the point of *human* facrifice, is only this; the knowledge of *one*, that gives *merit and effect*, to all the reft.

Secondly, It is objected, that the atonement made by Jefus Chrift, reprefents God as punifhing the *innocent* and acquitting the *guilty*; or, as punifhing the innocent *inftead* of the guilty.

But this proceeds all upon miftake: for the atonement made by Jefus Chrift, though it procures pardon for the guilty, yet it does not acquit them, or excufe them from any punifhment, or fuffering for fin, which *reafon could impofe upon them.* Natural religion calls men to repentance for their fins: the atonement made by Jefus Chrift does not acquit them from it, or pardon them without it; but calls them to a *feverer* repentance, than natural religion alone prefcribes.

God therefore does not by this proceeding, fhew his *diflike* of the *innocent* and his *approbation* of the *wicked*.

God

For how can God be thought to punish our bleſſed Saviour out of *diſlike*, if his ſufferings are repreſented of ſuch infinite merit with him? Or how can he ſhew thereby his *approbation* of the guilty, whoſe repentance is not *acceptable* to him, till recommended by the infinite merits of Jeſus Chriſt?

As to the fitneſs of our Lord's ſufferings, as God and man; and the *nature* and *degree* of their worth; reaſon can no more enter into this matter, or *prove* or *diſprove* any thing about it, than it can enter into the ſtate of the whole creation, and ſhew, how it could, or could not, be in the whole, better than it is.

For you may as well aſk any of your *ſenſes*, as aſk your *reaſon* this principal queſtion, *Whether any ſupernatural means be neceſſary for the atonement of the ſins of mankind?* Or, ſuppoſing it neceſſary, whether the *mediation, death*, and *interceſſion* of Jeſus Chriſt, as God and man, be that true ſupernatural means?

For as the fitneſs or unfitneſs of any *ſupernatural* means, for the atonement of ſin, muſt reſult from the *incomprehenſible relation* God bears to ſinners, as it muſt have ſuch *neceſſity*, and *dignity*, as this relation *requires*, it neceſſarily follows, that if God acts according to *this relation*, the *fitneſs* of his actions cannot be according to our comprehenſion.

Again: Suppoſing ſome *ſupernatural means* to be neceſſary, for deſtroying the guilt and power

of

of sin; or that the *sufferings*, and *intercession*, of the Son of God incarnate, is that true supernatural means, it necessarily follows, that a revelation of such, or any other *supernatural* means, cannot possibly be made obvious to our reason and senses, as the things of human life, or the transactions amongst men are; but can only be so revealed, as to become just occasions of our *faith, humility,* and *pious resignation,* to the divine wisdom and goodness.

For, to say that such a thing is *supernatural,* is only saying, that it is something, which, by the *necessary state* of our own nature, we are as incapable of knowing, as we are incapable of seeing *spirits.*

If therefore supernatural things are by the letter of scripture ever revealed to us, they cannot be revealed to us as they are in their *own nature:* for if they could, such things would not be *supernatural.*

If an *angel* could appear to us, as it is in its own nature, then we should be *naturally* capable of seeing angels; but, because our nature is not *capable* of such a sight; therefore, when *angels* appear to men, they must appear, not as they are in themselves, but in some *human* or *corporeal* form.

It is just thus, when any *divine* matter is revealed by God; it can no more possibly be revealed to us, as it is in its *own nature,* than an *angel* can appear to us, as it is in its own nature;

but

but such supernatural matter can only be revealed to us, by being represented to us, by its likeness to something, that we already *naturally* know.

Thus revelation teaches us this *supernatural* matter; that Jesus Christ is making *perpetual intercession for us in heaven*: for Christ's *real state,* or *manner* of existence with God in heaven, in regard to his church, cannot, as it is in its *own nature*, be described to us; it is in this respect ineffable, and incomprehensible. And therefore, this high and inconceivable manner of Christ's existence with God in heaven, in regard to his church, is revealed to us under an idea, that gives us the truest representation of it, we are capable of.

But if any one should thence infer, that the Son of God must therefore either be always upon his knees, or *prostrate* in some humble form of a supplicant, he would make a very weak inference.

Because this revealed idea of Christ, as a perpetual Intercessor in heaven, is only a comparative representation of something, that cannot be *directly* and *plainly* known as it is in its own nature; and only teaches us, how to believe something, though imperfectly, yet *truly* of an incomprehensible nature.

Again: When it is by the letter of scripture revealed to us, that the blessed Jesus is the one *Mediator* between God and man; that he is the *Atonement*, the *Propitiation*, and *Satisfaction* for
our

our sins: these expressions only teach us *as much* outward knowledge of so great a mystery, as human language can represent. But they do not teach us the perfect nature of Christ's state between God and sinners. For that being a *supernatural* matter, cannot by any outward words be revealed to us as it is in its *own nature*, any more than the *essence* of God can be made *visible* to our eyes of flesh.

But these expressions teach us thus much with certainty, that there is in the *state* of Christ between God and sinners, something infinitely and inconceivably beneficial to us; and *truly answerable* to all that we mean by *mediation, atonement, propitiation,* and *satisfaction*.

And though the *real, internal manner*, of this mediation and atonement, as it is in its own nature, is *incomprehensible*, yet this does not lessen our knowledge of the truth and certainty of it, any more than the *incomprehensibility* of the divine nature, lessens our certainty of its real existence.

And as our idea of God, though consisting of incomprehensible perfections, helps us to a real and certain knowledge of the divine nature; and though all mysterious, is yet the solid foundation of all piety; so our idea of Jesus Christ, as our *Mediator* and *Atonement*, though it be incomprehensible as to its real nature, yet helps us to a *certain* knowledge of Christ, as our *Mediator* and *Atonement*; and, though full of mystery, is yet

yet full of motives to the highest piety, love, and gratitude unto God.

All objections therefore, raised from any difficulties about the nature of *atonements, propitiations,* and *satisfactions,* as these words are used in common language, are vain, and entirely groundless.

For all these objections proceed upon this supposition, that *atonement,* or *satisfaction,* when attributed to Jesus Christ, signify neither more nor less, than when they are used as terms in *human laws* or in *civil* life; take away this supposition, and all objections are entirely removed with it.

To return: I have granted this writer his great principle, *That the relations of things and persons, and the fitness resulting from thence, is the sole rule of God's actions:* and I have granted it upon this supposition, that it thence follows, that God must act according to his *own nature*; and therefore nothing could be fit for God to do, but what had the reason of its fitness in his own nature: and if so, then the *rule* of his actions could not fall within our comprehension. And consequently, *reason alone,* could not be a competent judge of God's proceedings; or say, what God might, or might not, require of us: and therefore I have, plainly turned his main argument against himself, and made it fully confute that doctrine, which he intended to found upon it.

But

But though I have thus far, granted the *nature* and *relations* of things and beings, to be the rule of God's actions, because that plainly supposes, that his *own nature* must be the rule of his actions; yet since our *author*, and other modern opposers of revealed doctrines of religion, hold it in another sense, and mean by it, I know not what *eternal, immutable* reasons and relations of things, *independent* of any being, and which are a *common rule and law of God and man*, I entirely declare against it, as an erroneous and groundless opinion.

Thus, when this writer says, *If the relations between things, and the fitness resulting from thence, be not the sole rule of God's actions, must he not be an arbitrary being?* As he here means some *eternal, immutable relations, independent* of God; so, to suppose, that God cannot be a *wise* and *good* being, unless such eternal, independent relations, be the *sole rule* of his actions, is as erroneous, as to affirm, that God cannot be *omniscient*, unless *mathematical demonstrations* be his *sole manner* of knowing all things. And it is just as reasonable to fix God's knowledge *solely* in mathematical demonstrations, that we may thence be assured of his *infallible knowledge,* as to make I know not what independent relations of things, the *sole rule* of his actions, that we may thence be assured, he is not *arbitrary*, but a wise and good being.

And we have as strong reasons to believe God

to be, in the highest degree, *wise* and *good*, without knowing on what, his wisdom and goodness is *founded*; as we have to believe him to be *omniscient*, and *eternal*, without knowing on *what* his *omniscience* is founded; or to *what*, his eternity is owing. And we have the same reason to hold it a vain enquiry, to ask what obliges God to be *wise* and *good*, as to ask what obliges him to be *omniscient*, or *eternal*.

And as it would be absurd to ascribe the *existence* of God to *any cause*, or found it upon any *independent relations* of things, so it is the same absurdity, to ascribe the infinite wisdom and goodness of God to *any cause*, or found them upon any independent relations of things.

Nor do we any more *lose* the notion, or *lessen* the certainty of the divine wisdom and goodness, because we cannot say on *what* they are founded, than we *lose* the notion of God, or render his existence *uncertain*, because it cannot be founded on any thing.

And as in our account of the existence of things, we are obliged to have recourse to a being, whose existence must not be ascribed to *any cause* because every thing cannot have a cause, no more than every thing can be created, so in our account of *wisdom* and *goodness*, there is the same necessity of having recourse to an infinite wisdom and goodness, that never *began* to be, and that is as different as to its *manner* of existence, from all other wisdom and goodness, that have a beginning,

ginning, as the *existence* of God is *different* from the existence of the creatures.

* But if it be necessary to hold, that there is an infinite wisdom and goodness that *never began* to be, then it is as necessary to affirm, that such wisdom and goodness can no more be *founded* upon the *relations* of things, than the *unbeginning existence* of God can be *founded* upon the existence of things. And to seek for any *reasons* of a wisdom and goodness that was always in the *same infinite* state, is like seeking the cause of that which can have no cause, or asking *what* it is that *contains* infinity.

* When therefore this writer saith, *Infinite wisdom can have no commands, but what are founded on the unalterable reason of things* ;† he might as justly have said, an *infinite Creator* can have no power of creating, but what is founded on the *unalterable nature* of creatures.

* For the *reason* of things, is just as unalterable, as the *nature* of creatures. And if the reasons and relations of things are nothing else but their *manner* of existence, or the *state* of their nature, certainly the relations of things must have the same *beginning*, and the same *alterable* or unalterable nature, as the things from whence they flow. Unless it can be said, that a thing may exist in *such a manner*, though it does not exist at all.

When

† Page 247.

When therefore he says again, *That the will of God is always determined by the nature and reason of things* ;† It is the same as if he had said, the *omnipotence* of God is always determined by the *nature* of *causes* and *effects*. For as all causes and effects are what they are, and *owe* their *nature* to the omnipotence of God, so the relations of things are what they are, and owe their nature to the wisdom and will of God.

Nor does this dependance of the relations of things on the will of God, destroy the nature of relations, or make them doubtful, any more than the existence of things depending on the *power* of God, destroys the certainty of their existence, or renders it doubtful. For as God cannot make things to exist, and not to exist at the same time, though their existence depends upon his power, so neither can he make things to have such relations, and yet not to have such relations at the same time, though their relations depend upon his will.

So that the ascribing the relations of things to the will of God, brings no uncertainty to those duties of life, which flow from such relations, but leaves the state of nature with all its relations, and the duties which flow from them, in the greatest certainty, so long as nature itself is continued; and when that either *ceases entirely*, or is only *altered*, it is not to be wondered at, if all its relations cease, or are altered with it.

Our

† Page 65.

Our author says, *Dare any one say, that God's laws are not founded on the eternal reason of things?†*

*I dare say it with the same assurance, as that his *existence* is not founded on the *eternal existence* of things. And that it is the same extravagance to say, that God's laws are founded on the *eternal reasons* of things, as to say, that his *power* is founded on the *eternal capacities* of things. For the *capacities* of things have just the same *solidity* and *eternity*, as the relations of things have, and are just such *independent realities* as they are: and are just the same *proper materials* to found the omnipotence of God upon, as the relations of things are, to found his infinite wisdom upon.

And as we can say, that the *omnipotence* of God in preserving and supporting the creation, will certainly act *suitably* to itself, and *consistent* with that omnipotence which first made things be what they are, and put nature into such a state as it is in; so we can say, that the *infinite wisdom* of God in giving laws to the world, will act *suitably* to itself, and *consistent* with that wisdom which at first made the nature and relations of the rational world be what they are.

But then as the *omnipotence* of God, though it acts suitably to the state of the creation, and the nature of causes and effects, which it first ordained, yet cannot be said to be founded upon the nature of causes and effects, because neither causes nor effects have *any nature*, but what they owe to

† Page 125.

omnipotence; so the infinite wisdom of God, though in giving laws to the world, it acts *suitably* to the natures and relations of rational beings, yet cannot be said to be *founded* upon such relations, because such relations are the *effects* of the divine wisdom, and owe their existence to it.

And the *reason* or *relations* of things shew God's *antecedent* wisdom, and are effects of it, just as the nature of *causes* and *effects* shew his *antecedent* power, and are the effects of it. And as he is infinitely powerful, but not from the nature of causes and effects; so he is infinitely wise, but not from the *reason* and *nature* of things.

Again; if God is *infinite* wisdom, then his wisdom cannot be founded on the relations of things, unless things *finite*, and relations that began to be, can be the foundation of that wisdom which is infinite, and could not begin to be.

Therefore to ask, *what* it is founded upon, when it can have no foundation upon *any thing*, is asking, what an *independent* being is dependent upon, or *how* that began, which could have no beginning?

And to ask the reason or foundation of *any one* of the divine attributes, is the same as asking the reason or foundation of them all. And to seek for the reason or foundation of all the divine attributes, is seeking for the cause of God's existence.

And as we do not come to God's existence, till we come to the *end* of *causes*, so nothing that is divine, can be attributed to any cause.

Nor

Nor is it any more a contradiction to say, there is something whose nature is without any cause or foundation of its existence, than to say, something exists without ever *beginning* to exist. For as nothing can have a beginning, but as it proceeds from some cause; so that which can have no beginning, can have no cause. If therefore the divine wisdom ever *began* to be *infinite*, and we could know when that beginning was, we should have some pretence to search for that, upon which its infinity was *founded*; but if it never could begin to be, then to seek for its reason, or foundation, is seeking for its beginning.

This writer affirms, that God's wisdom and goodness must be founded on the nature and reason of things, otherwise it could not be proved, that God was not an *arbitrary being*.

* Now to seek for reasons to prove that God is not an arbitrary being, that is, a being of the *highest freedom* and *independency*, that does every thing according to his *own will* and *pleasure*, is as vain, as to seek for reasons to prove, that *all things are not* the effect of his *will*. For if every thing besides God, received its existence from him; if every thing that exists, is the effect of his will, and he can do nothing, but because he wills the doing it, must he not be free and arbitrary in as *high a manner*, as he is powerful?

This *writer* says, *It is not in our power to love the deity, whilst we consider him to be an arbitrary being, acting out of humour and caprice.*†

But

† Page 31.

But if God's *will* is as *essentially* opposite to *humour* and *caprice*, as his omnipotence is to *weakness and inability*; then it is as absurd to suppose, that God must act according to humour and caprice, because he acts according to his own will, as to suppose that he must act with inability, because he acts by his omnipotence.

And if the will of God, *as such*, is in the highest state of perfection, then we have the *highest reason* to love and adore God, because he is arbitrary, and acts according to his *own all-perfect will*. And if it be asked, what it is that makes the will of God *all-perfect*, it may as well be asked, what it is that makes him omnipotent, or makes him to exist. For, as we have not found out a God, till we have found a being that has no *cause*; so we have not found the *will* of God, till we have found a *will*, that has no *mover*, or *director*, or *cause* of its perfection. For that *will* which never began to be, can no more be any thing, but what it is in itself, than it can begin to be.

That which makes people imagine, that *will alone* is not so adorable, is because they consider it as a blind imperfect faculty that wants to be directed. But what has such a will as this to do with the *will* of God?

For if the will of God is as *perfect* a *will*, as his omniscience is a *perfect knowledge*, then we are as sure, that the will of God cannot want any direction, or *will* any thing amiss, as we are, that his

his omniscience cannot need any information, or fall into any mistake. And if the *will* of God wanted any direction or government, it is impossible it should have it; for having no superior, it could only be so governed, because it *willed* it, and therefore must be always under its own government.

All the perfection therefore that can be ascribed to God, must be ascribed to his *will*, not as if it was the production of his will, (for nothing in God is produced) but as eternally inherent in it.

And as God's will has thus all the perfection of the divine nature, and has no rule, or reason, or motive to any goodness, that comes from it, but its own *nature* and *state* in God: so this great will is the only law of all creatures, and they are all to obey and conform to it, for this reason, because it is the will of God.

* Nothing has a *moral* reason, or fitness to be done, but because it is the will of God that it should be done.

* It may be asked, Is there then no *reason* or *nature* of things? Yes; as certainly as there are things. But the nature and reason of things, considered *independently* of the divine will, have no more *obligation* in them, than a *divine worship* considered independently of, and without any regard to the *existence* of God. For the *will* of God is as absolutely necessary to found all *moral obligation* upon, as the existence of God is necessary to be the foundation of religious worship. And
the

the fitness of moral obligations, without the *will* of God, is only like the fitness of *religious* worship without the *existence* of God.

And it is as just to say, that he destroys the *reason* of religion, who founds it upon the nature and existence of God, as to say, he saps the foundation of moral obligations, who founds them upon the will of God. And as religion cannot be solidly defended, but by shewing its connexion with, and dependence upon God's existence; so neither can moral obligations be asserted with reason, but by shewing them to be the will of God.

It may again be asked, Can God make that fit in itself, which is in *itself absolutely* unfit to be done?

This question consists of improper terms. For God's will no more makes actions to be fit *in themselves*, than it makes *things* to exist *in, or of themselves*. No things, nor any actions have any *absolute* fitness, of and in *themselves*.

A *gift*, a *blow*, the making a *wound*, or *shedding* of *blood*, considered in themselves, have no *absolute* fitness, but are fit or unfit according to a variety of accidental circumstances.

When therefore God by his will makes any thing fit to be done, he does not make the thing fit in *itself*, which is just in the *same state* considered in *itself*, that it was before, but it becomes fit for the person to do it, because he can only be happy, or do that which is fit for him to do, by doing the will of God.

For inſtance, the *bare eating* a fruit, conſidered in *itſelf*, is neither fit nor unfit. If a fruit is appointed by God for our food, then it is as fit to eat it, as to preſerve our lives. If a fruit is poiſonous, then it is as unfit to eat it, as to commit ſelf-murder. If eating of a fruit is prohibited by God, then it is as unfit as to eat our own damnation.

But in none of theſe inſtances is the eating or not eating, conſidered in *itſelf fit* or *unfit*: but has all its fitneſs, or unfitneſs, from ſuch circumſtances, as are entirely owing to the will of God.

Suppoſing therefore God to require a perſon to do ſomething, which according to his preſent circumſtances, *without* that command, he ought not to do, God does not make that which is *abſolutely* unfit in *itſelf*, fit to be done: but only adds *new circumſtances* to an action, that is neither fit, nor unfit, moral, nor immoral in *itſelf*, but becauſe of its circumſtances.

Again, it is objected, *If there is nothing right or wrong, good or bad, antecedently and independently of the will of God, there can then be no reaſon, why God ſhould will, or command one thing, rather than another.*

It is anſwered, *firſt*, That all goodneſs, and all poſſible perfection, is as *eternal* as God, and as eſſential to him as his exiſtence. And to ſay, that they are either *antecedent* or *conſequent*, *dependent* or *independent* of his will, would be equally abſurd. To aſk therefore, whether there is
not

not something right and wrong, antecedent to the will of God, is as abfurd, as to afk for fome antecedent caufe of his exiftence. And to afk, how God can be good if there is not fomething good independently of him, is afking how he can be infinite, if there be not fomething infinite independently of him. And to feek for any other *fource* or *reafon* of the divine goodnefs, befides the divine nature, is like feeking for fome external caufe and help of the divine omnipotence.

The goodnefs and wifdom, therefore, by which God is wife and good, and to which all his works of wifdom and goodnefs are owing, are neither *antecedent*, nor *confequent* to his will.

Secondly, Nothing is more certain, than that all *moral obligations* and *duties* of creatures towards one another, *began* with the exiftence of moral creatures. This is as certain, as that all corporeal qualities and effects, *began* with the exiftence of bodies.

As therefore nothing has the nature of a caufe or effect, nothing has any quality of any kind in bodies, but what is entirely owing to matter fo created and conftituted by the *will* of God; fo no actions have any *moral qualities*, but what are wholly owing to that ftate and nature in which they are created by the will of God.

* Moral obligations therefore of creatures have the fame *origin*, and the *fame reafon*, that natural qualities and effects have in the corporeal world, *viz.* the fole will of God. And as in a different

different state of matter, bodies would have had different qualities and effects; so in a different state of rational beings, there would be different moral obligations, and nothing could be right or good in their behaviour, but what began then to be right and good, because they then began to exist in such a state and condition of life. And as their state and condition could have no other cause or reason of its existence, but the sole will of God, so the cause and reason of right and wrong in such a state, must be equally owing to the will of God.

The pretended *absolute independent fitnesses,* or *unfitnesses* of actions therefore *in themselves,* are vain *abstractions,* and philosophical *jargon,* serving no ends of morality, but only helping people to wrangle and dispute away that sincere obedience to God, which is their only happiness. But to make these imaginary *absolute fitnesses* the *common law* both of God and man, is still more extravagant. For if the *circumstances* of actions give them their *moral nature,* surely God must first be in our circmstances, before that which is a law to us, can be the same law to him.

And if a father may require that of a son, which his son, because of his *different state,* cannot require of his brother; surely that which God may require of us, may be as different from that which a father may require of a son, as God is different from a father.

Again, if God is as much under a law as we are, then he is as much under authority;
for

for law can no more be without authority, than without a law-giver. And if God and we are under the *fame law*, we muft be under the *fame authority*.

* But as God cannot be under any law in common with us his creatures, any more than he can be of the fame rank or order with any us; fo neither can he be under any law at all, any more than he can be under any authority at all.

And though God is not to be looked upon as an *arbitrary being*, in the fenfe of this author, who will not diftinguifh arbitrary from *humour* and *caprice*; yet in a true fenfe of the word, when applied to God, he muft be affirmed to be an arbitrary being, that acts only from himfelf, from his *own will*, and according to his *own pleafure*.

And we have no more reafon to be afraid to be left to a God without a law, or to be left to his will and pleafure, than to be left under the protection and care of a being, that is all love, and mercy, and goodnefs. For as the exiftence of God, as fuch, necefiarily implies the exiftence of all perfection; fo the will of God, as fuch, necefiarily implies the *willing* every thing, that *all perfection* can will.

And as the exiftence of God, becaufe it contains all perfection, cannot for that reafon have any external caufe; fo the will of God, becaufe it is *all perfection*, cannot, for that reafon, have any external *rule* or *direction*. But his own will is wifdom, and his wifdom is his will. His goodness is arbitrary, and his arbitrariness is goodness.

But this writer does not only thus bring God into this state of law and obligation with us, but makes farther advances in the same kind of errors.

Hence, says he, *we may contemplate the great dignity of our rational nature, since our reason for* kind, *tho' not for degree, is of the* same nature *with* that of God's.†

Here you see *our reason*, that is, our *faculty* of reasoning, (for reason cannot be called *ours* in any other respect,) has no other difference from reason as it is in God, but that of degree. But what greater absurdity can a man fall into, than to suppose, that a being whose existence had a beginning but a few years ago, differs only in a degree from that which could not possibly have a beginning; or that a *dependent* and *independent* being, should not be different in *kind*, but *only* in degree?

For to say, that the faculties of a dependent and independent being, may be of the same kind, is as flat a contradiction, as to say, the same kind of thing may be dependent, and independent.

Reason belongs to God and man, just as *power, existence, life,* and *happiness*, belong to God and man; and he that can, from happiness being common to God and man, prove our happiness to

† Page 24.

to be of the *same kind* and nature with God's, may also prove reason in God and man to be of the same kind.

This writer indeed says, *Our happiness is limited*, because *our reason is so*; and that God has *unlimited happiness*, because *he alone has unlimited reason*.†

But if that which is *necessarily limited*, is different from that which is *necessarily unlimited*, then we have proof enough from this very argument, that a reason *necessarily* limited cannot be of the *same kind* with that reason, which is *necessarily* unlimited. Unless it can be said, that limited and unlimited, finite and infinite, beginning and unbeginning, have no contrariety in *kind*, but only differ, as a *short* line differs from a *long* one.

* The truth of the matter is this; reason is in God and man, as power is in God and man. And as the divine power has some degree of likeness to human power, yet with an *infinite* difference from it: so that perfection which we call *reason* in God, has some degree of likeness to reason as it is in man, yet is *infinitely* and beyond all conception different from it.

* And as our enjoyment of power is so limited, so imperfect, so superficial, as to be scarce sufficient to tell us, what power is, much less what omnipotence is; so our share of reason is so small, and we enjoy it in so imperfect a manner,

† Page 24.

ner, that we can scarce think or talk intelligibly of it, or so much as define our own faculties of reasoning.

CHAP. II.

Shewing from the relation *between God and man, that human reason cannot be a competent judge of the* fitness *and* reasonableness *of God's proceedings with mankind, either as to the* time, *or* matter, *or* manner *of an external revelation.*

AS our author has laid it down for an undeniable rule of God's actions, that he must, if he be a wise and good being, act according to the relation he stands in towards his creatures; I proceed upon this principle to prove the incapacity of *human reason*, to judge *truly* of God's proceedings in regard to divine revelation.

For if the fitness of actions *results from the nature and relations* of beings, then the *fitness* of God's actions, as he is an *omniscient Creator* and *Governor*, to whom every thing is *eternally foreknown*, over beings endued with *our freedom of will*, must be to us incomprehensible.

* We are not so much as capable of comprehending by our reason, the *possibility* of this relation, or how the fore-knowledge of God can consist with the free agency of creatures. We know

know that God fore-knows all things, with the same certainty as we know there is a God. And if *self-confcioufnefs* is an infallible proof of our own exiftence, it proves with the fame certainty the freedom of our will. And hence it is, that we have a full affurance of the confiftency of God's fore-knowledge with freedom of will.

* Now this *incomprehenfible* relation between an *eternally fore-knowing Creator and Governor*, and his free creatures, is the *relation* from whence arifes the fitnefs of God's providence over us. But if the *relation* itfelf is incomprehenfible, then thofe actions that have their fitnefs from it, muft furely be incomprehenfible. Nothing can be fit for God to do, either in *creation* or *providence*, but what has its fitnefs founded in his *fore-knowledge* of every thing that would follow, from *every kind* of *creation*, and *every manner* of providence: but if nothing can be fit, but becaufe it is according to *this fore-knowledge* of *every thing* that would follow from *every kind* of creation, and *every manner* of providence; then we have the utmoft certainty, that the fitnefs of God's actions as a *fore-knowing Creator*, and *Governor* of free agents, muft be founded upon *reafons* that we cannot poffibly know any thing of.

* And a child that has but juft learned to fpeak, is as well qualified to ftate the fitnefs of the laws of matter and motion by which the whole

whole vegetable world is preserved, as the wisest of men is qualified to comprehend, or state the fitness of the methods, which a *fore-knowing Providence* observes over free agents. For every reason on which the fitness of such a providence is founded, is not only *unknown* to us, but by a necessity of nature *impossible* to be known by us.

For if the *fitness* of God's acting in this, or that manner, is founded in his fore-knowledge of every thing that would *happen*, from every *possible way* of acting, then it is impossible for us to know the reasons, on which the fitness of his actions is founded, as it is impossible for us to be omniscient.

Who can tell what *different kinds* of rational creatures, distinguished by variety of natures, and faculties, it is fit and reasonable for God to create, because he eternally foresaw what would be the *effect* of such different creations? Who can explain the *fitness* of that vast *variety* there is amongst rational creatures of the *same species*, or shew that all their different faculties ought to be as they are? And yet the *fitness* of this providence has its *certain reason* in the divine fore-knowledge, and it could not be fit, but because of it.

Who can tell what *degree* of reason rational creatures ought to enjoy, or what degrees of *new* and *revealed* knowledge it is fit and reasonable for God to give, or not give them, because

cause they seem, or seem not to themselves to want it, are disposed, or not disposed to receive it? For as mankind cannot tell why it was fit and reasonable for God to create them of such a *kind*, and *degree*, as they are of; so neither can they tell how God ought, or ought not to add to their natural knowledge, and make them as *differently accountable* for the use of revealed rules of life, as for the use of their natural faculties.

And as the reason why God created them of *such* a *kind*, and with *such faculties*, was because of his own fore-knowledge of the *effects* of such a creation; so if ever he does reveal to them any *supernatural* knowledge, both the doing it, the *time*, the *matter*, and *manner* of it, must have their fitness in his own *eternal fore-knowledge* of the effects of such a revelation.

The reasons therefore on which the fitness of this or that revelation depends, *why* or *when*, of *what matter*, in *what manner*, and to whom it is to be made, must, from the nature and reason of things, be as unsearchable by us, as the reasons of *this* or *that* creation of rational beings, at such a *time*, of such a *kind*, in such a *manner*, in such a *state*.

This may help us to an easy solution of the unreasonable questions, which this writer puts in this manner.

" If

"If the design of God in communicating any thing of himself to men was their happiness, would not that design have obliged him, who at all times alike desires their happiness, to have at all times alike communicated it to them? If God always acts for the good of his creatures, what reason can be assigned, why he should not from the beginning have discovered such things as make for their good, but defer the doing it till the time of *Tiberius*; since the sooner this was done, the greater would his goodness appear?" †

And again "How is it consistent with the notion of God's being universally benevolent, not to have revealed it to all his children, when all had equal need of it? Was it not as easy for him to have communicated it to all nations, as to any one nation or person? Or in all languages, as in one?" ‡

Now all this is fully answered, by our author's own great and fundamental principle.

"For if the relations between things and persons, and the things resulting from thence, be the sole rule of God's actions," § as he expressly affirms; then the *sole rule* or reason of God's revealing any thing to any men, at any time, must have its *fitness resulting* from the divine fore-knowledge of the effects of *such* a revelation, at *such* a time, and to *such* persons. If God

† Page 393. ‡ Page 196. § Page 28.

God does not act thus, he does not act according to the relation betwixt a *fore-knowing Creator*, and his free creatures. But if he does act according to a *fitness resulting* from this *relation*, and makes, or does not make revelations, according to his own fore-knowledge of the fitness of times and persons for them; then to ask how a God, always equally good, can make a revelation at any time, and not make the *same* at *all* times, is as absurd as to ask, how a God, always equally good, can reveal that at one time, because it is a *proper* time for it, and not reveal it at every other time, tho' improper for it.

* God's goodness, directed by his own fore-knowledge of the *fitness* of times, and of the *state* and *actions* of free agents, deferred a certain revelation to the time of *Tiberius*, because he *fore-saw* it would then be an act of the *greatest* goodness, and have its *best effects* upon the world: to ask therefore, *what reason can be assigned*, why so good a revelation was not *sooner*, or even from the *beginning* made to the world, is asking, why God should act, according to his *own fore-knowledge* of the *state* and *actions* of *free agents*, and order all things, according to a fitness resulting from such a fore-knowledge?

These questions suppose, that if God shewed his *goodness* to mankind by a revelation at such time, he must be *wanting* in goodness before that time, because he did not make it *sooner*;
whereas

whereas if his deferring it till *such* a time, was owing to his *fore-knowledge* of the actions and state of free agents, and because it would then have its *best effects*, then God is proved to be equally good before he made it, for this very reason, because he did not make it before its *proper* time: and he had been wanting in goodness, if he had not *deferred* it till that time.

Now this appealing to God's fore-knowledge of the state and actions of *free agents*, as the cause of all that is particular in the *time* and *manner* of any revelation, and deducing its fitness from thence, cannot be said to be *begging the question*, but is resolving it directly according to the *rule*, which this writer lays down for God to act by: that " the relations between things and persons, *and* the fitness resulting from thence, must be the sole rule of God's actions."

But if this is the *sole rule*, then God in giving any revelation, must act as the *relation* betwixt a *fore-knowing* Creator and his *free* creatures requires; and his actions must have their *fitness resulting* from his fore-knowledge of the *state* and *actions* of free agents. And if this is God's sole rule, then to ask why *this* or *that* revelation *only* at *such* a time, is to ask why God *only* does that which is *fit* for him to do? And to ask, why not the same revelation at any other time, is asking why God does not do that, which it is *not fit* for him to do?

This writer asks, " How it is consistent with the

the notion of God's being univerfally benevolent, not to have revealed it to all his children, who had equal need of it?" But if they had *equal need* of it, yet if they were not *equally fit* for it, but prepared only to have their *guilt* increafed by it, and fo be expofed to a greater damnation; then God's goodnefs to them is manifeft, by withholding fuch information from them, and referving it for thofe that would be made happier by it.

Judas, Pontius Pilate, and the *Jews* that called for our Saviour's crucifixion, had *equal need* of a Saviour with thofe that believed in him. *Chorazin* and *Bethfaida* wanted the light of the gofpel as much as thofe that received it. And if the reft of the world had been, at that time, as much indifpofed for the light of the gofpel, as they were, God's goodnefs had been greater to that age, if he had referved the light of the gofpel till a better age had fucceeded.

So that this argument, founded on the *equal need* of all, or former ages, has no force, unlefs it could be fhewn, that the fame revelation made to any of thefe former ages, would have produced all thofe good effects, which God forefaw would follow, from its being referved for fuch a *particular time* and *ftate* of things and perfons.

He afks again, " Was it not as eafy for God to have communicated it to all nations, as to any one nation or perfon? Or in all languages, as in any one?" This argument is built upon this fuppofition, that God does things becaufe they are *eafy*, or forbears things becaufe they are *difficult* to be performed. For it can be no argument, that God ought to have revealed fuch things to *all* nations or perfons, becaufe it was as *eafy* to him, as to do it to *any one* nation or perfon; unlefs it be fuppofed, that the *eafinefs* of a thing is a reafon why God does it, and the difficulty of a thing a reafon why he does not do it. But if this fuppofition be very abfurd, then the argument founded upon it muft be liable to the fame charge.

But if God does things, not becaufe they are eafy, but becaufe they are infinitely good and fit to be done, then the reafon why God has afforded different revelations, to different ages and perfons, is this, that his *manner* of revealing every thing, might be worthy of his own *foreknowledge* of the effects of it, and that every thing that is particular in the *time* or *manner* of any revelation, might have its *fitnefs refulting* from the *relation* betwixt a good God and his creatures, whofe *changing* ftate, *different* conduct, tempers and actions, are all eternally fore-known by him.

Again, it is objected, that a divine revelation muft either be the effect of *juftice*, or elfe of *mercy* and *free goodnefs*; but in either of thefe cafes it ought to be *univerfal*; for juftice muft be done to all. But if it is the effect of *mercy* and *free goodnefs*,

nefs, this writer asks, "How a being can be denominated merciful and good, who is so only to a few, but cruel and unmerciful to the rest? †

It is answered, That there is neither *justice* in God without mercy, nor *mercy* without justice; and to ascribe a *revelation* to either of them separately, in *contradistinction* to the other, has no more reason in it, than to ascribe the *creation* separately either to the *wisdom* or *power* of God, in contradistinction to the other.

Secondly, A divine revelation is not owing barely to the *justice* or *free goodness* of God, but to the goodness, mercy, and justice of God, governed and *directed* by his eternal fore-knowledge of all the effects of every revelation, at any, or all times.

* God ordains a revelation in this, or that manner, time, and place; not because it is a *justice* that he cannot refuse, not because it is a matter of *favour* or *free goodness*, and therefore may be given in any manner at pleasure; but because he has the whole *duration* of human things, the whole *race* of mankind, the whole *order* of human changes and events, the whole *combination* of all causes and effects of human tempers, all the actions of free agents, and all the consequences of every revelation, plainly in his sight; and according to this eternal fore-knowledge, every revelation receives every thing that is *particular* in it, either as to *time, matter, manner,* or *place*.

All

† Page 401.

* All complaints therefore about that which is *particular*, or *seemingly* partial in the time and manner of any revelation, are very unjustifiable; and shew, that we are discontent at God's proceedings, because he acts like himself, does what is best and fittest to be done, and governs the world, not according to our weak imaginations, but according to his own infinite perfections.

* We will not allow a providence to be *right*, unless we can comprehend the reasonableness of all its steps; and yet it could not possibly be right, unless its proceedings were as much *above* our comprehension, as our wisdom is *below* that which is infinite.

For if the *relations* of *things*, and *persons*, and the fitness resulting from thence, be the *rule* of God's actions; then all the revelations that come from God, must have their fitness resulting from the relation his fore-knowledge bears to the *various states*, *conditions*, *tempers*, and *actions* of free agents, and the various effects of every manner of revelation.

But if God cannot act worthy of himself in any revelation, unless he acts according to a fitness resulting from this relation; then he must act by a *rule* that lies out of our sight, and his providence in this particular must be incomprehensible to us; for this very reason, because it has that very fitness, wisdom and goodness in it, that it ought to have.

CHAP.

CHAP. III.

Shewing how far human reason is able to judge of the reasonableness, truth, and certainty of divine revelation.

THE former chapter has plainly shewn, from the state and relation between God and man, that we must be strangers to the true reasons on which a divine revelation is founded, both as to its *time, matter,* and *manner*.

But it is here objected, " If God by reason of his own perfections must be thus mysterious and incomprehensible, both in the matter and manner of divine revelation; how can we know what revelations we are to receive as divine? How can we be blamed for rejecting this, or receiving that, if we cannot comprehend the reasons on which every revelation is founded, both as to its matter and manner?"

If a man may be blameable, or commendable, for his right or wrong belief of a God; then a man may be accountable for a right or wrong belief of such matters, as are in their own nature too mysterious for his comprehension. And tho' a man knows the reasons of a divine revelation, either as to its *matter* or *manner,* as imperfectly as he knows the divine nature; yet he may be as liable to account for believing *false revelations,* as for *idolatry*; and as full of guilt

for

for rejecting a *true revelation*, as for denying the only *true God*.

Secondly, Tho' we are insufficient for comprehending the *reasons*, on which the particular *matter* or *manner* of any divine revelation is founded; yet we may be so far sufficient judges, of the reasons for *receiving* or not *receiving* a revelation as divine, as to make our conduct therein justly accountable to God.

For if God can shew a revelation to proceed from him, by the *same undeniable* evidence, as he shews the *creation* to be his work; if he can make himself as visible in a *particular extraordinary* manner, as he is by his *general* and *ordinary* providence; then, tho' we are as unqualified to judge of the mysteries of a *revelation*, as we are to judge of the mysteries in *creation* and *providence*; yet we may be as fully obliged to receive a revelation, as to acknowledge the creation to be the work of God; and as highly criminal for disbelieving it, as for denying a general providence.

Adam, *Noah*, *Abraham*, and *Moses*, were very incompetent judges, of the reasons on which the particular revelations made to them were founded; but this did not hinder their sufficient assurance, that such revelations came from God, because they were proved to come from God in the same manner, as the creation is proved to be the work of God.

And as *Adam* and *Noah* must see every thing wonderful, mysterious, and above their comprehensions, prehenfions, in thofe new worlds into which they were introduced by God; fo they could no more expect, that he fhould require nothing of them, but what they would enjoin themfelves, than that their own *frame*, the *nature* of the creation, the *providence* of God, or the *ſtate* of human life, fhould be exactly as they would have it.

And if their pofterity will let no *meſſages* from heaven, no *prophefies* and *miracles* perfuade them, that God can call them to any duties, but fuch as they muſt enjoin themfelves; or to the belief of any doctrines, but fuch as their own minds can fuggeſt; nor to any methods of changing their prefent ſtate of weaknefs and diforder for a happy immortality, but fuch as fuit their own *taſte*, *temper*, and way of reafoning; it is becaufe they are grown fenfelefs of the myſteries of creation and providence with which they are furrounded, and forget the awful prerogative of infinite wifdom, over the weakeſt, loweſt rank of intelligent beings.

* And as we can only know what is worthy of God in creation, by knowing what he has created; fo we can no other way know what is worthy of God to be revealed, but by a revelation. And he that pretends independently of any relation, to fhew *how*, and in what manner God ought to make a revelation worthy of himfelf, is as great a *viſionary*, as he that fhould pretend independently of the creation, or without learning

ing any thing from it, to shew how God ought to have proceeded in it, to make it worthy of himself. For as God alone, knows how to create worthy of himself, and nothing can possibly be proved to be worthy to be created by him, but because he has already created it; so God alone knows what is worthy of himself in a revelation, and nothing can possibly be proved worthy to be revealed by him, but because he has already revealed it.

Hence we may see how little this *writer* is governed by the *reason* and *nature* of things, who proceeds upon this as an undeniable principle, that we could not know a revelation to be divine, unless we knew, antecedently to revelation, what God could teach or require of us by it. Thus, says he, "Were we not capable by our own reason of knowing what the divine goodness could command, or forbid his creatures, antecedently to any external revelation, we could not distinguish the true instituted religion, from the *many* false ones."†

Just as wild and visionary, as if it was said, Were we not capable by our reason of knowing what kind or orders of beings God *ought* to create *independently* of any thing we learn from the creation, we could never prove this or that creation to proceed from him. Did we not, antecedently to facts and experience, know by our own reason what ought to be the method and manner

† Page 66.

ner of divine providence, we could never prove that the providence which governs nations and persons is a divine providence.

Again, He proceeds to shew, that a revelation from God cannot contain any thing, but what human reason can prove from the nature of things; because if God could require any thing more of us, than what our own reason could thus prove, he must require *without* reason, and then there is an end of all religion.

Now this argument proceeds thus; If God does not act according to the *measure* of *human* reason, he cannot act according to *reason itself.* If he requires any more of us, than what we *think* the nature of things requires of us, then he cannot act according to the nature of things. If his wisdom is in any matters of revelation *greater* than ours; if it is not in every thing he reveals *measurable* by ours, it cannot be wisdom at all, much less can it be infinite wisdom.

That is, if he is *more powerful* than we are, he cannot be *omnipotent*; if he is *more perfect* than we are, he cannot be *all perfection*; if he acts upon *greater*, or *higher*, or *more* reasonable motives than we do, he cannot be a *reasonable* being.

Now if these absurdities are not plain and manifest to every common understanding, it is in vain to dispute about any thing; but if they are, then it is as plain, this writer's great argument against Christianity, and first principle of his *rational religion,*

ligion, is in the fame ftate of undeniable abfurdity.

Thus fays he, "Natural religion takes in all thofe duties which flow from the reafon and the nature of things."† That is, natural religion takes in all thofe things that bare human reafon can difcover from the nature of things. This is granted; but what follows? Why, fays he, " Confequently, was there an inftituted religion which differs from that of nature, its precepts muft be arbitrary, as not founded on the nature and reafon of things, but depending on mere will and pleafure, otherwife it would be the fame with natural religion."‡

Here you fee all the abfurdities juft mentioned, are exprefly contained in this argument, God is all *humour* and *caprice*, if his revelation is not ftrictly, in every refpect, the fame with human reafon. That is, he is *without* wifdom, *without* reafon, if his wifdom and reafon exceed ours. He has *no reafon*, nor *wifdom*, if his reafon and wifdom are *infinite*.

Secondly, This argument, if it were allowed, leads directly to *atheifm*. For if a revelation cannot be divine, if it contains any thing myfterious, whofe fitnefs and neceffity cannot be explained by human reafon, then neither *creation* nor *providence* can be proved to be divine, for they are both of them more myfterious than the Chriftian revelation.

And

† Page 114. ‡ Page 16.

And if every thing is *arbitrary*, whose *fitness and experience* human reason cannot *prove* and *explain*, then surely an *invisible over-ruling providence* that orders all things in a manner, and for reasons, known only to itself; that subjects human life, and human affairs, to what changes it pleases; that confounds the best-laid designs, and makes great effects arise from folly and imprudence; that gives not the race to the swift, nor the battle to the strong; that brings good men into affliction, and makes the wicked prosperous; surely such a providence must be highly arbitrary.

And therefore if this argument is to be admitted, it leads directly to *atheism*, and brings us under a greater necessity of rejecting divine providence, on the account of its mysteries, than of rejecting a revelation that is mysterious in any of its doctrines. And if, God cannot be said to deal with us as rational agents, if he requires any thing of us, that our reason cannot prove to be necessary; surely he cannot be said to deal with us as rational agents, if he over-rules our persons and affairs, and disappoints our counsels, makes weakness prosperous, and wisdom unsuccessful, in a *secret* and *invisible* manner, and for reasons and ends that we have no means of knowing.

* There is nothing therefore half so mysterious in the Christian revelation, as there is in that *invisible* providence, which all must hold that believe

lieve a God. And tho' there is enough plain in providence, to excite the adoration of humble and pious minds, yet it has often been a rock of *atheism* to those, who make their own reason the measure of wisdom.

Again, Tho' the *creation* plainly declares the glory, and wisdom, and goodness of God; yet it has more mysteries in it, more things whose fitness, expedience, and reasonableness, human reason cannot comprehend, than are to be found in scripture.

If therefore he reasons right, who says, " If there may be some things in a true religion, whose fitness and expedience we cannot see, why not others: nay, why not the whole; since that would make God's laws all of a piece ? And if the having of these things is no proof of its falshood, how can any things fit and expedient (which no religion is without) be a proof of the truth of any one religion?"† *If, I say, this is the right reasoning, then it may be said,* " If there are things in the creation whose fitness we cannot see, why not others: nay, why not the whole; since that would make God's works of a piece? And if the being of such things as these in the creation, is not a proof of its not being divine, how can the fitness and expedience of any creation prove that it is the work of God?

Thus does this argument tend wholly to *atheism*, and concludes with the same force against

† First address to the inhabitants of London, Page 57.

against *creation* and *providence*, as it does against revelation.

Either therefore there is nothing in the work of the creation, whose fitness and expedience cannot be proved; nothing in God's providence over whole nations, and particular persons, whose fitness and expedience cannot be explained and justified by human reason, or else neither creation nor providence can be ascribed to God.

The credibility of an external divine revelation with regard to human reason, rests wholly upon *such external* evidence, as is a sufficient proof of the divine interposition. If there be no such external evidence possible; if God has no ways of acting so *peculiar* to himself, as to be a *sufficient* proof to human reason of his action; then no revelation can be sufficiently proved to be a divine, external revelation from God.

I appeal therefore to the miracles and prophecies on which Christianity is founded, as a sufficient proof, that it is a divine revelation. And shall here consider, what is objected against the sufficiency of this kind of proof.

1. It is objected, That miracles cannot prove a *false*, or *bad* doctrine, to be *true* and *good*; therefore miracles, *as such*, cannot prove the truth of any revelation.

But though miracles cannot prove falſe to be true, or bad to be good; yet they may prove, that we ought to receive ſuch doctrines, both as true and good, which we could not know to be true and good without ſuch miracles. Not becauſe the miracles have any influence upon the things revealed, but becauſe they are God's teſtimony to the truth of that which he reveals.

But our author brings a farther objection againſt this uſe of miracles.

"If, *ſays he*, evil beings can impreſs notions in mens minds as ſtrongly as good beings, and cauſe miracles to be done in confirmation of them; is there any way to know to which of the two, notions thus impreſſed are owing, but from their internal marks of wiſdom and goodneſs?"

This objection ſuppoſes, that no miracles, can be a ſufficient proof of the divinity of a revelation; becauſe we do not know the extent of that power, which evil ſpirits have, of doing miracles. But this objection is groundleſs. For, granting that we do not know the extent of that power which evil ſpirits may have; yet if we know *enough* of it to affirm, that the *creation* is not the work of evil ſpirits; if we can ſecurely appeal to the creation, as *a ſufficient proof* of God's action and opperation; then we are ſecure in appealing to miracles, as a ſufficient proof of a divine revelation.

For, if the creation muſt be allowed to be the

works

work of God, notwithstanding any *unknown degree* of power in evil spirits; if we can as certainly ascribe it to God, as if there were no *such* spirits; then miracles may be as full a proof of the interposition of God, as if there were no such spirits in being.

I do not ask, Whether the *same divine* perfection is necessary to foretel such things as are foretold in scripture, and work such miracles as are there related, as is necessary to *create?* I do not ask, Whether any power less than divine can do such things? I only ask, Whether there is any certainty, that the creation is the work of God? Whether we can be sure of the divine operation, from the existence of that creation? Or, Whether we are in *doubt* or *uncertainty* about it, because we do not know the *degree* of power, that may belong to evil spirits.

For if it can be affirmed, that the creation is the work of God, notwithstanding our uncertainty about the degree of power that may belong to evil spirits; then we have the same certainty, that the *prophecies* and *miracles* recorded in scripture, are to be ascribed to God, notwithstanding our uncertainty of the power of evil spirits.

For every reason for ascribing the creation to God, is the same reason for ascribing such miracles and prophecies to God; and every argument against the certainty of those miracles and prophecies coming from God, is the same argument against the certainty of the creation's being the work of God; for there cannot be more or less certainty in one case than in the other.

For, if evil spirits have so the creation in their hands, that by reason of their power over it, no *miracles* can prove the operation of God, then the operation of God cannot be proved from the creation itself.

For the creation cannot be proved to be the operation of God, unless it can be proved that God *still presides* over it.

And if *all that* which is extraordinary and miraculous may be accounted for, without the interposition of God; then nothing that is ordinary and common according to the course of nature, can be a proof of the action of God. For there can be no reason assigned, why that which is *ordinary* shall be ascribed to God, if all that is, or has been, or can be miraculous, may be ascribed to evil spirits.

Either therefore it must be said, that there are, or may be miracles, which cannot be the effects of evil spirits; or else nothing that is ordinary and common can be a proof of the operation of God. For if nothing miraculous can be an undeniable proof of God's action, nothing created can be a proof of it.

The matter therefore stands thus: There are, and may be miracles, that cannot be ascribed to evil spirits, without ascribing the creation to them; and which can no more be doubted to come from God, than we can doubt of his being the

the Creator of the world. There may be miracles therefore, which, are as full a proof of the *truth* of that which they atteſt, as the creation is of the *fitneſs* of that which is created.

And though the *matter* of a revelation is to be attended to, that we may fully underſtand it, and be rightly affected with it; yet the reaſon of our receiving it, muſt reſt upon that *external authority*, which ſhews it to be of God.

And the authority of miracles, ſufficiently plain and apparent, are of themſelves a full reaſon for receiving a revelation, which both as to its *matter* and *manner*, would not be approved by us without them.

The hiſtory of magical wonders, and extraordinary things done by evil ſpirits, is no objection againſt the ſufficiency of that proof, that ariſes from miracles. For the queſtion is not, whether nothing that is extraordinary can be done by evil ſpirits, but whether nothing that is miraculous can, be a proof of its being done by God. For theſe two caſes are very conſiſtent. It may be very poſſible for evil ſpirits, to do things extraordinary in *ſome circumſtances*, as were people enter into contracts with them, and reſign themſelves up to their power, and yet that miracle may in *other circumſtances*, be a ſufficient proof of their being done by God.

And as miracles are the higheſt and moſt undeniable evidence of the truth and divinity of any external revelation; ſo Chriſtianity ſtands fully diftinguifhed from all other religions, by the higheft and moft undeniable evidences; fince it has all the proof that the *higheft ftate* of miracles can give, and every other religion is without any fupport from them.

And though this writer, with a boldnefs worthy of himfelf, often puts all *traditional religion* upon a level; yet he might have fhewn himfelf as much a friend to truth as fobriety, by afferting, that all *arguments* are equally conclufive, all *tempers* equally virtuous, all *defigns* equally honeft, and all *hiftories* and *fables* equally fupported by evidences of fact.

To give you one inftance more of this writer's extravagant and inconfiftent notions.

He makes *reafon*, or *natural religion*, to be God's *internal revelation*, differing *only* from *external revelation in the manner of its being communicated*. He rejects *external revelation* as unworthy of God, becaufe it has not been fufficiently made known at *all times*, and in *all places*; yet he fets up an internal revelation, as worthy of God, which has never been made known to any *one man* of any *time* or *place* in the world. For what one man ever knew that *reafon* was God's *internal revelation*, to which nothing could be added by any external revelation?

It is a mighty complaint with our author againft Chriftianity, that fo much happinefs fhould be deferred till the time of *Tiberius*, and that it fhould be communicated to no greater a part of the world, than Chriftianity hath been. But
is

is not this a *judicious* complaint in the mouth of a pérson, that is setting up a religion, that has been communicated to no body but himself.

I know nothing that can be said for our author, in excuse of so much confusion and self-contradiction, unless it be the particular hardships of his *sect*. The *free-thinking few*, he says, *are forced into an outward compliance*; and that which *forces* a man into a state of hypocrisy, may force him into a great deal of confusion and self-contradiction.

To return: I have from a consideration of the state of man, and the several relations which God stands in towards his creatures, shewn that it is utterly impossible for human reason to be a competent judge of the fitness, or unfitness, of all that God may, or may not require of us. The two following chapters shall state the nature and perfection of reason, as it is a faculty, or principle of action in human nature.

CHAP. IV.

Of the state and nature of reason, as it is in man; and how its perfection in matters of religion is to be known.

THIS writer and others, who take to themselves the names of *free-thinkers*, make their court to the world, by pretending to vindicate the right that all men have, to judge and act according

cording to their own reason. Though, I think, the world has no more to thank them for on this account, than if they had pretended to assert the right that every man has, to see *only* with his *own eyes*, or to hear *only* with his *own ears*.

For their own reason always did, does, and ever will, govern rational creatures, in every thing they determine, either in speculation or practice. It is not a matter of *duty* for men to use their own reason, but of *necessity:* and it is as impossible to do otherwise, as for a being that cannot act but from choice, to act without choice.

Man is under the same necessity of acting from his own choice, that *matter* is of not acting at all; and a being, whose principle of action is reason and choice, can no more act without it, or contrary to it, than an extended being can be without extension.

All men therefore are equally reasonable in this respect, that they are, and must be, by a *necessity* of nature, equally directed and governed by their own reason and choice.

* The dispute therefore betwixt Christians and *unbelievers*, concerning reason, is not, whether men are to use their *own reason*, any more than whether they are to see with their *own eyes*; but whether every man's reason must needs guide him, by its *own light*, or must cease to guide him, as soon as it guides him by a light borrowed from revelation ? This is the true state of the question, not whether reason is to be followed, but when it

is

is *best* followed? Not whether it is to be our guide, but how it may be made our *safest guide?*

* The *free-thinkers*, therefore, rather appeal to the passions, than reason of the people, when they represent the clergy and Christianity as enemies to reason, and themselves as friends and advocates for the use of reason.

* For Christians oppose unbelievers, not because they *reason*, but because they reason *ill*. They receive revelation, not to suppress the natural power, but to give new and heavenly light to their reason; not to take away their right of judging for themselves, but to secure them from false judgments.

Christians therefore do not differ from unbelievers in the *constant use* of their reason, but in the *manner* of using it: as *virtuous* men differ from *rakes*, not in their desire of happiness, but in their manner of seeking it.

It appears from what has been said, that every man's own reason is his only principle of action, and that he must judge according to it, whether he receives, or rejects revelation.

Now although every man is to judge according to the light of his own reason, yet his reason has very little light that can be called its own. For, as we derive our nature from our parents, so that which we generally call *natural knowledge*, or the light of nature, is a knowledge and light that is made natural to us, by the same authority,

which

which makes a certain language, certain cuſtoms, and modes of behaviour, natural to us.

Nothing ſeems to be our own, but a bare capacity to be inſtructed, a nature fitted for any impreſſions; as liable to be made a *Hottentot*, by being born among Hottentots, as to be a *Chriſtian*, by being born among Chriſtians.

It is not my intention by this to ſignify, that there is not a good and evil, right and wrong founded in the nature of things: but only to ſhew, that we find out this right and wrong, not by any inward ſtrength, that our natural reaſon of itſelf affords, but by ſuch external means, as people are taught articulate language, or the rules of civil life.

Men do not prefer virtue to vice, from a philoſophical contemplation of the fitneſs of the one, and the unfitneſs of the other; but becauſe it is a judgment as early in their minds, as their knowledge of the words, virtue and vice.

And it can no more be reaſonably affirmed, that our knowledge of God and divine things, our opinions of the excellency of this, or that virtue, and of the immortality of our ſouls, are the effects of our natural light; than it can be reaſonably affirmed, that our living in ſociety, and our articulate language are owing to the light of nature.

For, as all mankind find themſelves in this ſtate before any reaſoning about it; as education, and human authority have taught us language,

and

and accuftomed us to the rules and manners of a focial life: fo education, and the fame authority, have planted in our minds, certain notions of God and divine things, and formed us to a belief of our foul's immortality, and the expectation of another life.

And mankind are no more left to find out a God, or the fitnefs of virtue, by their own reafon, than they are left by their own reafon, to find out who are their parents, to find out the fitnefs of fpeaking an articulate language.

Now if this is the ftate of reafon, as it is in man; if this is all the light that we have from our own nature, a bare capacity of receiving good or bad impreffions, right or wrong opinions and fentiments, according to the ftate of the world we fall into; then we are but poorly furnifhed, to affert the *abfolute perfection* of our own reafon.

If our light is little more than the opinions and cuftoms of thofe amongft whom we live, and it be fo hard for a man to arrive at a greater wifdom, than the common wifdom of the *country* which gave him birth and education; how unreafonably do we appeal to the perfection of our reafon, againft the *neceffity* and *advantage* of divine revelation?

* If we are nothing without the affiftance of men; if we are a kind of foolifh, helplefs animals, 'till education and experience have revealed to us the wifdom and knowledge of our fellow-creatures; fhall we think ourfelves too wife and full of of our own light, to be farther enlightened with a wisdom revealed to us by God himself?

This gentleman, speaking of education, saith, "Education is justly esteemed a second nature; and its force is so strong, that few can wholly shake off its prejudices, even in things unreasonable and unnatural."

All that I shall add to this account, is, that we are by the condition of human life, necessarily subjected to this *second nature*, and cannot avoid coming under its power.

And here let me ask this pleader for the sufficiency of the light of nature, how those that resign themselves up to the light of their *own nature*, shall know, whether it is their *first*, or their *second* nature that directs them?

Here are, it seems, *two natures*; they may be as different as good and evil; yet as they are both *natures*, both *internal light*, how shall a man know which he follows? He does not know which was first, or why he should call one first, and the other second; they are both internal, and without any thing to distinguish them. And as he is not to resist the motions of nature, or stifle its directions; so he must be as obedient to the directions of the second, as of the first nature, because he does not perceive their difference, nor has any means to distinguish their operations.

He therefore that asserts the light of nature to be a sufficient unerring guide in divine matters,

ters, ought either to shew, that our *second* nature is as *safe* a guide as the first; or that though it is nature, yet it has no *natural powers* over us.

For since every man is *necessitated* to take upon him a second nature, which he does not *know* to be a second, or *when* it began, or *how far* it has proceeded, or how *contrary* it is to his first nature; he that would prove the light of nature to be so perfect, that nothing can be added to it, is obliged to prove, that our second nature, which we receive by education, has the same degree of perfection. For so far as our second nature is different from the first, so far it has changed the first; and if we are to follow nature exclusive of revelation, we may take *revenge, self-murder, incontinence, sensuality, pride, self-conceit,* and a *contempt* of all things sacred, to be the true dictates of nature.

For it often happens to people, to be thus educated; so if education is a second nature, and nature is to be esteemed a *true* and *perfect* guide; a man thus educated, has all his vices made so many glorious laws of nature; and thro' the strength of his natural light, he condemns humility, self-denial, and devotion, as foolish bigotry.

This writer says, " Natural religion, *that is, the religion of nature,* is a perpetual standing rule for men of the meanest, as well as the highest

eſt capacities, and carries its own evidence with it, thoſe internal, inſeparable marks of truth.† *But if education is a* ſecond nature, *and, as this writer affirms,* has the force of a ſecond nature even in things unreaſonable and unnatural; *then this ſecond nature has not only its natural religion, which is alſo* a perpetual ſtanding rule for men of the meaneſt, as well as the higheſt capacities; which carries its own evidence with it, thoſe internal, inſeparable marks of truth; *but it may alſo have a natural religion, both* unreaſonable and unnatural; *ſince education has the force of nature even in things of this kind."*

Again: If education has this force of nature even in things unreaſonable and unnatural; if it is alſo abſolutely neceſſary for all men to come under the power of ſome ſecond nature; what can be more vain, than to pretend to ſtate the light, or rectitude of human nature, ſince it muſt be for the moſt part in every man, as the uncertainty, variety, happineſs or unhappineſs of education has rendered it?

And our author can no more tell, what man would be without education, or what nature would do for thoſe who had no foreign inſtruction, than he can tell what ſort of beings dwell in the moon. And yet he that does not know this, how can he know what the light of nature is in itſelf?

* Again

† Page 243.

* Again to declare the light of nature so perfect, as to be incapable of all improvement even by divine revelation, is no less an extravagance, than to declare the education of mankind to be perfect in the same degree.

* For if nature not only wants, but cannot possibly avoid education; if this necessary unavoidable education becomes another nature, undiscernible from the first; then nothing can possibly be affirmed of the perfection of the light of nature, but what must be affirmed in the same degree of the perfection of education. And he that affirms that mankind have had, at all times, and in all places of the world, the same sufficient, perfect light of nature, must affirm, that mankind have had, at all times, and in all places of the world, the same perfect, unerring education.

* When therefore it is just, for all people to abide by the absolute perfection of their education, the infallible light of their second nature, as the unerring standard, of all that is moral, religious, and divine; then it may be just to appeal to the natural light of all men, of all ages, and all places, as a sufficient teacher of all that ought, or ought not to be a matter of religion.

* For till it can be shewn, that men are not liable to a second nature from education; the state of nature must differ all over the world, and in every age of the world, just as the light, and advantages of education, have differed in the several parts, and ages of the world.

* In a word, the religious and moral light of our firſt nature, is juſt as great as the firſt ſtrength of infants; and the religious and moral light of our ſecond nature, is juſt as perfect as our education, and as much of our own growth, as the firſt language that we are taught to ſpeak.

May not therefore one juſtly wonder, what it is that could lead any people into an imagination of the abſolute perfection of human reaſon? There ſeems no more in the ſtate of mankind, to betray a man into this fancy, than to perſuade him, that the reaſon of infants is abſolutely perfect. For ſenſe and experience, are as full and ſtrong a proof againſt one, as againſt the other.

But it muſt be ſaid for theſe writers, that they decline all arguments from facts and experience, to give a better account of human nature; but with the ſame juſtice, as if a man was to lay aſide the authority of hiſtory, to give you a truer account of the life of *Alexander*.

Their objection againſt revelation is founded upon the pretended ſufficiency and perfection of human reaſon, to teach all men all that is wiſe, and holy, and divine, in religion. But how do they prove this perfection of human reaſon? Do they appeal to mankind as proofs of it? Do they produce any body of men in this or any other age, that without any aſſiſtance from revelation, have

attained

attained to this perfection of religious knowledge? This is not so much as pretended to; the history of such men is entirely wanting. And yet the want of such a fact as this, has even the force of demonstration against this pretended sufficiency of natural reason.

Because it is a matter not capable of any other kind of proof, but must be admitted as certainly true, or rejected as certainly false, according as fact and experience bear witness for or against it.

* For an enquiry about the light, and strength, and sufficiency of reason, to guide and preserve men in the knowledge and practice of true religion, is a question, as *solely* to be resolved by *fact and experience*, as if the enquiry was about the *shape* of man's body, or the *number* of his senses. And to talk of a light and strength of reason, natural to man, which fact and experience have never yet proved, is as egregious nonsense, as to talk of natural senses, or faculties of his body, which fact and experience have never yet discovered.

From the bare consideration of a rational soul in union with a body, and bodily passions, we can neither prove man to be *strong* nor *weak*, *good* nor *bad*, *sickly* nor *sound*, *mortal* nor *immortal*: all these qualities must discover themselves, as the *eye* discovers its degree of *sight*, the *hand* its degree of *strength*.

To enquire therefore, whether men have by nature

nature light sufficient to guide, and keep them in the true religion; is the same appeal to fact and experience, as to enquire, whether men are *mortal, sickly,* or *sound:* or how far they can *see* and *hear.*

-* As therefore these gentlemen are, in this debate, without any proof, or even pretence of proof, from experience, so their cause ought to be looked upon to be as vain and romantic, as if they had asserted, that men have senses naturally fitted to hear sounds, and see objects at all distances, tho' experience has, from the creation to this time, proved the quite contrary.

For he that asserts the sufficiency of reason, to guide men in matters of religion, is not only without any positive proof from experience on his side, but has the history of all ages, for near six thousand years, fully demonstrating the quite contrary.

If some other enquirers into human nature, should affirm, that there is in mankind a *natural instinct,* sufficient to make every man, at all times, love every other man, with the *same degree* of affection, as he loves himself; I suppose such an opinion would be thought too absurd to need any confutation. And yet all the absurdity of it would lie in this, that it affirmed something of the *sufficiency* of a natural quality in man, which could not be supported by a single instance of any one man, and was contrary

trary to the experience and hiſtory of every age of the world.

Now this is exactly the caſe of theſe gentlemen: their opinion has neither more or leſs abſurdity in it: they only affirm ſuch a ſufficiency of reaſon to be natural to all men, as cannot be ſupported by a ſingle inſtance of any one man, that ever lived, and is fully contradicted by the experience and hiſtory of every age ſince the creation of the world.

By what has been ſaid, I hope the reader will obſerve, that this enquiry about the perfection or imperfection, the ſtrength or weakneſs, of reaſon in man, as to matters of religion, reſts *wholly* upon fact and experience; and that therefore all ſpeculative reaſonings upon it, are as idle and viſionary, as a ſick man's dreams about health; and are as wholly to be rejected, as any ſpeculative arguments that ſhould pretend to prove, in ſpite of all facts and experience, the *immortality*, and *unalterable* ſtate of human bodies.

Our author himſelf ſeems ſenſible, that the argument drawn from facts and experience, preſſed hard upon his cauſe; and therefore has given the beſt anſwer to it, he can yet think of.

" It cannot, *ſays he*, be imputed to any defect in the light of nature, that the *Pagan* world ran into idolatry; but to their being entirely governed by prieſts, who pretended communication with their gods, and to have thence their revelations,

lations, which they imposed upon the credulous, as divine oracles."

The justness of this assertion will fully appear by the following illustration.

" It cannot be imputed to any defect in the
" health and soundness of man's natural consti-
" tution, that the world has, in all ages, been
" over-run with distempers; but to their being
" entirely governed by physicians, who pretend-
" ed to I know not what secret knowledge of
" medicines, which they imposed upon the sick-
" ly, as infallible remedies."

For, as a perfect state of health, conscious to itself of a sufficiency of natural strength to keep clear of all diseases, seems to be out of all danger from physicians; so had mankind been ever conscious to themselves, of a sufficient natural knowledge of what is true or false in religion; such *as enabled men of the meanest capacity to distinguish between religion and superstition*,† what room had there been for frauds and impostures herein?

" Can the superstition of the *Pagans* be imputed to any defect or insufficiency in the light of reason, when it was wholly owing to their abandoning that divine light; and in defiance of it, running into senseless traditions?"‡

But how came it, that they ran into senseless traditions? What was it that admitted these traditions as just and good? Why, it was that faculty

† Page 3.   ‡ Page 37.

culty which judges of every thing, and which this writer recommends as an unerring guide. And to say, a man's superstition is not owing to any defect or weakness of his reason, but to his admitting senseless traditions, is as vain, as to say, a man's false reasoning is not owing to any weakness of his reason, but to his proceeding upon foolish and absurd arguments.

He proceeds thus: "It is certainly no good argument against the sufficiency of the divine light of nature, that men could not err, except they left it, and followed vain traditions,"†

This observation has just the same sense and acuteness in it, as if it had been said, *It is certainly no good argument against* the sufficiency of the divine healthfulness *of human nature, that men could not be sickly, except they left it.* and *fell into various distempers:* or, *against the* sufficiency of the divine strength of natural courage, that men could not be timorous, till they left it, and followed vain fears. For, to prove that reason is sufficient, because every thing that is absurd, is contrary to reason, is like proving our healthfulness to be sufficient, because all distempers are contrary to it: or our courage to be sufficient, because fears and cowardice are contrary to it.

Vol. VI.   F   Besides,

---

† Second Address, page 39.

Besides, how is it that men leave their reason? Why, just as ignorant men leave their knowledge; as dull people leave their wit, or cowards leave their courage. The first part of this paragraph tells you of a sufficiency of the divine light of nature: well; What has this divine light of nature done? What sufficient effects has it had? Why, it has covered all the world with darkness.

Again: Supposing that all mankind, even the wisest nations, have for this six thousand years been thus imposed upon, not knowing how to distinguish idle tales and senseless traditions from true religion; is not this a noble foundation for this writer to build the *sufficiency of the divine light of nature upon?* For supposing it had been in the greatest degree insufficient, what other effect could have followed from it, but only this, that *all mankind,* even the *wisest nations,* should have been over-run with error? And is it not strange, that effects should bear no proportion to their causes; that the same things should follow from the *sufficiency* of the divine light of nature, which must have followed from its greatest *insufficiency?*

* And must not the enemies of *reason* and *free-thinking* be forced to confess, that this writer hath chosen an excellent guide for himself; since he so fully acknowledges, that no one yet has been rightly guided by it? Must not his present undertaking be granted to be
the

the effect of cool and sober deliberation, since it only calls people of *all,* even the *meanest, capacities,* to such an use of their reason, as the wisest of men and nations have always been strangers to?

C. H A P. V.

Shewing that all the mutability *of our tempers, the* disorders *of our passions, the* corruption *of our hearts, all the* reveries *of the imagination, all the* contradictions *and* absurdities *that are to be found in human life, and human opinions, are in effect the mutability, disorders, corruption, and absurdities of* human reason.

IT is the intent of this chapter to shew, that altho' common language ascribes a variety of faculties and principles to the soul, imputing this action to the blindness of our *passions,* that to the inconstancy of our *tempers;* one thing to the heat of our *imagination,* another to the coolness of our *reason;* yet, in strictness of truth, every thing that is done by us, is the action and operation of our reason, and is to be ascribed to it, as the sole principle from whence it proceeded, and by which it is governed and effected.

And the different degrees of reason are in men, as the different degrees of love and aversion;

as the different degrees of wit, parts, good nature, or ill nature, are in man.

And as all men have naturally more or less of these qualities, so all men have naturally more or less reason: and the bulk of mankind are as different in reason, as they are in these qualities.

As love is the same passion in all men, yet is infinitely different; as hatred is the same passion in all men, yet with infinite differences; so reason is the same faculty in all men, yet with infinite differences.

And as our passions not only make us different from other men, but frequently and almost daily different from ourselves, loving and hating under great inconstancy; so our reason is not only different from the reason of other men, but is often different from itself; by a strange inconstancy, setting up first one opinion, and then another.

So that when we talk of *human reason*, or a reason *common* to mankind, we talk of as *various*, *uncertain*, and *unmeasurable* a thing, as when we talk of a *love*, an *aversion*, a *good nature*, or *ill nature*, common to mankind; for these qualities admit of no variation, uncertainty, or mutability, but such as they directly receive from the *reason* of mankind.

For it is as much the reason of man that acts in all these tempers, and makes them to be just

what

what they are, as it is the reafon of man that demonftrates a mathematical propofition.

Was our reafon fteady, there would be juft the fame fteadinefs and regularity in our tempers; did not reafon fall into follies and abfurdities, we fhould have nothing foolifh or abfurd in our love or averfion. For every humour, every kind of love or averfion, is as ftrictly the *action* or *operation* of our reafon, as judgment is the act of our reafon.

And the tempers and paffions of a child, differ only from the tempers and paffions of a man, as the reafon of a child differs from the reafon of man.

So that our paffions and tempers, are the natural real effects of our reafon, and have no qualities, either good or bad, but fuch as are to be imputed to it.

A laudable good nature, or a laudable averfion, is only reafon acting in a *certain manner:* a criminal good nature, or a criminal averfion, is nothing elfe but reafon acting in another certain manner.

But ftill it is reafon, or our underftanding that is the *only agent* in our bad paffions, as well as good paffions; and as much the *fole agent* in all our paffions and tempers, as in things of mere fpeculation.

So that the ftate of reafon in human life, is nothing elfe but the ftate of human tempers and paffions;

passions; and right reason in morality, is nothing else but right love, and right aversion.

All *that* therefore which we commonly call the weakness, blindness, and disorder of our *passions*, is in reality the weakness, blindness, and disorder of our *reason*. For a right love, or wrong love, denotes only reason acting in a *certain, particular* manner.

So that if any thing can be said of love, aversion, good nature, or ill nature, as common to mankind; the same may be said of reason, as common to mankind.

For the distinction of our reason from our passions, is only a distinction in language, made at pleasure; and is no more real than the *desire* and *inclination* are really different from the *will*. All therefore that is weak and foolish in our passions, is the weakness and folly of our reason; all the inconstancy and caprice of our humours and tempers, is the caprice and inconstancy of our reason.

It is not properly *avarice* that makes men sordid; it is not *ambition* that makes them restless; it is not *bribery* that makes men sell their consciences; it is not *interest* that makes them lye, and cheat, and perjure themselves. What is it therefore? Why it is that *absolutely perfect* faculty, which our author sets up as the *unerring* standard of all that is *wise, holy,* and *good*; it is *reason*, the *use of reason, human reason*, that does all this.

For

For whether any thing be fit to be done, it is as he says, " reason alone which must judge ; as the eye is the sole judge of what is visible, the ear of what is audible, so reason of what is reasonable."

Every thing therefore that is done, every thing that is chosen in human life before any thing else, is as strictly chosen by reason, as every thing that is seen, is seen by the eye ; and every thing that is heard, is heard by the ear.

To suppose that reason permits itself to be governed by passions or tempers, but is not the *immediate agent* of all that is done by them, is as absurd, as to suppose that reason permits itself to be governed by the *hand* when it is writing falsly, or the *tongue* when it is talking profanely, but it is not the immediate, direct agent of all that is written and spoken by them.

* *Brutes* are incapable of immorality, because none of their actions are the actions of *reason:* every thing therefore that is immorality, baseness, or villainy in us, must be the act of our reason, otherwise it could no more be immoral, than the actions of brutes.

* If therefore, as this author often saith, reason be the only faculty that distinguisheth us from brutes ; it necessarily follows, that those irregularities, whether of humour, passions, or tempers, which cannot be imputed to brutes, must be solely attributed to that faculty by which we are distinguished from brutes; and consequently, every thing that is foolish, vain, shameful, false, treacherous, and base, must be the acts of our reason; since if they were the acts of any thing else, they could have no more vanity, falseness, or baseness, than hunger and thirst.

It is not my intent to condemn our common language, which talks of reason and the passions, as if they were as different as a *governor* and his *subjects*.

These forms of speech are very intelligible and useful, and give great life and ornament to all discourses upon morality.

But when persons ascribe to reason, as a *distinct faculty* of human nature, I know not what *absolute perfection*, making it as immutable, and incapable of any addition or improvement, as God himself: it is necessary to consider reason, not as it is represented in common language, but as it is in reality in itself.

Notwithstanding therefore in common language, our passions, and the effects of them, are usefully distinguished from our reason, I have here ventured to shew, that all the disorders of human nature, are in effect the disorders of human reason, and that all the perfection or imperfection of our passions is the perfection or imperfection of our reason.

Our follies and absurdities of every kind are as necessarily to be ascribed to our reason, as the *first immediate* cause of them, as our wisdom and discretion are to be ascribed to it in that degree.

The

The difference between reason assenting to the properties of a *square*, and reason acting in motions of desire or aversion, is only this, that in the latter case, it is reason acting under a sense of its own good or evil, in the former case, it is reason acting under a sense of *magnitude*.

And as the relations of magnitude, as they are the objects of our reason, are only the objects of its assent or dissent; so good and evil, as they are objects of our reason, are only the objects of its *desire* or *aversion:* and as the assent or dissent, in matters of speculation, whether right or wrong, is solely the act of our reason; so desire or aversion, in human life, whether right or wrong, is equally the act of our reason.

We often say, that our passions deceive us, or persuade us; but this is no more strictly so, than when we say, our *interest* deceived, or a bribe blinded us. For bribes and interest are not active principles, nor have any power of deception; it is only our reason that gives them a false value, and prefers them to a greater good.

It is just so in what we call the deceit of our passions: they meddle with us no more than bribes meddle with us; but that pleasurable perception, which is to be found in certain enjoyments, is by our reason preferred to that better good, which we might expect from self-denial.

We say again, that our passions paint things in false colours, and present to our minds vain appearances of happiness.

F 5 But

But this is no more strictly true, than when we say, our *imagination* forms castles in the air. For the imagination signifies no distinct faculty from our reason, but only reason acting upon our own ideas.

So when our passions are said to give false colours to things, or present vain appearances of happiness, it is only our reason acting upon its own ideas of *good* and *evil*, just as it acts upon its own ideas of *architecture*, in forming castles in the air.

So that all *that* which we call different faculties, tempers, and passions, strictly speaking, means nothing else, but the various acts of one and the same rational principle, which has different names, according to the objects that it acts upon, and the manner of its acting.

In some things it is called speculative, in others it is called practical reason. And we may as justly think our speculative reason is a different faculty from our practical reason, as that our aversions, or likings, are not as fully to be ascribed to our reason, as syllogisms and demonstrations.

* It was truly reason that made *Medea* kill her children, that made *Cato* kill himself, that made Pagans offer human sacrifices to idols; that made *Epicurus* deny a providence, *Mahomet* pretend a revelation; that made some men sceptics, others bigots; some enthusiasts, others profane; that made *Hobbes* assert all religion to be human invention, and *Spinosa* to declare trees, and stones,

and

and animals to be parts of God; that makes free-thinkers deny freedom of will, and fatalists exhort to a reformation of manners; that made *Vaux* a conspirator, and *Ludlow* a regicide; that made *Muggleton* a fanatic; and *Rochester* a libertine. It was as truly reason that did all these things, as it is reason that demonstrates mathematical propositions.

Medea and *Cato* acted as truly according to the judgment of their reason at that time, as the confessor that chuses rather to suffer, than deny his faith.

Had not *Medea* and *Cato* thought it best to do what they did, at the time they did it, they would no more have done it than the *confessor* would chuse to suffer rather than deny his faith, unless he had judged best so to do.

And when we say reason governs the passions, it means no more, than that reason governs itself; that it acts with deliberation and attention, does not yield to its first judgments, but uses second, and third thoughts.

So that guarding against the passions, is only guarding against its own first judgments and opinions; that is guarding against itself.

To all this may, perhaps, be objected, that our passions arise from bodily motions, and depend upon the state of our blood and animal spirits, and therefore what we do under their commotions, cannot be attributed to our reason.

F 6   It

It is readily granted, that the body has this share in our paffions and tempers: but then the ame thing muft be granted of the body, in all the acts and operations of the mind. So that if our defires and averfions cannot be imputed to our reafon, becaufe of the joint operation of the animal fpirits in them; no more can fyllogifms and demonftrations be attributed to our reafon, becaufe the operation of bodily fpirits concurreth in the forming of them.

For the moft abftract thought, and fpeculation of the mind, has as truly the *conjunct* operation of bodily fpirits, as our ftrongeft defires or averfions. And it is as much owing to the ftate of the body, that fuch fpeculations are what they are, as it is owing to the ftate of the body, that fuch paffions are what they are.

For the motions of the bodily fpirits are infeparable from, and according to, the ftate and action of the mind: when reafon is in fpeculation of a trifle, they concur but weakly; when reafon fpeculates intenfely, their operation is increafed. And fometimes the attention of the mind is fo great, and has fo engaged and called in all the animal fpirits to its affiftance, that the operations of our fenfes are fufpended, and we neither fee, nor feel, till the attention of the mind has let the fpirits return to all the parts of the body.

Now will any one fay, that thefe intenfe thoughts are lefs the acts of the mind, becaufe they have a greater concurrence of bodily fpirits,

than

than when it is acting with indifference, and so has a lesser quantity of bodily spirits?

Yet this might as well be said, as to say, that the assent or dissent, in speculation, is the act of our reason; but liking or disliking, loving or hating, are not the acts of our reason, because they have a greater concurrence of bodily spirits.

For, as the mind is in a different state when it desires good, or fears evil, from what it is when it only compares two triangles; so the motions of the bodily spirits, have only *such* a difference, as is *correspondent* to these two states of the mind. They act and join as much in comparing the triangles, as in the desire of good, or fear of evil. And the mind is just as much governed by the body, in its passions, as in its calmest contemplations.

For as the gentle operation of the animal spirits is then correspondent to the state and action of the mind; so in all our passions, the strong and increased motion of the animal spirits, is equally correspondent thereto.

So that reason is no more the agent, in our tempers and passions, than in our dry and sedate speculations.

It may happen, that a man may have as great an eagerness in solving a mathematical problem, as another hath to obtain any great good, or avoid any great evil.

But

But may it therefore be said, that it is not reason that solves the problem, because the bodily spirits are so active in it?

To draw now some plain consequences from the foregoing account.

First, If reason be the *universal agent* in the natural man; if all the difference among *such* men, is only such a difference as reason makes, then nothing can be more extravagant, than to affirm any thing concerning the degree of perfection, or imperfection of reason, as *common* to man. It is as wild and romantic, as to pretend to state the measure of folly and wisdom, of fear and courage, of pride and humility, of good humour and ill-humour, *common* to mankind: for as these states of the mind, are only so many different states of reason; so no uncertainty belongs to them, but what, in the *same degree*, belongs to *reason*.

Secondly, Granting that all matters of religion must be agreeable to *right*, *unprejudiced* reason; yet this could be no ground for receiving nothing in religion, but what *human* reason could prove to be necessary; for *human* reason is no more *right*, *unprejudiced* reason, than a sinner is *sinless*, or a man an *angel*.

Granting again, that a man may go a great way towards rectifying his reason, and laying aside its prejudices; yet no particular man can be a *better judge* of the rectitude of his *own reason*, than he is of the rectitude of his own *self-love*,

the

the brightness of his own *parts*, and the depth of his own *judgment*.

For there is nothing to deceive him in *self-love*, in the opinion of his *own merit, wit,* and *judgment,* but what has the same power to deceive him, in the opinion of his own reason. And if, as our author says, " It be the fate of most sects to be the fondest of their ugliest brats."† None seem so inevitably exposed to this fatality, as those whose religion is to have no form, but such as it receives from their own hearts.

Thirdly, A man that has his religion to chuse, and with this precious privilege, that he need not allow any thing to be matter of religion, but what his own reason can prove to be so, is in as fair a way to be governed by his *passions*, as he that has his *condition* of life to chuse, with the liberty of taking that which his own reason directs him to.

Does any one suppose, that nothing but *reason* would direct him in the choice of his condition? Or that he would make the better choice, because he proceeded upon this maxim, that nothing could be right, but that which was agreeable to his *own reason?* Or that his tempers, his prejudices, his self-love, his passions, his partiality, would have no influence upon his choice, because

† Page 184.

cause he had resigned himself up to his *own reason?*

Now it is just the same in the choice of a religion, as in the choice of a condition of life: as it is not a matter of speculation, but of *good* and *evil*; so if it is left to be determined by our *own reason*, it rather appeals to our *tempers*, than employs our reason; and to resign ourselves up to our own reason, to tell us what ought, or ought not to be a matter of religion, is only resigning ourselves up to our tempers, to to take what we *like*, and refuse what we *dislike* in religion.

\# In a word; when *self-love* is a proper arbitrator betwixt a man and his adversary; when *revenge* is a just judge of meekness; when *pride* is a true lover of humility; when *falshood* is a teacher of truth; when lust is a fast friend of chastity; when the *flesh* leads to the spirit; when *sensuality* delights in self-denial; when *partiality* is a promoter of equity; when the *palate* can taste the difference between sin and holiness: when the *hand* can feel the truth of a proposition; then may *human reason* be a proper arbitrator between God and man, the sole, final, just judge of all that ought, or ought not to be a matter of a *holy, divine,* and *heavenly* religion.

Lastly, If this be the state of reason, then to pretend, that our reason, is too perfect to be governed by any thing but its own light, is the same

extra-

extravagance, as to pretend, that our love is too pure to be governed by any thing but its own inclinations, our hatred too juſt to be governed by any thing but its own motions. For if all that is baſe and criminal in love, all that is unjuſt and wicked in hatred, is to be imputed to our reaſon; then no perfection can be aſcribed to our reaſon, but ſuch as is to be aſcribed to our love and hatred.

An Extract from Mr. LAW's

SERIOUS ANSWER

To Dr. TRAPP's Four Sermons,

On the Sin, Folly, and Danger of being righteous over-much.

1.* MIGHT I follow the *bent* of my own mind, I should be wholly employed in setting forth the infinite love of God to mankind in Christ Jesus, and endeavouring to draw all men to the belief and acknowledgment of it. This *one great mercy* of God, which makes the *one* happiness of all mankind, so justly deserves all our thoughts and meditations, so highly enlightens, and improves every mind that is attentive to it, so removes all the evils of this present world, so sweetens every state of life, so inflames the heart with the love of every divine and human virtue, that he is no small loser, whose mind is, either by writing or reading, detained from the view and contemplation of it.

2. When

2. When the myſtery of divine love was firſt manifeſted to the world, it produced its proper effects. It put an end to all *ſelfiſhneſs and diviſion*; for all that believed were of one heart and one ſpirit, and had all things common.† And indeed, under the real influence and full belief of this great myſtery of divine love, there ſeems to be no room left for any thing elſe amongſt Chriſtians, but returns of love to God, and flowing out of love towards one another.

3. * It is ſo difficult to enter into controverſy without being, or at leaſt ſeeming in ſome degree unkind to the perſon one oppoſes, that it is with great reluctance I have entered upon my preſent undertaking; having nothing more deeply riveted in my heart, than an univerſal love and kindneſs for all men, and more eſpecially for thoſe whom God has called to be my fellow-labourers, in promoting the ſalvation of mankind. But however unwilling, yet I find myſelf obliged to conſider and lay open many grievous faults in the Doctor's diſcourſe; and to ſhew to all Chriſtians, that the deareſt intereſts of their ſouls are much endangered by it.

4. * And this I muſt do with great plainneſs and ſincerity in the love of truth, and under the direction of charity, ſaying nothing in the ſpirit of an *adverſary*, ſparing nothing thro' *reſpect of perſons*, ſacrificing nothing to the taſte or temper of the world, but ſetting every thing in that

† Acts ii. 44.

that naked light, in which the Spirit of God represents it to my own mind.

5. The Doctor undertakes to stir up, and alarm mankind with the *sin, folly* and *danger* of being *righteous over-much*. The text from which he has the title of his discourses is very unhappily chosen, and must be looked upon rather as a severe reproach, than any kind of justification of it. The text is indeed in the writings of *Solomon*, and as it stands there, has no hurt in it; because as the royal preacher sometimes introduces fools, and sometimes infidels making their speeches, so there is a necessity of supposing that to be the case in the Doctor's text; not only from the context which plainly shews there are two persons introduced, the one *for*, the other *against* righteousness; but because the words, otherwise, cannot be taken in a sense that is tolerable, or consistent with the common *notions* of piety.

6. Is it not therefore strange, that the Doctor should think it right, to limit, explain, and model both the letter and spirit of the gospel by such a saying in the writings of *Solomon* as must be ascribed to the spirit and mouth of an infidel? Is it not stranger, that such a text, so offensive to piety, should have not only been so long dwelt upon in the Doctor's three churches, but sent abroad into the world, as a proper key to all the practical sayings, parables, and doctrines of Jesus Christ?

7. Supported

7. Supported by this text, the Doctor endeavours to deter and fright Christians from the sin, folly and danger of being righteous over-much, and from what he calls the baneful plague of enthusiasm. But then it is matter of just complaint, that he does all this, without ever shewing in any part of his discourse, wherein true righteousness, or the right and sober spirit of piety consists. And if he supposed all his readers to be already well acquainted with the nature, and extent of Christian holiness, there would then have been little occasion for his present undertaking.

8. But the Doctor overlooks this important matter. He neither supposes them to have this knowledge, nor endeavours to help them to it; but in a flow of zeal, reflects at large upon all attempts towards a piety, that is not *modern, common*, and according to the present fashion of religion in the world. Thus, you every where find severe reflections cast upon pretenders to piety, pretended spiritualists; great accusations of excesses, extraordinaries and by-paths; but no where a word or a hint, in favour of those, who would only be so extraordinary, and so much out of the *common* paths, as the blessed saints and martyrs of the primitive church were. No where are *such people* told, that he wishes them *God speed*, that *their zeal* is much wanted both amongst *clergy* and *laity*, and that the gospel suffers because we know not where to find living examples

ples of its purity and perfection. No where are they told, that he writes not against them, that he loves their spirit, and should be glad to add new fervours to it: nor what Christian perfection is, what a holiness of body, soul and spirit it requires; how powerfully all are called to it, how earnestly all ought to aspire after it, and how sadly mistaken, what enemies to themselves they are, who for the sake of any, or all the things in the world, die less purified and perfect, than they might have been.

9. If we had to do with *one single* person sincerely good, yet seeming to carry matters too high in some part of his duty, and intended privately to dissuade him from such heights; yet even this, thus privately done and to a person of piety, would be exceeding *dangerous* and *unjustifiable*; unless we took the utmost care at the same time, to *keep up* the pious zeal of his mind, to shew him wherein true perfection consisted, and to encourage his utmost endeavours after it.

But if this caution, instruction and encouragement, cannot be omitted without great hurt to religion, when we speak only to a person of piety, and in private, about any religious *extremes*, what must be said of the Doctor's conduct? Who to the world dead in trespasses and sin, preaches up the *sin, folly* and *danger* of *being* righteous over-much? To the world *eating and drinking and rising up to play*, he harangues

upon

temperance, abstinence, mortification and severity of life! To the world asleep, insensible, and careless, not only of the purity and perfection, but of the first principles of the gospel, he boldly and rashly approaches all appearances of holiness, that are uncommon and extraordinary! To *no* part of the world does he represent or propose the *perfection* of the gospel, or recommend it as that, which deserves all that they can do, or suffer for the sake of it.

This, therefore, I am obliged to point out, as a *fundamental defect* in the Doctor's discourse, and such as renders it an evil *temptation*, a dangerous *snare*, and fatal *delusion* to all those who do not read it with a full, and thorough dislike.

10. * Coldness, indifference, and a lifeless, outward compliance with the duties of religion: a slavery to ease, softness, and sensual pleasures: a criminal conformity to the spirit, fashions, and corruptions of the world; unmortified passions; conniving at favourite sin; deep roots of pride, partiality, and self-love: an unawakened conscience; an insensibility of their corrupt, unreformed, unregenerate state: a proneness to be content and satisfied with poor beginnings, names and appearances of virtue; is perhaps the state of more than two *thirds* of those that are looked upon to be the religious amongst us.

Now the Doctor's discourse has a direct and natural fitness to lull all these people asleep, to suppress upon the madness, danger, and folly of too much suppress all stirring and intentions of amendment, to keep up and nourish every disorder of their hearts, to increase their blindness, and awaken nothing in them, but a *hurtful* *zeal* to censure and condemn all those that are endeavouring to practise the *uncommon* piety of the gospel.

There is scarce a reader amongst this number of people, whether he be *layman* or *clergyman*, but will find this effect from the Doctor's instructions; he will begin to take *fresh comfort* in his state, to think himself *happy* for having had no aspirings after high improvements in piety; he will not only be content with his corruptions, but be fixed and hardened against all *inward* and *outward* calls to a solid piety; he will approve of the deadness and insensibility of his own heart, and acquiesce in it, as his just security, from the *sin* and *folly* and *danger* of being *righteous over-much*.

11. Again, others there are, I make no doubt in all parts of the kingdom, both amongst clergy and laity, men and women, rich and poor, whose consciences are greatly awakened, who see the general apostacy from the religion of the gospel, whose souls are wanting and wishing nothing so much, as to know how all that they *are*, all that they *have*, and all that they *do*, may be one continual sacrifice, and service of love unto God; to know how, and in what manner, and to what extent, and by what means, they may and ought

to *be perfect, even as their Father which is in heaven is perfect.*

Now, who can help looking with *love* and *compassion* upon those poor souls, longing for that which has been so long lost; asking after that, which scarce any one will tell them any thing of, and wanting to enter upon paths where there are few or no footsteps to be seen, nor any travellers in motion?

Had these awakened souls lived in the first ages of the church, nay, I may say in almost any till these very last ages of it, their zeal had not been in vain: they could have been at no loss to know *how* they were to proceed in their heavenly purpose; because they would have been immediately directed to some living examples of the perfect spirit of the gospel, who were publicly known and acknowledged by all to be such, who had the same undisputed right, to point out the Christian profession, as *John* the Baptist had to preach up *mortification* and *self-denial*. Every age, and every sex, priests and people of all conditions, had their known standards to resort to, where every one was sure to be guided, assisted, and encouraged to live up to that height of holiness.

12. But now how does the Doctor deal with this sort of people? What *love, assistance,* and *encouragement* does he reach out to them? Why, truly, he considers them as a *deluded, weak,* or *hypocritical,* or *half-thinking* people, that disturb

the Christian church with their projects; who are to be set right by returning to the instructions of common sense. He ridicules every step they must take in their intended progress, by adding absurdities of his own invention to it. There is nothing for such people throughout his whole discourse, but reproaches, and discouragement.

Are they desirous of all that *self-denial*, all such *mortification* of bodily appetites and sensual passions, as may best fit them to be temples of the Holy Spirit? He ridicules them, as holding the sinfulness of *smelling a rose*.

Do they begin to discover the *deep corruption* of their nature, the superficialness and weakness of their virtues, and to fear they have as yet scarce come up to the righteousness of the *Scribes* and *Pharisees?* He tells them " The great enemy of souls adapts his temptations to all sorts of tempers and dispositions. Those who are disposed to be good and virtuous, if he cannot prevail with them to be vicious, commonly so called, he labours to make them over virtuous, that is vicious, tho' not commonly so called; and so involves them in dangers and mischiefs.

Are they such as are desirous of reforming their own lives, by bringing all their actions to the standard of the gospel, and wholly intent upon their own advancement in merely *practical piety?*

To

To these he shews, that they are in the very paths that lead, and always did lead to *fanatic madness*.

Thus says he, "To what a height of *fanatic madness* in *doctrines*, as well as practice are some advanced, who set out at first with the appearance of more than ordinary sanctity in *practice only?*" And again, " I do say that in all ages enthusiasts have been *righteous over-much*; they began with the last mentioned, and ended with the other; *and is it not so now?*"

13. Further, are there others, who begin to feel the *mystery* of their redemption discovered in their own souls, so that they hunger and thirst after the manifestation of the divine life in them, desiring that Christ may be wholly formed and revealed in them, that they may *put on* Christ, *be* in him *new creatures*, led by his spirit, *growing* in him as branches in the vine, hearing the word of God written and spoken in their hearts, in his light *seeing* light, and *tasting* in the inward man *the powers of the world to come?*

* For such as these, the Doctor has this instruction: "That there is, says he, such a thing as the operation of the Holy Spirit upon our souls, tho' we cannot distinguish it from the operations of our own minds, is not only granted, but insisted upon by all sincere and sober Christians. But what *reason*, what *scripture*, is there for this inward *seeing, hearing, feeling?*"

* According

*According therefore to the Doctor's divinity both reason and scripture require, that the true Christian be *inwardly blind*, *inwardly deaf*, and void of all inward *feeling*. For if neither scripture nor reason will allow of any inward senses, then they must both of them require an *inward insensibility*. But as scripture from *Genesis* to the *Revelation*, is full of proofs of these inward senses, I shall not now produce them: I shall here only observe that *hardness of heart* is a well known phrase of scripture, and every where *signifies* some degree of *blindness*, *deafness*, and loss of *feeling*. I suppose it will not be said that it signifies blindness, or loss of *outward eyes* and *ears*, or feeling: neither does it signify a want of *human reason*, or natural *sagacity*; for *learned*, *polite*, and *ingenious* men, are full as subject as others to this hardness of heart. Therefore the scripture is as open, as plain and express in declaring *for inward senses*, as it is in declaring against such a thing, as *hardness* of *heart*. Hardness of heart is that to the inward senses, which a deep, or as we call it, *dead sleep*, is to the *outward*. It keeps our inward eyes, and ears, and feeling all locked up.

14. A broken and a contrite heart unlocks our inward senses, and makes us see, and hear, and feel the things, which could no more be seen, heard or felt before, than a man in a deep sleep can hear, and see, and feel the things, that are said and done about him.

Water

Water frozen into a rock of ice, is very different from the same water melted, warmed, and moving under the influence of the sun and the air.

Now this difference between water *flowing*, full of *light* and *air*, and the same water frozen into a dark, hard rock of ice, is but a small resemblance of the difference between a *hardened* heart, and the *same heart* become broken.

15. But I return to the Doctor. His further instruction to this sort of people stands thus. They are told by him, " that their high notions of spiritual improvements have this effect: on the one hand, they lead to *presumption*, on the other to *desperation*." " He has been told, *he says*, that some have been actually thrown into despair. They have been made stark mad, and received into *Bedlam* as such. *And then he cries out,* Was the religion of Jesus Christ intended to make people mad? Is this for the honour of Christianity."

* I shall not here question the Doctor's information. I shall only observe, that when our Saviour was upon earth, there were two sorts of *mad* people about him; the *one sort* ran about in disorder, tore their cloaths and cut their own flesh; the other sort raved in malice, threw dust into the air, stopped their ears, and cried out *crucify him, crucify him*.

* It may be asked, which of these two sorts of people were in the most disordered and distempered

pered state? Whose madness was the most shocking, that of the lunatics, or that of the *High Priests, Scribes,* and *Pharisees?* Those who only mangled their own bodies, or those that thirsted after the blood of Christ, and would have no rest till they saw his body nailed to the cross? To me the *lunatics,* seem to be in a *less degree* of disorder; and the reason is this, because I see that our Saviour could heal them, but not the Priests, Scribes, and Pharisees.

Now is it reasonable, on account of the *madness* of these Priests, Scribes and Doctors of the law, to say, " Is this for the honour of the *Jewish law?* Were the *law and the prophets intended to make people mad?*" If the Doctor knows how to excuse the law and the prophets, tho' these great students of them were in such a desperate state of *madness,* then Christianity may be blameless; tho' here and there a Christian (so called) may be fit for *Bedlam.*

16. Again, are there others, who desire to bring the whole form of their lives under rules of religion, to let the spirit of the gospel give laws to the most ordinary, indifferent, innocent and lawful things and enjoyments; so that, as the apostle speaks, *whether they eat or drink, or whatever they do,* they may *do all to the glory of God?*

These people are told by the Doctor, that " Wholly abstaining from things indifferent and innocent in themselves, as forbidden and unlawful,

ful, is a signal instance of being righteous overmuch; and so on the other hand, is making things indifferent to be necessary, and matters of duty."

What is here said has some truth in it, and might be useful in its proper place, and under right limitations. But as it here stands, it is a grievous *snare* and *deceit* to the reader. For it is to signify to him, that *wholly abstaining from* things in themselves indifferent, cannot be made a *matter* of true religious advancement; but is a blameable instance of excess. If the Doctor had meant only to teach, that we should not abstain from things indifferent, as if they were in *themselves unlawful*, he should have told his readers that he meant no more. He should have told them, that such things might be abstained from justly, upon a better principle, and so become very expedient and edifying; and that he did not condemn the abstaining from such things, when it was done upon a motive of piety, or for the better fulfilling any duty; but only when it was done from a superstitious notion, of the things being in themselves sin.

Had he done this, he had prevented the *snare* and *deceit* that is now in his assertion: but then he would at the same time have made it useless, and insignificant to the design of his discourse, and would have left a door open for such advances in piety, as he is now opposing.

17. It might easily be shewn, if this was the place for it, that no one can truly fulfil the two first and greatest of all laws, that of loving God with all our heart, and that of loving our neighbour as ourselves, unless he be willing and glad, in many instances, *wholly* to *abstain* from things in themselves indifferent and innocent.

St. *Paul*'s doctrine is this: *All things are lawful for me, but all things are not expedient.* This sets the matter right on both sides. It leaves things in their own state of indifference, and yet carries us to a higher rule of acting. It directs us wholly to abstain from, some things innocent in themselves, and to do things because they are *expedient*; because by so doing, we shew a higher love of God, and a greater desire of doing every thing to his glory; because we thereby attain a greater conquest over all our inward and outward enemies, and in a greater degree help forward the edification of our neighbour.

18. Let us look at St. *Paul*'s doctrine and examples in the two following remarkable instances.

First where he declares it to be *lawful* for those that preach the gospel to live by the gospel, and yet makes it matter of the greatest *comfort* and joy to himself, that he wholly abstained from this *lawful* thing: and declares, it were better for him to die, than that this *rejoicing* should be taken from him. He appeals to his daily and nightly labouring with his own hands, that so he might preach the gospel freely, and not be chargeable

chargeable to those that heard him. And this he said he did, not for want of authority to do otherwise, but that he might make himself an example unto them who followed him.

* What awakening instructions are here given to us of the clergy, in a matter of the greatest moment! How ought every one to be frighted at the thought of desiring or seeking a second living, or of rejoicing at great pay where there is but little duty, when the apostle's rejoicing consisted in this, that he had passed thro' all the fatigues and perils of preaching the gospel without any pay at all! How *cautious*, nay, how *fearful* ought we to be, of going so far as the *secular* laws permit us, when the apostle thought it more desirable to lose his life, than to go so far as the general laws of the gospel would have suffered him!

* It is *looked upon* as *lawful*, to get several preferments, and to make a gain of the gospel, by hiring others to do duty for us at a lower rate.—It is looked upon as lawful, to quit a cure of souls of a small income, for no other reason but because we can get another of a greater.——It is looked upon as lawful, for a clergyman to apply the revenue of a church, which he serves, to his own use, tho' he has more than a sufficient competency of his own, and much more than the apostle could get by his labour.— It is looked upon as lawful, for the clergy to live in state and equipage, to buy purple and fine linen out of the revenue of the church.——It is looked upon as lawful, for clergymen to enrich their families, and bring up their children in the fashionable vanities of a worldly and expensive life, by money got by preaching the gospel of Jesus Christ.

* But now *supposing* all these to be *lawful*, what *comfort* and *joy* might we treasure up for ourselves, what benefit and edification should we give to our neighbour, if we wholly abstained from all these things, not by working day and night with our hands, as the great apostle did, but by limiting our wants and desires according to the plain demands of nature, and a religious self-denial?

The other instance of the apostle's I appeal to is that, where he says, it is good neither to eat " flesh, nor drink wine, nor any thing whereby thy brother stumbleth and is offended.. And again, if meat make my brother to offend, I will eat no flesh while the world standeth, that I may not offend my brother." Hence it appears, that to abstain from things indifferent, as if they were in themselves sinful, is wrong; but to *abstain* from them upon other motives, may be matter of necessary duty and edification. But since the Doctor has not looked at this matter in the twofold view in which only it can be justly apprehended, he cannot well be excused from that *half thinking*, which he so much reproaches in others.

19. But I must further observe, that there is yet more of *snare* and *deception*, in what the

Doctor

Doctor has here said of this matter. For the reader may thereby be easily brought into a belief, that things in themselves indifferent, are not *proper subjects* of religion, or means of advancing in piety; and that he need not bring himself under *any laws* of religion, concerning such things.

Whereas nothing can be more contrary to truth, or more hurtful to piety than such a belief. " Eating, drinking, sleeping, dressing, resting, labour, conversation, trade, diversion, and money, are in themselves indifferent."

But it is in the religious, or irreligious use of these that some people *live* up to the spirit of the gospel, and others *wholly die* to it. And it is from strict laws of religion, made concerning these indifferent things, that the spiritual life of every one is to be built up.

And it is for want of religious laws in the use of these things, that the spirit of the gospel cannot get possession of our hearts. For our souls may receive an infinite hurt, and be rendered incapable of all true virtue, merely by the use of innocent and lawful things.

* What is more innocent than rest and retirement? And yet what more dangerous than sloth and idleness? How lawful is the care of a family? And yet how are many people rendered incapable of all virtue, by a wordly, sollicitous temper? How lawful is it for us, to eat and drink in such quantity and quality, as may render the body healthful

healthful, and useful to the soul? And yet what danger is there in eating and drinking if we are not under this strict law of religion, to seek *only* health; and not the pleasure of various tastes in our food? What *sensuality* of discourse shall we not every day fall into, unless it be a fixed law to us, to speak of no other joy in our food, but that which is expressed by our grace before, and after our meals?

How indifferent a thing, and innocent in itself, is *dress?* And yet what more hurtful and abounding with sin? It reaches and affects the heart and soul both of the wearer and beholder. Its evils are innumerable; it has destroyed, and does destroy like a pestilence.

Now how can all these evils, which arise from the use of these things indifferent and lawful in themselves be avoided, but by making every thing in our *common* and *ordinary* life to be matter of conscience, which is to have its *rule* and *measure* and *end* from the spirit of religion? And indeed what other end is there in religion, but to govern every motion, and desire of our hearts? To make all the actions of our common life pure and holy, by being done in strict conformity to the will of God, and under the light and guidance of his Holy Spirit? So that the very outward *form* of our lives, and the *whole manner* of our living in the world, whether in estates, shops, or farms, whether in eating, drinking, or dressing, may make it known to all the world, that

we

we do every thing in the name of Jesus Christ, suitably to that high vocation wherewith we are called.

20. No folly of life whatever can be rightly removed but by being thus wholly cut up by the roots, by making every thing subject to the spirit of religion.

That which is to direct our *prayers*, and govern us at church, must with the same strictness direct our conversation, and govern our dealings in common life. We must dress with the same spirit that we give *alms*, or go to *prayers*; that is, we must no more dress to be seen and admired by others, than we must give alms, or make prayers for the same reasons.

And when religion has its seat in our hearts, and is the work of God's spirit in us, this acting according to its direction in *all things*, will be so far from seeming to be a hard lesson, that it would be a pain to act otherwise. It is no hardship to a *miser* to do *every* thing suitably to the greedy desires of his heart. The ambitious man is not troubled with acting always agreeable to his ambition. If these persons are in trouble or distress, or under any dejection, you can only comfort the one with honour and power, and the other with filthy lucre and gain.

21. Yet the Doctor complains of the *Treatise upon Christian Perfection*, because Christians in *sickness, distress, and dejection* of *spirit*, are there directed to seek for comfort and refreshment in God

God alone! Our blessed Lord is very short and yet very full upon this article. He only says, *Be of good comfort, I have overcome the world.* And the Doctor might as well be angry at the gospel for having made no mention of worldly amusements proper for sick and distressed Christians, as at the treatise of Christian Perfection, for not having done the same.

If I should see a sick man smelling a rose, I should not reprove him. But if he wanted comfort in his state, I would no more direct him to *any thing,* but the great and solid comforts that are to be found in the love, and goodness of God, than I would direct him to another Saviour, than Jesus Christ.

* For to tell Christians that in *some kinds* of trouble, they might justly seek for relief in reading a *play,* or wanton *Bucolic,* instead of the *gospel;* would be the same absurdity, as to have told people in our Saviour's time, that in some sorts of distress, they might justly have recourse to *Simon Magus,* instead of Jesus Christ.

22. But now to look back a little. I have considered the bulk of those Christians that are the most likely to be the Doctor's readers, under two characters. The one as living some way or other in a partial, false, superficial, or half state of piety; the other as an awakened people, called by the Spirit of God to come out of the common corruption of the times. I have shewn that the Doctor's discourse (where it is not disliked) must

do

do great hurt, and have dreadful effects upon those two sorts of people; the one sort it seals up in a false security, sleeping in the chambers of death, without any oil in their vessels; the other it frightens, and discourages from their pious intentions of trimming their lamps with all diligence, and living upon the watch for the midnight call of the bridegroom's voice.

That I may therefore do all the good I can to both these sorts of people, that I may awaken the one from their false security in their form of godliness, and encourage the other to proceed with all earnestness, after every degree of Christian holiness; I shall before I proceed any further, lay down a short account of the whole *ground* of the Christian religion, that every one may clearly see, why we want the Christian religion to save us, what it is to do for us; and how it is done.

23. [I] Man was created a living image of the Holy Trinity, Father, Son, and Holy Ghost.

" 2. This whole visible world, as far as the stars, or any corporeal being reaches, takes up that extent of space, where *Lucifer* and his angels before their fall, had their glorious kingdom. So far as this visible frame of nature extends, so far was the extent of that kingdom.†

" 3. That the *place* or *extent* of this world, was the place or extent of their kingdom, is probable from

---

† N. B. This, with several of the particulars that follow are probable, but not supported by scripture. This is the theory of *Jacob Behme,* ingenious, but quite incapable of proof.

from the two following ~~reasons~~: first, because the place of this world is now their habitation. For we 'must by no means suppose that God brought them from some other region into this world, only to tempt man. No: but they are here *now*, because they were created to dwell *here*. For fallen angels do not leave the *place* of their sin and fall: they live in the *defilements* and *disorders* of their spoiled kingdom; and in that place they find their hell and torments, where they extinguished their light and joy. Secondly, because the whole extent of the world, and every thing in it, *sun, moon, stars, fire, air, water,* and *earth, stones, minerals*, must all be *dissolved*, and pass thro' a *purifying fire*. Therefore all these things are polluted, and have in them some disorder from the fall of the angels; and we may see *how far* the place of their kingdom extended, by the extent of those things that are to be *dissolved* and *purified*.

" 4. When the angels had, by their rebellion, lost the divine life within themselves, and brought their *whole outward* kingdom into darkness and disorder, so that as *Moses* speaketh: " Darkness was upon the face of the deep;" that is, the whole extent of the place of this world; then in the place where they were fallen, and out of the *materials* of their ruined, angelical kingdom, did God begin the *creation* of this present, material, temporary, visible world.

" 5. In

" 5. 'In the beginning, faith *Moses*, God created the heaven and the earth.' Here, at this *instant*, ended the devil's power, over the place or kingdom in which he was created. As foon as the whole of his outward, difordered kingdom was thus divided into a *created heaven and earth*, all was taken out of his hands, he was fhut out of every thing, and he and all his hoft became *poor prisoners* in their left kingdom, that could only *wander about* in chains of darknefs, looking with impotent rage at the *created heaven and earth*, which was fprung up in their own place of habitation.

" 6. Thus was this *outward kingdom*, of the whole extent of this world, taken out of the hands of *Lucifer* and his angels. All its darknefs, difharmony, and diforder, was by the *creation* reftored to a low refemblance of its firft ftate, and put into that form of fun, ftars, fire, air, light, water, and earth, in which we now fee it.

" 7. Into this world thus created out of the *ruins* of the kingdom of the fallen angels, was man introduced on the fixth day of the creation, to take his place as lord and prince of it; to have power over all outward things, to difcover and manifeft the wonders of this new created world, and to bring forth fuch an *holy offspring*, as might fill up the place of the fallen angels. And when certain periods of time had produced thefe great effects, then this *whole frame* was by the laft *purifying fire*, to have been raifed from its paradifaical saical state, into that *first heavenly* brightness and glory, in which it stood before the fall of *Lucifer*.

" 8. But the first man, thus created to be a prince of a new, angelical kingdom, stood not out his trial.

" 9. He came into this world in that *same glorious* body in which after the resurrection, he shall *be like the angels in heaven*. For no other body, but that which was at *first* created shall rise in Jesus Christ. He only restores that which was lost. The resurrection will only take away what *sin* and *death*, and *earth*, had added to the *first created* body.

" 10. In this glorious body, did the first man stand in this world, incapable of receiving any hurt, or *knowing* evil from outward nature. The *Holy Ghost* was the *light* that illuminated all both within and without him.

" 11. Had he fixed his will to be *eternally* what he was, had he desired only to eat of the tree of life, to live by the word of God, he had been established and confirmed an eternal angel, or divine man.

" 12. But his imagination wandered after the secrets of this outward world, after the knowledge of such good and evil, as wrought an entire change in his nature.

" He turned from the tree of life to the forbidden fruit. And so he fell as deep into an *earthly life*, and the miseries of the earth, as the

devil

devil fell into a *hellish life*, and the miseries of hell.

" 13. And here we may see as in a glass, what it is that earthly desires *now do* to every son of *Adam*. They do all that which they did to the first man. They carry on, keep up, and continue that *same* death in us which he died in paradise.

" 14. Thus it was, that *Adam* lost the *light* of the Son of God, and the breath of the Holy Spirit. And this was the *immediate death* that he died in paradise; a death much more grievous than that which is to bring us all to our graves. It was a death that extinguished all that was divine and holy in human nature, just as the sin of angels turned them into devils. Now in looking at *this death*, we have the clearest view, of what our regeneration by the *second Adam* means. For what can it be, but the restoration of that divine life which was lost in *Adam* the *first*? For will any one say, that Christ is not in as high a degree, the *restorer* of our nature, as *Adam* was the *destroyer* of it? Now tho' this great truth, seated in the very heart of the Christian religion, speaks at once the whole nature of regeneration; yet many learned men either not seeing or not *loving*, or being afraid *to own* it, have been forced, not only to mistake, but wholly to sink the most glorious article of the Christian faith? And instead of telling us the height and depth of the blessing of having the nature and life of Christ

derived

derived into us, they can only teach us, what kind of word regeneration is—that it is a figurative expression—and that our Saviour may be justified, for having made use of it. What learned pains do people take, to root up the belief of our having a new life in Christ? They run from *book* to *book*, from *language* to *language*; they consult all criticks, search all lexicons, to shew us, that according to the rules of true criticism, regeneration *need signify* no more than the *federal* rite of baptism. Nay, what is still worse, they appeal to the poor notions of the blind, infatuated Jews! They produce the opinions which they had of a regeneration talked of, and a baptism used amongst them, when they rejected and crucified our Saviour, to teach us, what we are to understand by our divine birth in Christ Jesus! But if this be the use of learning among ourselves, we need not look at *Rome*, or the ancient Rabbies of the *Jewish Sanhedrim*, to see what miserable work learning can make with the holy scriptures. For it is sure the true Messiah it not *rightly owned*, nor the Christian religion *truly known*, till the soul is all love, and faith, and hunger, and thirst after this new *life*, and real formation of Jesus Christ in it: till without fear of *enthusiasm* it seeks, and expects all its redemption from it. But to return.

"15. Man, thus dead to the divine life, thus destitute of the Son, and *Holy Spirit*, thus fallen into an *earthly nature*, under the dominion of an earthly world, which would afford him for a while a miserable life, and then leave him to a more miserable death; could do no more to replace himself in paradise, or to regain his first nature, than the devil could do to restore himself to his lost glory.

"16. But in this state the *infinite mercy* of God met him. That love which at *first breathed*, a holy and divine soul into him, now again breathed a spark, or ray of divine light into him in the declaration of a *serpent bruiser:* which spark of life should in time do all that which *Adam* should have done; that is, should bring forth a *generation* of men, that should become *Sons of God*, and take possession of that kingdom from which the angels had fallen.

"17. Here began the merciful mystery of man's redemption; for this seed of divine life, was the Holy Jesus, who from that time, stood in the place of the first man.

And from that time it may be said in a true sense that the *incarnation* of the Son of God began; because he was from that time entered again into the human nature, as a seed of its salvation, tho' not made manifest, till he was born in the Holy Virgin *Mary*. And in this sense St. *John* says of him, *that he was the true light which lighteth every man, that cometh into the world*. Because every man has from him this light, which if it is duly attended to, is our certain guide to

Christ,

Christ, born in the fulness of time, and sacrificed for us upon the cross.

"18. What we want from Christ, as our Redeemer, is manifest by that which he gives to us, namely a redemption from the *hell* that is in our souls, and from the death and corruption that is in our bodies.

"19. We are no more created to be in the sorrows, and anguish of an *earthly life*, than the angels were created to be in the *darkness* of hell. It is as contrary to the *will* of God towards us, that we are out of paradise, as it is contrary to the design of God towards the angels, that some of them are *out* of heaven, prisoners of darkness.

The sickness, pain and corruption of our bodies, is brought upon us by ourselves, in the same manner as the dark, hideous forms of the devils are brought upon them. * How absurd, and even blasphemous would it be, to say, with the scripture and the church, that we are by *nature, children of wrath, and born in sin,* if we had that nature which God at first gave us? What a reproach upon God to say, that this world is a *valley of misery,* a shadow of death, an habitation of *disorders, snares, evils,* and *temptations,* if this was an original creation, or that state of things in which God created us? Is it not as consistent with the goodness of God, to speak of the *misery* and *disorder* that holy angels find above, and of the vanity, emptiness and sorrow of the *heavenly state,* as to speak of the misery

sery of *men*, and the sorrows of *this world*, if man and the world were in that order, in which God at first had placed them?

"20. But by the mercy of God in Christ, this prison of an earthly life, is turned into a state of purification. It is made a time and place of putting off our *filthy* garments, and of *slaying* and *sacrificing* that man of sin that is hid under them. And God suffers the sun to shine upon us, and the elements to afford us nourishment, for no other end, but that we may all have time and opportunity to hear the call of the Son of God, to be *born again*, to be renewed by the *Holy Spirit*, and be made capable of that kingdom, from which *Lucifer* and his angels fell."

24. Look at our Saviour's sermon on the *mount*, and indeed at all his instructions, and you will find them pointing at nothing else on our *side*, but a *denial* of ourselves, and a *renunciation* of the world. And indeed how could it be otherwise! For if we want a Redeemer, only because we have *wandered* out of paradise, and could not get back to it ourselves; if we are overcome by this world, only because our first father *sought* after it, what wonder is it that he who is to replace us in paradise, should call us to a *renunciation* of the world?

25. * Vain man, taken with the *sound* of heavenly things, and *prospects* of future glory, yet at the same time a *fast friend* to the interests of flesh and blood, would fain compound matters between
God

God and mammon. He is very willing to acknowledge a *Saviour*, that died on the cross to save him. He is ready to receive outward *ordinances* and *forms* of worship, and to contend with zeal for the observance of them. He likes heaven, and future glory on these conditions. He is also ready to put on *outward morality*, to let religion polish his manners, that he may have the credit and ornament of a *prudential piety*, and a *decency* of life. This does no hurt. But to lay the axe to the *whole root* of our disease, to cut all those *silken cords* asunder, which tie us to the world, and the world to us, to deny every temper and passion that cannot be made holy, wise and heavenly; to die to every gratification which keeps up, and strengthens the folly, vanity, pride, and blindness of our *fallen nature*; to leave no little morsels of sensuality, avarice and ambition for the *old man* to feed upon, however well-covered under his mantle; this, tho' it be the very essence of religion, is what he flies from with as much aversion as from *heresy* and *schism*. Here he makes learned appeals to reason and common sense to judge betwixt him, and the gospel; which is just as wise, as to ask the learned *Greek*, and the worldly *Jew*, whether the *cross* of Christ be not foolishness, and a just rock of offence: or to appeal to flesh and blood about the narrow way to that kingdom of heaven, into which itself cannot possibly have an entrance.

26. * To

26. * To seek for any thing in religion, but a *new nature* fitted for a new world, is knowing neither it, nor ourselves. *To be born again*, is to be fit for Paradise in whatever part of the universe we live. *Not to be born again*, is continuing where the sin and death of *Adam* left us, whatever church, or sect of religion we have fellowship with. All ways and opinions, all forms and modes of worship, stand on the outside of religion. They certainly are helps to the kingdom of God, when we consider them only as the *gate* to that *inward life*, which we want. But this is unquestionably true, that our *salvation* consists wholly in our inward renewal by the Holy Ghost. When this begins, our salvation begins; as this goes on, our salvation goes on; when this is finished, our salvation is finished. This alone saves the soul, because this alone restores the first paradisaical, divine nature, which is the true image of God, and which alone can enter into the kingdom of heaven.

27. If we had only a *notional knowledge* that our first father had sinned, and knew no more of his *sinful condition* than history tells us of it; if we had only *instituted types* and *figures* to keep up the remembrance of it in our minds, we should be never the worse for his sins. We should have no hurt by *owning* ourselves to be children of a sinful father, if his nature, *life* and *spirit* were not propagated in us. So, if we have

only a *notional belief* that Jesus is become the *second Adam*, to redeem, and regenerate the fallen nature; if we know this only in the *notion* and history kept up in our minds by *outward* figures and *ordinances:* tho' we contend ever so much for this belief of a Saviour, and write *volumes* in defence of it; yet he is not our Saviour, till his nature, life and spirit, be in us. If there be any man in the world, in whom the *nature* of *Adam* is not, he has no *sin* from *Adam*. If there be any man in whom the life of Jesus is not, he has no *righteousness* from him. We must have life and righteousness in the same *truth* and *reality* in us from the second *Adam*, as we have sin and death in us from the first.

28. The whole matter is this: Christ, by the overshadowing of the Holy Spirit, became in the *Virgin Mary*, of the same nature with that *first man*, which was created in Paradise; who according to the *purpose* of God, was to have been the father of an holy *race* of men. But seeing the first *Adam* failed in this *design* of God, the wisdom of God provided a *second Adam*, who was born in the *same degree* of perfection, in which the first man was created. To this holy paradisaical human nature the *Son* of God was personally united. And thus Christ the second *Adam*, took the place of the first, and stands as the second father of all the sons of *Adam*. Now as we are *earthly*, corrupt, and *worldly* men, by having the *nature* and *life* of the first *Adam* propagated

gated in us, so we must become *holy* and heavenly men, by having the life and nature of the second *Adam* derived into us; or as the scripture speaks, by being *born again*. Jesus Christ therefore helps us by a *second* birth, to such an *holy*, and *undefiled* nature, as he himself received in the *blessed Virgin*, and which we should have received in *Paradise* from our *first father*.

Thus by faith in Christ we put *on Christ*, he is formed in us; we eat his *flesh* and drink *his blood*, and have his *nature* and *life* in us.

Thus we are real members, living branches, and new born children of God.

29. * Look now at *yourselves*, at the *world*, at *religion*, in this true light, and surely you must see the desirable nature of every virtue, and every degree of it, which the gospel sets before you. Surely you must awake into a strong abhorrence of every thing that the fall has brought upon you; whether it be in your *souls*, your *bodies*, or the state of the world into which you are fallen. To renounce the poor interests of a worldly life, to be content with a *pilgrim's fare* in it, to live looking and longing after that which you have lost; to have no more of covetousness, of pride, of vanity and ambition, than *John* the Baptist had; to live unto God in your *shops*, your *employments* and estates, with such thoughts and desires of going to your heavenly Father, as the lost son had when he saw his poor condition, eating *husks* among *swine*, is only a

proof that you are, like him, come to yourselves, that you begin to see *what*, and how, and where you are. Surely you can need no exhortations to run to your Redeemer, to beseech him to do every thing in you and for you that your corrupted heart, and polluted body are in need of. He now stands as near you, as full of love to you, as he did to *Lazarus* when he raised him from the dead. He is no farther from your call than he was from the call of blind *Bartimæus*.

30. * Surely it should be as needless to exhort you to look earnestly after every means of recovering your first glorious state, as to exhort the blind to receive their sight, the sick to accept of health, or the captive to suffer his chains to be taken off. For when you see your *misery* and your *redemption*, both of them so exceeding great, you see *something* that must needs penetrate the depth of your soul, that leaves you no room to *doubt* about the nature of any virtue; no liberty to indulge *one vain* passion, or to think it any hardship that the gospel calls you to be *perfect*. For in this light every virtue of the gospel stands recommended to us, as *health, purity* and *sight* stand recommended to a *sick, noisome, blind leper*, who was shut up in a place that continually increased all his evils.

* It strips us of nothing, but the *uncleanness* of leprosies, the *miseries* of sores, pains and blindness. It takes nothing from the world which is
about

about us, but its poison and power of infecting us.

* So that to be called to the height of all virtue, however excessive it may seem to the *reasonings* of flesh and blood, is only being called away from every *misery* and *evil* that can be avoided by us.

31. * No virtue therefore has any *blameable extreme* in it, till it *contradicts* this general end of religion, till it *hinders* the restoration of the divine image in us, or makes us *less fit* to appear amongst the inhabitants of heaven. *Abstinence, temperance, mortification* of the senses and passions, can have no excess, till they hinder the purification of the soul, or make the body less subservient to it. *Charity* can have no excess, till it contracts that love which we are to have in heaven, till it is more than that which would lay down its life even for an enemy, till it exceeds that which the first Christians practised, when they had all things common; till it exceeds that of St. *John*, who requires him that has two coats, to give to him that has none; till it is loving our poor brethren more than Christ has loved us; till it goes beyond the command of loving our neighbour as we love ourselves.

32. See now how the Doctor instructs his readers on those two great articles, Christian *temperance,* and *charity*. To remove restraints of the first kind he says, Our Saviour came eating

ing and drinking, was prefent at weddings, and other entertainments. The Doctor may go on, and prove thefe indulgences to be good and pious, becaufe what our Saviour worked a miracle to promote muft needs be fo. And fo the adding another bottle, when friends are rejoicing, may be made a Chriftian duty.

But I muft vindicate the life and example of our bleffed Lord from the indignity done to it by the Doctor. Our bleffed Lord came indeed, as he fays of himfelf eating and drinking. But in what manner? In what fenfe, did he fay this of himfelf? Why it was in diftinction from *John the Baptift*, who came eating only one fort of food. And it was to fhew the *Jews* their great guilt in this refpect, that nothing could do them any good. For the mortification of the Baptift they condemned, as coming from the devil, and the condefcenfion of the holy Jefus in coming to their tables, they accufed as gluttony and winebibbing. Now the Doctor is plainly doing what our Lord accufed the *Jews* of; he with them condemns the mortification of the Baptift, as coming from the devil. But he differs from the *Jews* in this that he does not condemn, but *approves* of our Lord, as a *friend* to feafts, and merry meetings.

33. Our Saviour, fuitable to his gracious love, in coming into the world, fought the converfation of finners and publicans, becaufe he came to fave that which was loft, and becaufe he

knew

knew that some amongst such sinners were more moveable, than the proud sanctity of the learned Pharisees. But may we thence conclude, that the lives of such sinners were not blameable in his sight? Is not this as well, as to imagine he favoured the indulgence of feasting, and good fellowship, because he was found there? The holy Jesus conversed more freely, spoke of himself and of the kingdom of God more divinely to a wicked woman of *Samaria* than he appears to have done to his disciples. May we thence conclude, that he approved of a woman of that character, or thereby set his seal to the goodness, and lawfulness of her way of living? Is not this as well, as to make his presence at a wedding an approbation of the usual indulgences of such feasts?

34. O holy Jesus, thou didst nothing of thyself: thou soughtest only the glory of thy Father, from the beginning to the end of thy life. Thou spentest whole nights in prayer in mountains and desert places; thou hadst not where to lay thy head. Thy common poor fare with thy disciples was *barley bread* and *dryed fish*. Thy miraculous power never helped thee to any dainties or refreshment, tho' ever so much fatigued. But yet because this holy Jesus came into the world to save all sorts of sinners, and to shew that every kind and degree of sin could be taken away by him, therefore he came into all places, and entered into all sorts of companies. He did

not as the Baptist, tie himself to one sort of food. But he came eating and drinking. But why did he so? It was that he might reprove, and convert sinners at their own tables. He came not to indulge himself, or to find such gratifications as the Baptist abstained from; but to work miracles, to awaken sinners in the midst of their indulgences.

It is said, that wherever the King is, there is the court. But with much more reason may it be said, that wherever our Saviour came, there was the temple or the church. He came to *feasts* and *entertainments* with the same spirit, for the same end, and in the same divine power, as he went to raise a *dead corpse,* namely to shew forth the glory of God. Wherever he came, it was in the *spirit* and *power* of the Redeemer of mankind; every thing he did was only to destroy the works of the devil, to deliver man from his power, raise the dead, and give sight to the blind, and ears to the deaf. It made no difference to him, whether he did this in the temple, or in the streets, at a feast, or at a funeral. As he was every where God, so every place became holy to him. Lastly, if our Saviour, was present, at chearful entertainments, to shew his *approbation* of such indulgences, how came *John the Baptist,* that severe master of mortification to be a fit preparer of the way to the kingdom of heaven? Surely his voice must cry wrong, if such mortification was not right.

And if our Saviour disapproved of the severity
- of

of his life and manners, how came he to point him out as a burning and shining light? Thus much may serve to vindicate our Saviour's example from the shocking misapplication the Doctor has made of it.

35. Let us now see how he treats, and instructs the charitable Christian in these words.

" What, says the *half-thinker*, is not charity to the poor, a most excellent thing? And can I be too charitable? Can I therefore bestow too much upon the poor? I answer, tho' you cannot be too charitable, yet you may bestow too much upon the poor, to the ruin of your wife and children, which is not charity, but madness, and a great and *most grievous sin*. Did you never hear that *charity begins at home?* Did you never read that of St. *Paul? If any provide not for his own, and especially those of his own house: he hath deny'd the faith, and is worse than an infidel?*"

The Doctor's proverb I shall leave to himself; but the text of St. *Paul*, which he has as grosly misapplied, as he did our Saviour's miracle, I must take out of his hands. St. *Paul*'s words are quoted to prove, that it is madness, a great and grievous sin, for any one thro' charity to the poor to render himself unable to provide for his wife and children. Now the apostle in this place speaks no more about this sin, than he speaks against the sin of watching and prayer. Nay, what is more, there is not in all his writings, or in the whole New Testament, the *least supposition* or *hint* that such a sin ever was, or would be committed.

The apostle was singly speaking of *such women*, as were to be taken into the order of widows for the service of the church, and to be maintained by it. Verse 4. he says, that such widows as had children or nephews that could support them, were not to be maintained by the church. And to such sons and nephews who have mothers and aunts that thus want their assistance, he says, *If any one provide not for his own, especially for those of his own house,* i. e. If any sons or nephews have mothers or aunts become desolate widows, and take not care to assist them, especially if they live with them, such have renounced the piety of the gospel, and have not so much humanity as infidels.

36. This alone is the plain doctrine of the apostle, which the Doctor has grosly perverted, to the condemning of that which he never thought of. On the contrary, the scripture abounds with passages which might persuade us, that no family could ever be ruined by the alms and charity of its father; *I have been young, and now am old,* saith the psalmist, *Yet never saw I the righteous forsaken or his seed begging their bread.*

The liberal soul shall be made fat, and he that watereth shall be watered again. They that cannot believe this, want the faith of Christians. Had any one in the apostle's time reduced his wife and children to want, by his great charity to the poor, the apostle would have been so far from rebuking him, as a half-thinking fool, or exposing him

him to others, as guilty of madness, and grievous sin, that he would have told them, that he had consecrated himself and family to the church, that he and they were thereby become the dear objects of the church's care and love, since their present distress was brought upon them by a boundless love and compassion for the poor.

I will now put the following *case* in as high terms as the Doctor can well desire. Let it be supposed that some good *bishop*, possessed of as rich a *bishoprick* as that of *Winchester*, should through his extensive charity for the poor throughout the whole diocese, be forced to use the utmost frugality in family expences, and to bring up his children in employments of labour, to help themselves to food and raiment; one a carpenter, in which business our Saviour is said to have laboured in his youth; another a maker of tents, the trade of the great apostle: and the rest in the like manner. Let it be supposed, that when he died, he left only twenty pounds a year amongst them, not to be *possessed* by any one of them, but only to be used by every one as sickness or age made them stand in need of it, with this injunction, that it should be given to other sick and helpless people, when there was no such amongst themselves: Let it be supposed that by his life and conversation, he had filled his wife and children with the true and perfect spirit of the gospel, that they loved and rejoiced in his memory for all the good he had done to them, desiring nothing, but to go through the world, in the same *humility, piety, charity, love* of God, and *renunciation* of the world, as he had done. Will the Doctor say that this *bishop* had *ruined* his wife and children; that *half thinking* had betrayed him into a most *grievous sin,* that he had by this life *deny'd the faith,* and become *worse* than an infidel? I will venture to say, that if such a bishop should ever appear in this kingdom, he would bid fair to put an end to infidelity through all his diocese, though it were the largest in the nation. Now if the Doctor does not know of any one either among the *laity* or *clergy,* who is *ruining* his wife and children by a greater and more blameable charity than that of this bishop, it must be said, that he has been in too much haste, that his zeal has not proceeded from *knowledge*; and that he has been throwing *cold water* upon charity, before there was any flame in it.

37. I now proceed to shew in a more general way the blameable nature of the Doctor's discourse. The whole Christian world from the time of our Saviour to this day, has been praying, *Thy kingdom come, thy will be done on earth as it is in heaven.* Sacraments, divine worship, and the order of the clergy, are appointed as ministerial helps for this end, to raise, set up, and establish this kingdom of God on earth. The fall of a man brought forth the kingdom of this world; sin in all shapes is nothing else but the will of man, following the workings of a nature

broken

broken off from its dependency upon, and union with the divine will. All the evil and misery in the creation arises *solely* from this one cause: There is not the smallest degree of pain or punishment either within us, or without us, but is owing to this, viz. that man stands out of his place, is not *in*, and *under*, and *united* to God as he should be, as the nature of things requires. God created every thing to partake of his *own nature*, to have some share of his *own life*, and happiness. Nothing can be good or evil, happy or unhappy, but as it does or does not stand in the same *divine life* in which it was created, receiving in God, and from God, all that good that it is capable of, and so co-operating with, and under him, according to the nature of its powers and perfections. As soon as it turns to itself, and would as it were have a found of its *own*, it breaks off from the *divine harmony*, and falls into the misery of its own *discord*; and all its workings then are only so many sorts of torments. The redemption of mankind can then only be effected, the harmony of the creation can only then be restored when the will of God is the will of every creature. For this reason our blessed Lord having taken upon him a created nature, so continually declares against the doing any thing of himself, and always appeals to the will of God, as the only motive and end of every thing he did, saying, that it was his meat and
drink,

drink, to do the will of him that had sent him.

38. * What now can be so desirable to a sensible man, as to have the vain, disorderly passions of his heart removed from him, to be filled with such unity, love, and concord, as flow from God, to stand united to, and co-operating with the divine goodness, willing nothing, but what God wills, loving nothing, but what God loves, and doing all the good he can to every creature, from the principle of love and conformity to God. Then the kingdom of God is come and his will is done in that soul, as it is done in heaven. Then heaven itself is in the soul, and the life and conversation of the soul is in heaven. From such a man the curse of the world is removed; he walks upon consecrated ground, and every thing he meets, every thing that happens to him, helps forward his union and communion with God. For when we receive every thing from God, and do every thing for God, every thing does us the *same good*, and helps us to the same degree of happiness. *Sickness*, and *health, prosperity* and *adversity*, bless and purify such a soul; as it turns every thing *toward God*, so every thing becomes *divine* to it. For he that seeks God in every thing, is sure to *find* God in every thing. When we thus live wholly unto God. God is wholly ours, and we are then happy in all the happiness of God. This is the purity and perfection, that we pray for in the Lord's prayer, that *God's kingdom may come,*

come, and *his will be done in us, as it is in heaven.*

39. And this we may be sure is not only *necessary*, but *attainable* by us, or our Saviour would not have made it a part of our daily prayer. It may then justly be asked, have we yet obtained that, which we have been so long, and so universally praying for? Can we look upon the church of this nation, as drawing *near*, or even *tending* to this state of perfection? Can we be carried to any one parish, either in town or country where it can with truth be said of any *one pastor* and his *flock*, that there the kingdom of God is *coming* and his will *begins* to be done on earth, as it is done in heaven? Can we therefore find any *one parish*, where the *pastor* has not *great* reason to reject the Doctor's discourse, and to pray both for himself and his flock, that they may enter *much farther* into the spirit and practice of Christianity, than they have yet entered, that the gospel may have *much greater* power over them, than it hath yet had; and that they may all *see* what it is that has made so *divine*, and *powerful* a religion, so without its *proper effect* upon them? For if the case be thus, if we stand at this amazing distance from that state of perfection to which Christ has called us, do not *heaven* and *earth* seem to call upon *every minister* of the gospel, to take *some share* to himself of this *miserable state* of things, and to endeavour to convince both *himself*, and his *flock*, that they have not yet been Christians

in

in *true earnest*, that they have professed Christ with the tempers of *Jews* and *Heathens*, that they have not yet enough *renounced* the world, not enough *denied* themselves, not enough *emptied* their hearts of passions hurtful to piety, not enough *offered* and devoted themselves to God, not enough made the spirit of religion the spirit of their lives, not enough sought for strength and deliverance from sin, by a *firm* and *living faith* in Jesus Christ; not enough prayed and desired that they might be born again of God, so that Christ may be truly formed in them; not enough prayed and desired to be every where, and on all occasions under the perpetual influence and guidance of the Holy Spirit, that they may think and say, and do every thing by his holy inspiration; not enough looked to that first and great commandment, of loving God with our whole heart and strength: not enough endeavoured to keep the next, that of loving our neighbour, as ourselves; not enough renounced such fashions, customs, and conformities to the world, as corrupt the heart, and grieve and separate the Holy Spirit from it.

40. Now which way soever we consider the lamentable state of religion amongst us, no remedy can be procured by us of the *clergy*, but in this one way, that every *individual* of the order, from the highest to the lowest, begin in right earnest with himself, open the book of his own heart and life, and consider seriously,

in the presence of God, whether, according to his degree in the ecclesiastical function, the world has its *due* share of *salt* and *light* from him; whether all that is in the world, the *lust of the flesh, the lust of the eyes*, and the *pride of life* have been so openly, so constantly discouraged, and renounced by him, that the whole form of his life has been one kind, continual call to all orders of Christians, to set their affections on things above, to mind only the one thing needful, to have nothing at heart, but to be in Christ new creatures, seeking, intending, desiring nothing, thro' the pilgrimage of this life, but to live *unspotted from the world*, and to obtain every height of holiness, and heavenly affections, which becomes those who are to be called sons, and heirs of God with Christ Jesus.

41. If religion was at this time in a most flourishing state amongst us, abounding with such congregations as made up the primitive church, it would be great injustice to suppose that the clergy had not, under God, been the chief instruments of building it up to such a state of perfection. Seeing then an universal corruption of manners is on all hands confessed, to have overspread this Christian nation, and the true spirit of religion is hardly any where to be seen, nothing can be more reasonable than for every *clergyman*, wherever his lot is fallen, to suspect himself to have, in some degree, contributed to this common calamity, and to try to

discover

discover his own state, by such questions as these, laid *home* to his conscience. If Christianity has not done that to my flock which is the *only end* of it, is there nothing of this failure chargeable upon my conduct over it? Can my righteous Judge lay nothing to my charge on that account? Can my own heart bear me witness that I was not driven by *human passions*, but stayed and waited till the Holy Spirit called me to this office? Have I not undertaken the care of other souls, before I had any true and real care of my own? Have I not presumed to convert and strengthen others, before I was converted myself? To preach by hearsay of the grace, and mercy, and salvation of the gospel, whilst I myself was an obedient slave to sin? Have I not taken upon me to lay open the mysteries of God's love in Christ Jesus, before they had their *proper entrance* into my own soul? Have my own repentance, compunction, deep sense of the burden of sin, and want of a Saviour taught me how to make the terrors of the Lord known in the deep of every man's heart, and to awaken and pierce the consciences of sinners? Has, my own *true and living faith* in Christ my Saviour, my own experience of the atoning, cleansing, sanctifying powers of his precious blood, enabled me with great boldness to tell all sinners, that to the *faith which worketh by love*, Christ always and infallibly saith, what he said in the gospel,

Thy

Thy sins are forgiven; thy faith has saved thee; go in peace.

42. * Can my own heart, and God who is greater than our hearts, bear me witnefs that in my facred office I have not fought myfelf, or my own things, but the things of Jefus Chrift? If I have changed one flock or ftation for another, or added one cure to another, have I done it in *finglenefs of heart*, as unto the Lord and not for myfelf? Has all that I have fought or done of this kind, been only from this motive, that I might be more faithful to him that hath called me, and be more and more fpent and *facrificed* for the falvation of fouls? Have I neglected no means of fitting and preparing myfelf for the illumination of God's Holy Spirit, which alone can enable me in any meafure to fpeak to and work upon the hearts and confciences of men? Have I earneftly longed, and laboured after every kind and degree of inward and outward holinefs, and purity of *body, foul,* and *fpirit*, that my ftanding at the altar may be acceptable to God, and my prayers and interceffions for my flock avail much before him? Has my own felf-denial, renunciation of the world, and love of the crofs of Chrift, enabled me to preach up thofe duties in their full extent? Has my own ftrictly pious ufe of the things of this world, my own readinefs to affift every creature to the utmoft of my ability fitted me to call others to thefe things with power and authority? Have all ages and

and conditions of people under my care had their proper inftruction and warning from me, fo that I have fpared no folly, vanity, indulgence, or conformity to the world, that hurt mens fouls, and hinder their progrefs in piety? Have I done all that by my prayers and preaching, life and example, which Chrift expects from thofe whom he has enjoined to feed his fheep? Can my flock by looking at me fee what virtues they want? Can they by following me, be led to every kind and degree of Chriftian perfection! Laftly, has the will of God been the beginning and end, the reafon and motive, the rule and meafure, of my liking or difliking, doing or not doing every every thing among thofe people with whom I have lived as their minifter?

43. Thefe are a few of fuch queftions as the prefent ftate of religion in this *ifland* calls every minifter to try himfelf by. For as the order of the clergy is inftituted for no other end, but for the preferving of true piety in the world; fo when any age is more than ordinarily funk in vice and impiety, the *whole order* of the clergy, and *every member* of it, have great reafon not only to be deeply afflicted, but greatly affrighted at it, and to fufpect their own conduct, fince that which is their particular work, has had fo *little* fuccefs. They have great reafon to apprehend, that it is fome degeneracy of fpirit, fome general negligence, fome want of example, fome failure in doctrine, fome defect in zeal and care

of

of their particular flocks, that *too much* contributes to so *general a corruption* of manners. This does not suppose, that it is in the power of our order to regulate the manners of people as we please; it only supposes, that of all human means it has the *greatest effect*, and that when any nation or people are *very bad*, it behoves the clergy, who have any *right sense* of the nature of our order, any *true love* for our brethren of it, to awaken and stir up one another to a faithful diligence in our callings; not such as may secure us from public scandal, and the laws of the land, but such diligence as the nature of our office, the spirit of the gospel, and the present decay of religion call for. Let us beseech one another, deeply to consider the great need that this poor nation hath of a *zealous, pious, exemplary, disinterested* and *laborious* clergy; to consider the dreadful judgments of God, that may justly be expected to fall first upon our own heads, if this only remedy is not procured by all of us, according to the utmost of our ability. It is now no time for ease, indulgence or worldly repose; all is to be renounced, all is to be sacrificed. Our religion is founded on this doctrine.—That we are to be born again of the Holy Spirit;— that there is no sanctification of the heart, no illumination of the mind, no knowledge of divine mysteries, no love of holy things possible to be had, but in and by the motion and life of this Holy Spirit in us;—that its life, motion and power in us, increase according to our faith, prayers and desires of it.

44. * Is it not now a flat denial of all this to say, as do some, that the establishment of the gospel in the world, together with the assistances of *human learning*, and *languages*, has been the occasion why the assistance of the Holy Ghost is abated? For if we consult either scripture or experience, must it not be said, that *worldly peace* and *prosperity* want *as much* to be sanctified by the Holy Spirit, as *persecution* and *distress?* That *human learning* and *knowledge* need as *high degrees* of divine grace, as human ignorance? Is not the blindness and corruption of *men of letters*, as notorious as that of *unlearned* men? Does an *editor of Terence*, *Horace* or *Virgil*, receive such illumination from *plays* and *poetry?* Do *cardinals* and *pluralists* receive so much *unction* from human establishments, as to need less to be governed by the Holy Spirit of God? Or will we say, that a *critical study* of divided languages, and a religion established in worldly ease and peace, are not only in themselves free from danger and corruption, but have so much of the nature of the Holy Spirit in them, that they can be to us in *his stead*, and make his sanctifying operations upon us needed in a *less degree?*

45. On the part of God, our *redemption* in Jesus Christ, and our *sanctification* by the Holy Ghost, stand always in the *same degree* of *nearness* and *fulness* to all of us. There is hardly a chapter

ter in the New Testament that can be understood, but upon the supposition of this great truth. If Christ is less formed in us than he was in the first saints of the church, if we come not to the *perfect man, to the measure of the stature* of the *fulness of Christ*, it is not because Christ is now become only our Redeemer in an ordinary way; but it is because we have not so counted all things but *dung*, that we might win Christ, as the first saints did. If the Holy Spirit does not now in *such a degree* renew, quicken, move, and sanctify our hearts, and fill us with *such degrees* of divine light and love, as was done in the first age of the church, it is not because this sanctifying spirit has committed *some part* of his work to *human learning*, and so is become only our sanctifier in a lesser and *ordinary degree*, but it is because we ourselves have *forsaken this fountain of living waters, and hewed out broken cisterns* for ourselves; it is because we have grieved this Holy Spirit, *resisted* his motions, and under an *outward profession* of Christ have kept up that *old man, with his deeds*, which cannot be the habitation of the Holy Spirit.

* If therefore we have any true sense of the nature and weight of our ecclesiastical calling, any desire to do the *full work* of the ministry, to satisfy the necessities of our flocks; if we have any fear of being condemned as *useless* labourers in Christ's vineyard, it is high time to awake

from

from this dream of an ordinary and extraordinary sanctification of the Holy Spirit. It serves only to keep us *unsanctified,* shut up in death, in our own corrupted nature, to keep us *learnedly* content with our state, as if we were *rich and increased* in *goods*, and *had need of nothing*: and hinders us from knowing that we are *wretched* and *miserable, and poor, and blind and naked.*

46. * Several of the clergy, whose lot is fallen in this corrupt age, may be supposed to have taken upon them the sacred office, and to have lived in it, not enough according to the nature and spirit of it, merely through the *degeneracy* of the times, and from a consideration that they are well enough, according to the religion that now passes in the world. And perhaps there are few, if any of the order, however eminent for good works, whose virtues have not receiv'd *some abatement* from the same cause—This therefore may be added as another reason why all the clergy of this land must in the spirit of martyrdom awaken the world into a faith and love of the gospel. Now is the time that we must *give up* all our worldly regards, *forsake all that we have, that we must hate father and mother, wife and children, and brothers and sisters, yea and our own lives also,* or we cannot be faithful ministers of Jesus Christ. The same spirit which first planted the gospel, is now required to *recover* and *restore*

it

it amongst us. We must break off our chains of worldly prudence, and come forth in the spirit and power of the gospel: so live, and speak, and act, whether in the pulpit or out of it, that all who see and hear us may be forced to confess that God is in us of a truth. A *ministry* that have not this power, that have not *full proof*, both to themselves and others, that the Holy Spirit is thus *with them*, opening the kingdom of God in their own souls, and enabling them to preach it to others with spirit and power, are to answer to God for their want of it.

47. To ask whether the assistance of the holy Spirit is to be *ordinary* or *extraordinary*, is as needless a distinction, as to ask whether a *minister* of the gospel ought to be an ordinary or extraordinary man. The operation of the holy Spirit in us since the fall, is a supernatural power, and therefore in a just sense always extraordinary; because enabling us to be and do that, which the ordinary power of fallen nature is insufficient for. But it is more or less restored to us, as we are more or less fitted to receive it.

* The Christian religion has not had its proper effect, till it has so set up the kingdom of God among us, that *his will is done on earth, as it is done in heaven*.

* This is the perfection that every Christian is to *aspire* after. And if they who are to be taught, are to be thus emptied of all worldly pasfions, thus dead to the workings of self-will, that the Spirit of God may be all in all in them, what manner of men ought they to be, who are to *teach, promote, advance,* and *lead* the way to this purity and perfection? At what a distance ought he to be from every *appearance* of pride, that is to draw others to live and practife the profound humility of the bleffed Jefus? How ought he to humble his body, and be fteady in all kinds of self-denial, who would convince his flock, that *they who fow to the flefh reap* deftruction? How heavenly minded, how devoted to God, how attentive to the one thing needful, how unfpotted from the world ought he to be, who is to perfuade others that they cannot poffibly *ferve God and mammon?* How empty ought he to be of all *worldly* policy, all arts and methods of *ambition,* who is to fix it deep in the hearts of his hearers that *unlefs they become as little children, they cannot enter into the kingdom of God?* What open hands, and open heart ought he to have, what an extent of charity ought to be vifible in him, who is to bring his flock to this faith, that *it is more blessed to give than to receive?* How remarkably, undeniably plain, open, fincere, undefigning, and faithful fhould he be, who is to plant, and eftablifh fincerity, plainnefs, fimplicity, truth and innocence amongft his flock? There is fuch a neceffary fitnefs in thefe things, that the power of religion, muft be much prevented, when its precepts

cepts are recommended by such as excuse themselves from the plain and open practice of them.

48. * The office of the ministry is of the highest nature; it is a trust which no language can sufficiently express: and the unfaithful discharge of it is of all conditions in life the most dreadful. To be charged with the death and blood of souls, by that God who laid down his life to redeem them, is a condemnation that will carry more of guilt and punishment in it than any other. Would you know the office of a Christian pastor, you must look at the office of Christ. Would you know what manner of spirit he ought to be of, you must look at the Spirit of Christ. For the work of the ministry is only the work of Christ committed to other hands, who are to supply his absence, to be here in his stead, to be doing the same things, and with the same spirit that he did, till the end of the world.

* Nothing is so highly honourable as to bear a part in the priesthood of Christ, and be employed in the work of the ministry. But then it should be *well considered*, that it is only honourable in the *same sense*, as it is honourable to suffer as a martyr. It is an honour that is as different from all worldly figure and distinction, as the glory of Christ upon the cross is different from the triumph of an earthly prince. When therefore we think of the *honour* and *dignity* of the pastoral function, we should be careful to remember, that it is only the honour of dying a martyr, an honour

nour of humbling, abasing, and sacrificing ourselves with Christ, and continuing the exercise of his suffering-priesthood for the salvation of the world. The holy function is often considered only as an authoritative commission to minister in holy things. But it is much more than this. It is a call and command to act with the Spirit of Christ, to represent his purity, to continue his holiness, to bear a part of his sacrifice, and devote themselves for the good of others, as he did. A priest that has only his ordination to distinguish him, wants as much to make him a 'true priest, as *Judas* wanted to make him a true apostle. For tho' holiness alone gives no man a commission to exercise the pastoral office, yet all who are called to it, are as much ordained to a peculiar holiness, as to the administration of the sacraments.

49. For the sacred office is God's appointment, to continue through all ages, the spirit and power of Christ for reconciling men to God in the same manner and by the same means of holiness, sacrifice and devotion, which Christ exercised when he was upon earth. We need no other proofs of this, than this one saying of our Lord: *As my Father hath sent me, so send I you.* That is, for all the ends for which I am come into the world, for all the same ends I send you into it; to be there in my stead, to supply my absence, to carry on the work that I have begun, to act with my spirit, to continue the exercise of my

love

love, and labour, and suffering for the salvation of mankind. Now to be sent by our Lord for the same ends as he was sent into the world, is such an appointment of us to all kinds of holiness, as can never be rightly discharged, but by our devoting ourselves wholly and absolutely unto God.

Imagine that you had lived with our blessed Lord upon earth, that you had learned the dignity and divinity of his person, that you had seen the love which he bore to mankind, that you had entered into the glorious designs of his kingdom, which was to convert the inhabitants of the earth, poor creatures of flesh and blood, into sons of God and heirs of eternal glory.

Imagine that you had seen him after his resurrection, when he had redeemed the world, conquered sin, death and hell, and was about to take possession of his throne; imagine that then, you had seen him commission some of his followers to be priests and intercessors with God on earth, as he had been, to feed and nourish, and watch over his flock, as he had done, to go before them in such exemplary holiness, such love of God, such compassion for sinners, such contempt of the world, such poverty of spirit, such obedience, and resignation, as they had him for an ensample. Had you been present at all this, how would you then have felt these words, " As my Father hath sent me, so send I you?"

50. * What

50. " What sentiments of piety, what magnificence of spirit, what exalted holiness, would you have expected of those, who were called to succeed so great a master in so great a work? Could you think they could be fit for this office, unless they had *renounced* and *sacrificed* every thing for the sake of it? Could you think that any care but that of the church of God was proper for them? Would you not own that the conversion of sinners to God, ought to have been their only labour and pains? That they were to seek for no other happiness in this world, than such as their Lord and master had done, but consider themselves as called from the common affairs, ease and pleasures of life, to be in Christ's stead towards the rest of mankind, to conduct them safely to eternal happiness? Now when we consider the apostles in this light, as being the first that were entrusted with the *care of souls* from Christ himself, we can see no degree of zeal, no height of piety, no compassion for sinners, no concern for the honour of God, no contempt of suffering, no disregard of worldly interest, no watchings or mortifications, no fervours of devotion, to which we of the clergy are not equally obliged. For the salvation of mankind is still the same glorious, and necessary work that it was in their days; is still to be carried on by the same means, and is now in the hands of the clergy as it was then in theirs. If

it

it was their happiness and glory to be faithful to him that called them, to forget the little interests of flesh and blood, and have nothing at heart, but the advancement of God's kingdom, we shall fail both of happiness and glory if we seek it any other way. If an apostle considering the weight of reconciling souls unto God, is forced to cry out, *Who is sufficient for these things?* Shall we think any care but that which is the greatest, will make us stand uncondemned before God?

51. * It is a fatal deception to imagine, that the life of a minister of God is ever to be a life of ease and worldly repose. For tho' the temporal sword be not always drawn against them, nor they forced to flee from one city to another, yet the world, the flesh and the devil, are never so difficult to be resisted, as in temporal prosperity; nor have the ministers of Christ ever more occasion to put on all their armour, than when the world is given up to ease, and peace, and plenty. Swarms of vices steal in upon us in these seasons; the spirit and life of religion is in danger of being lost, and the salvation of souls is made more difficult, than in the most perilous times. And how is such a state of temptation to be resisted, such a torrent of vice to be suppressed, but by the clergy's shewing themselves *visible* and *notorious* examples of all the contrary virtues? When mankind are wallowing in debauchery, wantoning in pleasures, and given up

to vanity and luxury in all shapes, it is then the duty of the faithful minister, by his being crucified to the world, to proclaim himself a messenger of a crucified Saviour, and to make his own self-denying, mortified, and heavenly life, a plain, open, and constant reproof of all vain indulgences.

But to proceed, " To what a height of fanatic madness in doctrine as well as practice, says the Doctor, are some advanced, who set out at first with an appearance of more than ordinary sanctity only." Is not this calling upon the clergy to beware, how they admit these beginnings of a more than ordinary sanctity of life, either in themselves, or those committed to their care? Is it not plainly telling them, that they must stick *closely* and *steadily* to such sanctity of practice, as may be called *ordinary*, or else they will be in fanatic madness? Nay, it is no force put upon his words, to suppose, *a more than ordinary sanctity in practice only*, is marked out as the genuine, natural cause of *fanatic madness*, and therefore the cause is equally condemned with the effect. Had he meant that his reader should not have the same dislike of the one, as of the other, would he not have put in a word in favour of a *more than ordinary* sanctity of life? Would he not have said, that he did not intend to *blame that*, or at least not *so much* as the other? But not a word of this. A more than ordinary sanctity in *practice* only, and fa-

natic

natic *madness* are considered as cause and effect, and left in the same state of condemnation, to be equally guarded against, and avoided, by the reader.

52. I can't help here addressing myself with great affection to all my younger brethren of the clergy. According to the course of nature, you are likely to have the care of the church wholly upon your hands in a short time; and therefore it is chiefly from you that the restoration of true piety is to be expected in this nation. I beseech you, therefore for your own sakes, for the gospel's sake, for the sake of mankind, to devote yourselves wholly to the love and service of God. As you are yet but beginners in this great office, you have in your power to make your lives the greatest happiness, both to yourselves and the whole nation. You are entered into *holy orders* in degenerate times, where trade and traffic have seized upon all holy things; and it will be easy for you without fear to swim along with the corrupt stream, and to look upon him as an enemy or enthusiast, that would save you from being lost in it. But think my dear brethren, think in time what remorse you are treasuring up for yourselves, if you live to look back upon a loose, negligent, worldly life, spent among those whose blood will be required at your hands. Think on the other hand, how blessedly your employment will end, if by your voices, your lives, and labours, you put a stop

to the overflowings of iniquity, restore the spirit of the primitive clergy, and make all your flock bless and praise God, for having sent you among them. * Lay this down as an infallible principle, that *an entire, absolute renunciation* of all worldly interest, is the only possible foundation of that virtue which your station requires. Without this all attempts after an exemplary piety are in vain. If you want any thing from the world by way of figure and exaltation, you shut the power of your Redeemer out of your own souls, and instead of converting, you corrupt the hearts of those that are about you. Detest therefore with the utmost abhorrence, all desires of making your fortunes, either by preferments or rich marriages, and let it be your only ambition to stand at the top of every virtue, as visible guides and patterns to all that aspire after the perfection of holiness. Consider yourselves merely as the messengers of God, that are solely sent into the world, to bring the world to God.

53. I don't call you from a sober use of human learning, but I would fain persuade you to think nothing worthy of your notice in books and study, but that which applies to the amendment of the heart, which makes you more holy, more divine, more heavenly, than you would be without it. You want nothing, but to have the corruption of your natural birth removed, to have the nature, life, and spirit of Jesus Christ

Chrift derived into you. As this is all you want, fo let this be all that you feek from books, ftudy, or men. This is the only certain way to become eminent divines, inftructed to the kingdom of heaven. And above all, let me tell you that the book of all books is your own heart, in which are written and engraven the deepeft leffons of divine inftruction. Learn therefore to be deeply attentive to the prefence of God in your heart, who is always fpeaking, always inftructing, always illuminating that heart that is attentive to him: and be affured of this, that fo much as you have of inward attention to God, of love and adherence to his holy light and Spirit, fo much as you have of real, unaffected humility and meeknefs; fo much as you are dead to your own will, fo much as you have of purity of heart; fo much and no more, nor any further, do you fee and know the truths of God. Thefe virtues are the only eyes, and ears and fenfes, by which you will underftand every thing in fcripture, in that manner in which God would have it underftood, both for your own good, and the good of other people.

54. It was owing to this purity of heart, and attendance upon God, that an ancient widow named *Anna*, knew him to be the true Meffiah, whom the rulers, chief priefts, and doctors of the law, condemned as an impoftor. Had they, inftead of their adherence to critical knowledge and rabbinical learning, been devoted to God

in such purity of heart as she was, they had known as much of the kingdom of God, as she did. Place therefore all your hope, all your learned help and skill, in the ardent love and practice of *these virtues*. And then, you will be able ministers, holy priests, and messengers of God; your cleansed hearts, like so many purified mirrors, will be always penetrated, always illuminated by the rays of divine light, and you will no more need the critics, to tell you what God speaks to you in the scriptures. But of all men in the world, the critical dealers in words and particles, know the least of them, and make the vainest attempts to understand them.

Scripture confidered as a doctrine of *life, faith* and *salvation* in Jesus Christ, is a sealed or unsealed, an open or shut up book to every heart, in the same proportion as it stands turned to the world, or turned to God. Nothing understands God, but the Spirit of God; nothing brings the Spirit of God into any mind but the renouncing all for it, the turning wholly unto it, and the depending wholly upon it. * Human learning is by no means to be rejected from religion, for it is of the same use, and affords the same assistance to religion, that the *alphabet, writing* and *printing* does. But if it is raised from this kind and degree of assistance, if it is considered as a key, or the key to the mysteries of our redemption, instead of opening to us the kingdom of God, it locks us up in our own darkness. God
is

is an all fpeaking, *all working, all illuminating* effence, poffeffing the depth of every creature according to its nature; and when we turn from all impediments, this divine effence becomes as certainly the true light of our minds here, as it will be hereafter. This is not enthufiafm, but the words of truth and fobernefs; and it is the running away from this enthufiafm, that has made fo many great fcholars as ufelefs to the church as tinkling cymbals, and Chriftendom a mere *Babel* of learned confufion.

Some

Some ANIMADVERSIONS upon

Dr. TRAP's late REPLY.

HAD I the spirit of an *adversary*, or were inclined to find entertainment for the *satirical reader*, it would not be easy for me to overlook the opportunity which Dr. *Trap*'s Reply has put into my hands; but as I don't want to lessen any appearance of ability which the Doctor has shewn on this occasion; so whatever *personally* concerns him, either as a *writer*, a *scholar*, a *disputant*, a *divine*, or a *Christian*, shall have no reflection from me; and tho' by this means, some sort of readers may be less pleased, yet, the more Christian reader will be glad to find, that thus I must leave *two thirds* of his reply untouched; and as I neither have, nor (by the grace of God) ever will have any *personal contention* with any man whatever, so all the *triumph* which the Doctor has gained over me by that flow of wrath and contempt which he has let loose upon me, I shall leave him quietly to enjoy.

It would be no pleasure to me, nor benefit to the world, to discover that *malignity* of *spirit*, that *undistinguishing head*, that *diabolical calumny*, that
shameful

shameful ignorance, that *indecent sufficiency,* that *unbecoming presumption,* that *nauseous* dulness, that *ignorance* of *logic,* that *insensibility* of argument, that want of *grammar,* which he has so heartily laid to my charge; and if he has any readers that thank him for this, I shall make no attempt to lessen their number.

As I desire nothing for myself, or the reader, but good *eyes,* and a good *heart,* seriously attentive to things useful, and always open to the light and influence of the Holy Spirit of God, so I shall endeavour to say nothing but what is suitable to such a state of mind, both in myself and the reader.

* The thing of importance which I shall speak to, shall be with regard to what I have said to the clergy. The miserable state of religion, and the great corruption of manners, so incontestably apparent in this island, gave me a just occasion to desire all the clergy, from the highest to the lowest in the order, to consider their conduct, and see how free they were from the common corruption, and how justly every one could clear himself from having any share in this general depravity of manners. I was not insensible that this was a dangerous attempt, that would expose me to the resentment of not a few of my brethren: but as I wrote for no other end but to do as much good as I could to those who were capable of it, so I had no care but how to speak disagreeable truths, in as inoffensive a manner

as

as I could; how I have succeeded in this, is left to the world to judge. And as it is but too apparent, that the root of all the evil, which but too much spreads itself through the whole body of the clergy, is owing to a worldly, trading spirit, too visible from the top to the bottom of the order, so I pointed at it in the softest manner that I could, in the following words, grounded on a plain apostolical doctrine and practice.

St. *Paul,* I had observed, had said, it was lawful for those that preach the gospel to live by the gospel, and yet makes it matter of the greatest comfort to himself that he had wholly abstained from this *lawful thing*; and declares it were better for him to die than that *this* rejoicing should be taken from him. He appeals to his daily and nightly working with his own hands, that so he might preach the gospel *freely,* and not be chargeable to those that heard him. And this he said he did, not for want of authority to do otherwise, but that he might make himself an ensample unto them to follow him. Here, I say, " What awakening instructions are here given to us of the *clergy,* in a practical matter of the greatest moment? How ought every one to be frighted at the thoughts of desiring or seeking a *second living,* or of rejoicing at great pay where there is but little duty, when the apostle's rejoicing consisted in this, that he had passed thro' all the fatigues and perils of preaching the gospel without any pay at all? How cautious,

nay,

nay, how fearful ought we to be, of going so far as the secular laws permit, when the apostle thought it more desirable to lose his life, than to go so far as the very law of the gospel would have suffered him?

"It is looked upon as lawful to get several preferments, and to make a gain of the gospel, by hiring others to do duty for us at a lower rate. It is looked upon as lawful to quit a cure of souls of a small income, for no other reason, but because we can get another of a greater. It is looked upon as lawful for a clergyman to take the revenues of the church, which he serves, to his *own use*, tho' he has more than a competency of his own, and much more than the apostle could get by his labour. It is looked upon as lawful for the clergy to live in state and equipage, to buy purple and fine linen out of the revenues of the church. It is looked upon as lawful for clergymen to enrich their families, to bring up their children in the fashionable vanities, and corrupting methods of a worldly and expensive life, by money got by preaching the gospel of Christ. But supposing all this *lawful*, what comfort might we treasure up to ourselves, what honour might we bring to religion, what force might we give to the gospel, what benefit should we do to our neighbour, if we wholly abstained from all these lawful things? Not by working day and night with our own hands, as the great apostle did, but by limiting our

our wants and defires to the plain demands of nature, and a religious felf-denial."

Now, there are but two poffible ways of juftly replying to this; firft, either by fhewing that thefe obfervations are falfely drawn from the apoftle's doctrine and practice, that I have miftaken the fpirit of St. *Paul,* and the genius of the gofpel, that I am doing what the apoftle would not do, was he here in perfon, and reprefenting fuch things as corruptions, which the apoftle would be glad to fee flourifhing in the church of Chrift: Or, fecondly, that though thefe things are condemnable from the apoftle's doctrine and practice, yet they are not chargeable upon the temper and practice of the clergy of this land. But, though not a word to the purpofe could poffibly be faid, unlefs by one of thefe two ways, yet the Doctor fhuts his eyes to both of them, and then pronounces fentence upon me, " That a Quaker or Infidel could not well have reflected with more virulency upon the clergy of our church, than I have done in thefe expreffions."

Muft I then fuppofe, that the Doctor in his fermons never mentions any failings that concern his auditors? If he does, I defire to know, how he clears himfelf from virulently reflecting upon them? The Quakers and Infidels are ready enough, and able enough to fhew, that moft congregations of Chriftians are fadly fallen from the religion of the gofpel. But does the Doctor
forbear

forbear this charge, is he aſhamed to call his flock to a more Chriſtian life, or afraid to remind them of their departure from the goſpel, leſt he ſhould ſeem to join with Quakers and Infidels? Or, how can the Doctor be thought to have any *true love*, or *juſt eſteem* for thoſe Chriſtians, whom he is ſo often reminding of the corruption of their manners, ſo contrary to the religion of Jeſus Chriſt? Now, if the Doctor knows how to untie this knot, and to extricate himſelf from the charge of virulent reflecting upon his pariſhoners, as Quakers and Infidels do, then he has diſſolved his charge againſt me into a mere nothing.

* If it was a thing required of me, I know no more how to raiſe in myſelf the leaſt ſpark of ill-will towards the clergy, as ſuch, than I know how to work myſelf up into a hatred of the light of the ſun. It is as natural to me, to wiſh them all their perfection, as to wiſh peace and happineſs to myſelf here and hereafter; and when I point at any failings in their conduct, it is only with ſuch a ſpirit as I would pluck a brother out of the fire.

In that part of my anſwer, which is addreſſed to the younger clergy, I ſaid, " Lay this down for an infallible principle; that an entire, abſolute renunciation of all worldly intereſt, is the only poſſible foundation of that exalted virtue, which your ſtation requires; without this, all attempts after an exemplary piety are vain: *(and then, by way of limitation and explication of this, it thus immediately follows:*) If you want any thing from the world by way of *figure* and *exaltation*, you shut the power of your Redeemer out of your own souls, and instead of converting, you corrupt the hearts of those that are about you. Detest therefore, with the *utmost abhorrence*, all desires of making your fortunes, either by *preferments*, or *rich marriages*, and let it be your only ambition, to stand at the top of every virtue, as visible guides and patterns to all that aspire after the perfection of holiness," *p.* 61.

Now, one would imagine there was no part of the Christian world, however corrupted, where this doctrine would not be admitted at least in theory; or, that the gospel of Christ should be thought to be reproached, where such advice as this was given to young divines: and yet it is of this very advice, that Dr. *Trap* says, " he *hopes they* will have more *grace* and sense *than to follow it:* that it is *false doctrine, tending to the reproach and scandal of the Christian religion,*" p. 87.

Is it then come to this, that unless young divines chuse to serve mammon as well as God, their profession is a renouncing of grace and sense, and a reproach to religion? And must they that pretend to act in Christ's name, as successors in his office, take care that they renounce not the politics of the kingdom of this world? For my part, I thought it as consistent with the honour of the gospel, to give this advice, to suppress

all

all worldly views, as to refift the temptations of the devil.

Had *Martin Luther*, when he gave his reafons for withdrawing from the *Pope*, been able to have added this; that the advice here given, had been formally condemned by the *Pope* in a great council, the defenders of that church would have found it as hard to have made fuch a decree confiftent with the gofpel, as the felling of indulgencies: and it may well be fuppofed, that no Proteftant writer, when fetting forth the marks of antichrift, in that church, would have forgot to have made this condemnation to be one of them.

For who can fhew it to be fo contrary to the whole fpirit of the gofpel, to call in the *affiftance* of the faints, or to deny the cup to the laity, who can fhew this to put fo entire a ftop to falvation by the gofpel, as to condemn this *advice* to young divines, as a reproach to Chriftianity? For all the ends of the gofpel may be purfued, and men may arife out of the corruption of their nature, notwithftanding thefe two miftakes: but to condemn it as an error inconfiftent with grace and fenfe, a reproach to Chriftianity, for young divines to renounce worldly views, and devote themfelves wholly to God, is ftriking at the whole root of all holinefs, and a denial of the whole fpirit of the gofpel.

Our church requires all its candidates for holy orders, to make profeffion of their being moved and

and called by the Holy Ghost to enter into the service of the church: this, I should think, is proof enough, that the spirit of this world ought not to be alive in them, when they make this profession; and yet, if any young persons should come to be ordained, thus dead to all worldly views, thus wholly devoted to God, they ought according to the Doctor, to be rejected by the bishop, as being led by a spirit that has lost all *grace* and *sense*, and is a *reproach* to the Christian religion.

It is needless to quote particular texts of scripture, teaching the same that I have here taught; the whole nature of our redemption is a standing proof of the same thing; for we want to be redeemed for no other reason, but because we are born children of this world, and have by nature only the life, spirit and temper of this world, in us: this is our fall, our curse, our separation from God; and therefore we can have no redemption, but by a renunciation of all the workings of the life of this world in us, by a total dying to, and denying ourselves; because all that we are, as to our state, spirit and life in this world, is a life that carries us from God, a life that should not have been in us; 'tis a life begun by the fall, a life of sin and corruption, which cannot enter into heaven. Indeed the life that we have in this world, from *Adam*, is not to be *naturally* destroyed, nor are the necessaries and conveniences of life to be rejected,

nor

nor is any one to renounce his share in the employments that are useful to social life : the renunciation of this world reaches no farther than the renouncing the spirit, and inclinations of it. We may stand in our stations, when we stand in them as the servants of God, as citizens of the new *Jerusalem*, who have amongst earthly things, our conversation in heaven: we may keep our possessions, when we possess them as the things of God, and use them not as nature, but as the Spirit directs us; when we do thus, we have the poverty of spirit, which the gospel requires, and come up to the sense of that command given to the young man, *to sell all that he had, and give to the poor.*

But now, if our natural life is a corrupt, bestial, diabolical life brought forth by the fall, if we want to be born again of the Holy Spirit, because our natural birth is according to the spirit of this world; if nothing of the beast, or the devil, no kind or degree of envy, pride and vanity can enter into the kingdom of God, then it is plain, that all religion which leaves this nature unrenounced, which lets pride, wrath, and vanity subsist in us, which brings us to our graves in the same nature in which we were born, is not the religion that can save us. If this nature in all its most secret workings is not renounced, it matters not what we are, or what we have been doing, it signifies little in what chair we have sat, whether in *Italy*, or *England*, how long we have
been

been preachers, how many hereticks and fchif-
maticks we have oppofed, or how many books
we have written in defence of orthodoxy; it is
as vain to appeal to this, as to our having preached and *prophefied* in the name of Chrift: for if
this nature is allowed to live in us, all our good
works have been governed by it, they are animated with pride, and only ferve to gratify our
own natural paffions. When therefore the
Doctor calls upon young divines to have *more
grace* and *fenfe* than to be driven from thoughts
of advancing themfelves by *preferments and rich
marriages,* he would do well to confider, how
little fhort this is of calling them to break their
very baptifmal vow, of *renouncing the pomps and
vanities of the world.* And if young candidates
for holy orders, looking only at their baptifmal
vow, fhould be led into this degree of felf-denial
and detachment from the world, does the Doctor think, that the apoftles, from whom this
baptifmal vow is defcended, will rife up in the
day of judgment, and condemn fuch abufe of it?
Does he think, that there are any departed faints
that will join with him in faying, fuch a fpirit is
a *reproach* to the gofpel? What more favoura-
ble difpofition could the adverfary of mankind
wifh to fee, either in young or old divines, than
a wanting and defiring to have figure in the
world, either by preferments or rich marriages?
Would he find it difficult to enter into thofe
hearts, where the luft of the flefh, the luft of the
eyes,

eyes and the pride of life has thus entered? Or would he look upon such as but half fitted for him, in comparison of those who entered into holy orders in a spirit of self-denial, and renunciation of the pomps and vanities of the world?

* *John* the *Baptist* was but the preparer of the way for evangelical purity of life; but does, the Doctor think that if the *Baptist* was now to come amongst us, he would look at things as the Doctor does, that he would see such perfections and such corruptions, such orthodoxy and such enthusiasm as the Doctor sees; that this *burning and shining light* would see no *generation of vipers* but where the Doctor sees them; that he would preach no where but in churches; that he would spare no clergy, nor any church, but that which is established in this island; that he would complain of the hardships of our clergy, and the suffering spirit which they are forced to practise, that he would plead for a priestly liberty of coveting preferments and rich marriages, that he would recommend the Doctor's discourse of the *folly, sin, and danger of being righteous over-much*, as the true fruits of that spirit which first preached the gospel? He that can believe this, must believe that the Baptist was come to confess the errors of his first appearance in the world.

I shall therefore proceed to tell young divines, that a total renunciation of the spirit, and inclinations of this life, is the one thing necessary

to confecrate them to their holy office; that as
fure as the church of Chrift is not a kingdom of
this world, as fure as Jefus Chrift came to deliver us from this evil world, as fure as he requires us to be born again, and to forfake all and
follow him, fo fure is it that no one has the
call of the Holy Spirit to the miniftry, nor the
leaft ground of hoping to be led and governed
by it in his miniftry, till he at leaft prays, defires, and heartily endeavours to have all that
difregard of worldly profperity, figure, and diftinction, which the Spirit of Jefus Chrift, the
maxims of the gofpel, and the practice of the
apoftles fet before him. Till this renunciation
of the world is made, we cannot enter into the
miniftry at its *own door*, but like thieves and
robbers, climb over its walls; and then it will
be no wonder if we do no more good to the
church than thieves do the houfe they break open
and plunder. If a young minifter wants to act
the part of a fine gentleman, to go on in the common fpirit of the world, to cover a fecular fpirit
with an ecclefiaftic garb, and make his fortune in
the church, he muft be told that it is much fafer
to be a *publican* and a *finner*, than to be a *trader* in
fpiritual things; that he who with unfanctified
hands attends at the altar, is farther from the kingdom of God, than a *publican*.

Covetoufnefs is idolatry; it is a heathenifh, an-
tichriftian vice, tho' only trafficking in worldly
matters; but when it takes poffeffion of the altar,
and

and makes a trade of the myſteries of ſalvation. It has a blackneſs of vice which much exceeds that of the worldly miſer. The ſpirit of an ecclefiaſtic ſhould be the ſpirit of heaven, knowing nothing of this world, but how to eſcape its ſnares and temptations, burning in the love of God, and holding out light to all that aſpire after every perfection of the Chriſtian life.

* 'Tis too commonly thought, that when a young ſtudent has taken his degree, and ſhewn ſome ſigns of a genius for learning, he is well perpared to enter into the ſervice of the church. But alas! all the accompliſhments of human learning are but the ornaments of the *old man*, which leave the ſoul in it ſlavery to ſin, full of all the diſorders and corruptions of the fallen nature. If it were not thus, how could the errors of all churches have the greateſt ſcholars for their champions? All the learned Catholic world is amazed at the blindneſs, the perverſeneſs, the weakneſs, the ſophiſtry, the unfairneſs of *Proteſtant critics*. All the Proteſtant world is in the ſame degree of wonder at the ſame diſorders in *Catholic diſputants*. Is not this a demonſtration of the nature, power, and place of human learning? Of its great uſeleſſneſs to religion? Does not this enough ſhew, that it is the offspring of the old man, and his nature and qualities dwells in him, and is governed by him? Is not this a demonſtration, that the greateſt degrees of hiſtorical, verbal, critical knowledge are no real hinderance of

ſpiritual

spiritual blindness? That human learning is as different from divine light as heaven is from earth; and that considered in itself, it leaves us in our slavery to blind and corrupt passions? Now nothing can deliver a man from this state, but the Spirit of God derived into his soul, which alone can bring forth a new man created in Christ Jesus. Nothing can make way for this new birth, but a total dying to all that we are by our natural birth. 'Tis only *this separation* from things below, that can make us partakers of the truth and light that comes from above. Take away all selfishness from the Papist and the Protestant, let them be dead to the workings of the Spirit, and they will be as fully agreed about gospel truths, as they are in the form of a square or a circle. For nothing stands in the way of divine truth, or hinders its full entrance into us, but this selfishness, which adheres to every one who does not make it his first maxim, prayer, and endeavour to die to, and deny himself in all the tempers and inclinations of our fallen nature. This self-denial is the continual doctrine of our Lord; it is by him made the beginning of all conversion to God, and he that cannot, or will not begin there, can make no beginning of that life, to which he is called in Christ Jesus: therefore he that offers himself for holy orders, without this spirit of self-denial, is a miserable intruder; he only hardens and fixes himself in the corruptions of his own nature, and instead of becoming an inftrument of faving others, his very office makes his own falvation more dangerous.

I doubt not but fome will here charge me with pleading for poverty in the miniftry, and with enmity to that maintenance which they have both from the law and the gofpel. But this is fo far from being true, that I wifh every good minifter, whom the Spirit of God has called to this office, and governs in it, had much more of this world's goods than are needful for his own fubfiftence; becaufe it is certain, that fuch a one's money would all be put into the poor's bag, and he would as gladly adminifter to their temporal as to their fpiritual neceffities. I write againft nothing but *avarice, pride,* and *ambition,* and the making the provifions of the church *fubfervient* to thefe tempers. A provifion arifing from the gofpel, is *confecrated* by the gofpel, and is profaned by being touched and ufed by a worldly fpirit. And he who turns this provifion of the gofpel into a gratification of worldly paffions, fins againft the gofpel more than he that pays his tithes with reluctance.

I can eafily believe, there are clergy in this land, who labour in the gofpel, without having a fufficient fubfiftence from it; but may not much of this evil be charged upon *pluralities, commendams,* and fuch like fpiritual trading? If the inferior clergy had their labours only undervalued by the laity, they would be in a much better condition than they are.

When it is complained by what shameful *qualifications*, empty *titles*, and unworthy pretences, numbers of persons get loaded and dignified with variety of preferments; it is answered, that if preferments might not be thus crowded together, distinguished abilities and eminent labours for the service of religion, must go unrewarded.

As this answer is not fetched from the gospel, or the primitive church, so it is as little supported by reason. For if this eminent labour is truly pious labour, what state of life can so little want to be rewarded? How can imagination itself place a man more *above* the thoughts and desires of worldly advancement? If such a one is full of the spirit of the gospel, if his labours have been like those of an apostle, must he not like an apostle, be *dead* to the world? Can such a one look upon his labour as a *hardship*, because it has left him as low, and as far from the *pomp* of the world as it found him? Can he repine because the gospel has not proved a good *worldly bargain* to him? If the Spirit of God has begun, and directed all his labours, animated all his studies and designs, can such a one think it hard, that he has not by such labours purchased to himself a share in the state and pride of life?

* If by a *great divine*, is only meant a person well skilled in *critical contention*, who can artfully defend a set of notions, amongst which he happened to be born and bred, such a divine, I own, may be very *impatient*, and *much cooled* in his zeal,
unless

unless he finds himself well rewarded. But if an eminent divine is to be understood in a sense suitable to the gospel, he is that *particular person* that must needs have the greatest contempt and dislike of every thing, that has but the appearance of the pomp and vanity of this world in it. If therefore it was urged, that this conjunction of preferments and dignifying rewards was necessary to bring *ambitious scholars* into the church, or to keep them in it, there would be some sense, tho' no gospel in the pretence; but to talk of them as necessary to be the rewards of eminent piety and apostolic labour, is as absurd, as to say, that those who have truly put on Christ, who stand in the highest degree of a renewed nature, who best know and feel the blessing of a mortified, heavenly spirit, have less reason to be *content with food and raiment*, than those who stand in a lower degree of the Christian life; 'tis saying, that a *bishop*, because he has most of the spirit and office of an apostle, may well desire more of the *pride* and *figure* of this world, than the lower clergy, who have less of the apostolic spirit and perfection in them.

To want to stand in some degree of worldly figure, is the state of a *babe* in the Christian life, and therefore can no way become those, who are to lead others to fulness of stature in Christ Jesus.

A *great divine* is but a *cant* expression, unless it signifies a man *greatly advanced* in the divine life, whose

whose own experience and example is a demonstration of the *reality* of all the graces of the gospel. No divine has any more of the gospel in him, than that which proves itself by the spirit, and form of his life: if therefore poverty of spirit, a disregard of worldly figure, a total self-denial is any part of the gospel, an eminent divine, can have no wish with regard to the figure, pride and pomp of life, but to be placed out of every appearance of it: and if the highest in divine knowledge are not the foremost in poverty of spirit, and the outward humility of Christ and his apostles; if they desire to have a dignity of worldly figure, to have respect by any other means than by a divine evangelical spirit and conversation, and are not content with all the contempt that such a life can expose them to, they may be *great scholars*, but they are *little divines*, and are wanting in that which is the chief part of the ministers of Jesus Christ.

The next thing I said to the young clergy, was this; " Consider yourselves *merely* as the mes-
" sengers of God, that are sent into the world *solely*
" on his errand; and think it happiness enough
" that you are called to the same business for which
" the Son of God was born into the world." *p.* 81.

Now, I thought what I have said, was as unexceptionable, as unfit to be condemned by a professor of Christian theology, as if I had only recommended the loving of God with all our heart and soul, and mind and strength; and that

if

if any clergyman difliked it, he would be forced to keep his diflike to himfelf; but the Doctor is very open in his indignation at it; the fame anfwer, he fays, is to be given here, as before, *viz. that it is falfe doctrine, tending to the fcandal and reproach* of the Chriftian religion.

Our blefled Lord, when he fent the firft preachers of the gofpel into the world, faid unto them, *As my Father hath fent me, fo fend I you—go ye and teach all nations—and lo I am with you to the end of the world.* Now let it be fuppofed, that thefe firft preachers of the gofpel fully believed, that from the time of their appointment to this high office, they *were to confider themfelves merely as the meffengers of God, fent into the world folely on his errand,* and that *it was happinefs enough for them to be called to that bufinefs,* for which the Son of God was *born into the world;* if they had this belief, what follows? Why, according to the Doctor, that they fet out from the very firft in one of the greateft errors, had miftaken the nature and intent of their miffion, and had gone into the world upon a principle that *was falfe* in itfelf, and *fcandalous* and *reproachful* to the Chriftian religion.

But if this belief is not to be condemned in the firft clergy, I defire to know why thofe who claim their fucceffion from the firft, and expect the prefence of Chrift in and with their miniftry, are not to be called upon to be of the fame fpirit and belief with them, or how can it be a fcandal to the gospel, for the modern clergy to be as wholly devoted to the service of God, as the apostles were.

The Doctor sets it out as an extraordinary presumption in *such a man* as I am, to pretend to give advice to young divines, when it is so sufficiently done already by the *offices of our church, the charges, instructions and exhortations of our bishops at their visitation, and so many excellent ordination and visitation sermons*, p. 87. Now, granting the plenty and excellency of all these, yet I have some hope, my presumption may be found to be only like that of the *poor widow*, who after so many rich oblations of great people, presumed to put her little mite into the treasury. And if it be true, that the things suggested by me, are only such as have been already set forth by so many great bishops and excellent preachers, how will the Doctor come off for condemning it, as false doctrine, scandalous, and reproachful to the Christian religion?

Dr. *Trap* gives a reason for his condemning this advice, which is thus expressed: " It is, says he, false to say, that clergymen ought to mind nothing, in any degree, but their profession and duty, as clergymen; they are husbands, parents, men, as well as clergymen, and must in some measure be concerned in the affairs of the world. p. 88."

Part of this I own to be very true, *viz.* that they are men, and have the wants of human nature

nature which muſt be ſupplied; and for proof of this, the Doctor might have appealed to St. *Paul*, who, tho' miraculouſly called to be an apoſtle, and ſeparated from the world to be merely a meſſenger and apoſtle of Jeſus Chriſt; yet, after this high apoſtleſhip, worked at his trade, and often ſpent part of the day and the night in making tents: therefore, if all thoſe whom I have exhorted to conſider themſelves as ſet apart for the ſole ſervice of God, ſhould ſhew ſuch a degree of worldly care as St. *Paul* did, when he worked at his trade, they might yet juſtly be ſaid to act ſuitably to their ſtation, as the miniſters of God, that are wholly devoted to his ſervice; for who can ſay that St. *Paul* departed from his character, as a miniſter of God, when he laboured with his own hands, that he might glorioufly and freely preach the goſpel? For it was for the ſake of the goſpel, to promote and recommend the goſpel, to make his preaching the more ſuccefsful; it was to ſhew that he had fully renounced the world, and defired nothing from it, but for the glory of God. And thus have all the miniſters of the goſpel an example in St. *Paul*, how they may make their care of a livelihood a part of their ſervice to God.

But when the Doctor ſays, that clergymen are huſbands and parents, I muſt object a little; becauſe no ſcripture or antiquity ſhews me, that theſe characters *muſt* belong to a preacher of the goſpel; and therefore, when a clergyman exocuſes cufes himfelf from any heights of the minifterial fervice, by faying, *he has married a wife and therefore cannot come* up to them; it feems to be no better an excufe, than if he had faid, *he had hired a farm*, or *bought five yoke of oxen.*

I know very well, that the *reformation* has allowed priefts and bifhops not only to look out for wives, but to have as many as they pleafe, one after another: but this is only to be confidered as a bare allowance, and perhaps granted upon fuch a motive, as *Moses* of old made one to the *Jews*, for *the hardnefs of their hearts*, tho' *from the beginning it was not fo* ; and therefore when eulogiums are fometimes made from the pulpit on this matter, I think they had better have been fpared; an allowance granted to weaknefs is but an indifferent fubject to be made a matter of glory.

The Doctor fhould alfo have obferved, that my addrefs was made to the young clergy, and fuch as are only upon entering into holy orders, nine in ten of whom may be fuppofed to be neither hufbands nor fathers. He fhould alfo have remembered that our univerfities are full of clergy, who are obliged to live unmarried, that they may have proper leifure and freedom to attend their ftudies without impediment from worldly cares. And therefore, if I pointed at fuch a dedication of the clergy to the fervice of God, as *hufbands* and *fathers* cannot enter into, yet the matter is not blameable, becaufe here are

are ſo many that have not yet entered into this ſtate, but are at liberty to devote themſelves wholly to the ſervice of the goſpel. And therefore if to ſuch as theſe, I can ſo repreſent the weight, the duties, the heavenly nature of the prieſthood, as to prevent or extinguiſh in them all thoughts and deſires of being thus married to the world, what hurt have I done them, or the married clergy, or the goſpel of Jeſus Chriſt?

* *Celibacy*, when entered into from a principle of divine love, from a heart burning with the deſire of living wholly to God, is a ſtate that gives wings to all our endeavours, and fits the ſoul for the higheſt growth of every virtue: and if he that is conſecrated to the ſervice of the altar, feels not ſuch an aſcent of his ſoul towards heaven, as to have no wiſh, but that his *whole body, ſoul,* and *ſpirit,* may be preſented to God in its utmoſt degree of purity, he has his lamp much leſs kindled, than many of the laity, both men and women have had, in all ages of the church. Cuſtom has too great a power over our judgments, and reconciles us to any thing; but if a Chriſtian, who lived when Chriſtianity was in its glory, when the firſt apologiſts for it, appealed to the numbers of both ſexes, devoted to a ſingle life, as an invincible proof of the power and divinity of the goſpel; if a Chriſtian of thoſe days was now to come into the world, he would be more ſhocked at Reverend Doctors

making

making love to women, than at seeing a monk in his cell, kissing a wooden crucifix.

* The knowledge and love of the virgin state began with Christianity, when the nature of our corruption, and the nature of our redemption were so fully discovered by the gospel. Then it was, that a new degree of heavenly love was kindled in the human nature, and brought forth a state of life that had not been desired, till the son of the virgin came into the world. *John* the *Baptist* was the beginner of the gospel dispensation; this *burning and shining light* was in his person, the figure of *Judaism* ending in Christianity. In his outward state he was a *Jew*, in his inward spirit and character he belonged to the gospel. He came out of the wilderness burning and shining; to preach the kingdom of heaven *at hand*. This may shew us that heat and light from above, kindled in a state of great self-denial, are necessary to make us able ministers of the gospel; and that if we pretend to the ministry, without these qualifications, and come only burning and shining with the spirit of this world, we are as well fitted to hinder, as the Baptist was to prepare the way to the kingdom of heaven. Look at this great saint, all ye that desire to preach the gospel. He came forth in the highest degrees of mortification and chastity of life. But why did he so come? It was to shew the world that these virtues must form the spirit of every preacher of the gospel. His

character

character does not call you to a wilderness beyond *Jordan*, or to be cloathed with camel's hair. Such circumstances are particular to himself; but it calls you to his inward spirit of self-denial, to his death to the world, and all carnal love, if you would not only preach, but prove the perfection of the gospel: For if the *Baptist* was to be thus dead to the flesh and the world, that he might preach thus much, *the kingdom of heaven is at hand*; can less self-denial be required of those, who are to preach that which is much more, namely, that *the kingdom of heaven is come?*

* Now if this holy *Baptist*, when he had preached awhile upon penitence, and the kingdom of heaven *at hand*, had made an offering of his heart to some fine *young lady of great accomplishments*, had not this put an end to all that was burning and shining in his character? And if those clergy who date their mission from Jesus Christ himself, sent by him as he was by his Father, to stand as his representatives, applying the means and mysteries of salvation to all that desire to be *born again*; if they, whether they be vicars, rectors, arch-deacons, deans, or bishops, should look upon their office to be as sacred, and their station as high in the kingdom of God, as the *Baptist*'s was; if they should look upon love addresses to the sex, as unbecoming, as foreign, to their character, as to the *Baptist*'s, could any one say, that they took too much

much upon them, or paid too great a reverence to the holiness of the priesthood, which they derived from the very person and office of Jesus Christ?

* Our blessed Lord improved upon these two articles of mortification and chastity, and sets them before every preacher of the gospel in a yet fuller light. It is needless to shew how much he speaks of the nature and necessity of a total self-denial; but what he says of the virgin life, as to be chosen by those who are able to chuse it, for the kingdom of heaven's sake, *Matt.* xix. 12. is more than a volume of human eloquence in praise of it. What wonder is it, if after this, great numbers both of men and women were found in the first ages of the church, that chose to know no love, but that of God in a single life?

* St. *Paul* has done every thing to hinder a minister of Jesus Christ from entering into marriage, except calling it a sinful state, when he says, *He that is married careth for the things of the world, how he may please his wife*; and how could he more powerfully press the virgin life upon the clergy, than when he says, *He that is unmarried, careth for the things that belong to the Lord, how he may please the Lord.*

* I shall conclude this matter with a passage taken from the *Serious Call to a devout and Holy Life*; it is a quotation from *Eusebius*, who lived at the time of the first general council, when

the

the faith of our *Nicene Creed* was eſtabliſhed: his words are theſe, " There have been, ſaith he, inſtituted in the church of Chriſt, two ways or manners of living; the one raiſed above the ordinary ſtate of nature, and common ways of living, rejects wedlock, poſſeſſions, and worldly goods, and being wholly ſeparated and removed from the ordinary converſation of common life, is appropriated and devoted ſolely to the worſhip and ſervice of God, through an *exceeding degree of heavenly love*: they who are of this order of people, ſeem dead to the life of this world, and having their bodies only upon earth, are in their minds and contemplations dwelling in heaven; from whence, like ſo many heavenly inhabitants, they look down upon human life, making *interceſſions* and *oblations* for the whole race of mankind; and this, not with the blood of beaſts, or the fat, or ſmoak and burning of bodies, but with the higheſt exerciſes of true piety, with cleanſed and purified hearts, and with a whole form of life ſtrictly devoted to virtue: theſe are their ſacrifices, which they are continually offering unto God, and implore his mercy and favour for themſelves and their fellow-creatures. Chriſtianity receives this as the perfect manner of life.

" The other is of a lower form, and ſuiting itſelf more to the condition of human nature, admits of chaſte wedlock, the care of children and

and families, of trade and bufinefs, and goes through all the employments of life, under a fenfe of piety and fear of God: now, they who have chofen this manner of life, have their fet times for retirement and fpiritual exercife, and particular days are fet apart for their hearing and learning the word of God: and this order of people are confidered as in the fecond ftate of piety."†
Here you fee the perfection of the Chriftian life plainly fet out, and how it was, what numbers of private perfons, men and women, who had no fhare in the ecclefiaftical office, yet, by their perfection of life, were *holy and heavenly interceffors* for the whole race of mankind.
* Now, may we not fuppofe, that the clergy were in this number of people that were thus heavenly in the whole form of their life, thus devoted to God and the edification of the church, by embracing the perfect life of Chriftianity? If they were not, do they not ftand plainly condemned, fince *Chriftianity held this to be the perfect manner of life?* I fhall only add, that till fuch a degree of heavenly love, fuch a fenfe of the holinefs and heavenly nature of the facred calling, till fuch a defire of perfection is awakened in the clergy, as fhuts out all carnal love and worldly tempers from their hearts, they cannot be fuch priefts and interceffors with God, fuch patterns of holinefs, fuch kindlers of divine love

and

† Serious Call, &c. p. 134.

and heavenly defires amongſt men, as the nature of their office both intends and requires of them.

* If a candidate for holy orders dares not make this total donation of himſelf to God, to be an inſtrument of his good pleaſure only in the ſervice of the goſpel, if it is not his real ſtate, to wiſh nothing in this world but the moſt perfect purification of his nature, if he defires any thing in and by his office, but a concurrence with Jeſus Chriſt in the ſalvation of ſouls; if he has any reſerves of ſelf-ſeeking, or ſelf-advancement in the world, and fleſhly paſſions which he hopes to make conſiſtent with the duties of his profeſſion: if he is not ſeparated in will and defire from all that is not God, and the ſervice of God, he muſt be ſaid to want the beſt proofs of his being called by the Holy Ghoſt.

But the Doctor has a *ſecond reply*, *Whether you conſider the* divinity, *or the* ſenſe *of this, could* George Fox *himſelf have outdone it?* p. 48. This reply, confidered in itſelf, might have its place amongſt thoſe *algebraic quantities*, that are ſome degrees leſs than nothing; but with regard to the Doctor's purpoſe it has ſomething in it, for it is an appeal to that which is very powerful, which has ſuppreſſed many a good truth: it is an appeal to vulgar prejudice; and ſhews that the Doctor is not without his expectations from that quarter. And thus it is, that the Catholic artiſt in his country plays a *Martin Luther*, when he wants to re-

proach

proach that which he knows not how to confute. What degree of sense, or divinity *George Fox* was possessed of, I cannot pretend to say, having never read any of his writings; but if he has said any divine truths, I should be as well pleased in seeing them in his books, as in any of the fathers of the primitive church. For as the gospel requires me to be as glad to see piety, equity, strict sobriety, and extensive charity in a *Jew* or a *Gentile*, as in a Christian; as it obliges me to look with pleasure upon their virtues, and be thankful to God, that such persons have so much of true and sound Christianity; so it cannot be an unchristian spirit to be as glad to see truths in one party of Christians as in another; and to look with pleasure upon any good doctrines that are held by any sect of Christian people, and be thankful to God, that they have so much of the genuine truths of the gospel. * For if we have no complaint against those that are divided from us, but what proceeds from a Christian fear, that what they hold and practise will not be so beneficial to them, as our religion will be to us, must we not have the utmost readiness and willingness to find, own, and rejoice in those good doctrines and practices which they still retain? If a poor pilgrim, under a necessity of travelling a dangerous and difficult road, had, through his own perverseness lost the use of a leg, and the sight of one eye, could we be said, to have any charitable concern for his perverseness and misfortune, unless we were glad to see that he had one good leg, and one good eye still left, and unless we hoped and desired they might bring him at last to his journey's end? Now let every part of the church which takes itself to be sound and good, and is only angry at every other part, because they have *lessened the means* of their own salvation; let her but have thus much charity in her anger, and then she will be glad to see, in every perverse division, something like the one good leg, and the one good eye of the pilgrim, and which she will hope and wish may do them the same good.

* *Selfishness* and *partiality* are very base qualities, even in the things of this world; but in the doctrines of religion they are of a baser nature. Now this is the *greatest evil* that the division of the church has brought forth; it raises in every communion a selfish, partial orthodoxy, which consists in courageously defending all that it has, and condemning all that it has not. And thus all champions are trained up in defence of their own truth, their own learning, and their own church; and he has the most merit, who likes every thing, defends every thing among themselves, and leaves nothing uncensured in those that are of a different communion. Now how can truth, and goodness, and religion be more struck at, than by such defenders of it? If you ask why the great bishop of *Meaux* wrote so many learned books against all parts of the *reformation*, it is because he was born in *France*, and bred up

in

in the bosom of *mother church*. Had he been born in *England*, had *Oxford*, or *Cambridge* been his *alma mater*, he might have rivaled our great bishop *Stillingfleet*, and would have wrote as many learned folios against the church of *Rome* as he has done. And yet I will venture to say, that if each church could produce but one man a-piece that had the piety of an apostle, and the impartial love of the first Christians, in the first church at *Jerusalem*, a Protestant and a Papist of this stamp, would not want half a sheet of paper to hold their articles of union, nor be half an hour before they were of one religion. If therefore it should be said, that churches are divided, and made unfriendly to one another, by learning, a logic, a history, a criticism in the hands of partiality, it would be saying that which every particular church too much proves to be true. Ask why even the best amongst the Catholics are very shy of owning the validity of the orders of our church; it is because they are afraid of removing any odium from the reformation. Ask why no Protestants touch upon the benefit of celibacy in those who are separated from worldly business to preach the gospel, 'tis because that would be seeming to lessen the Roman error of not suffering marriage in her clergy. Ask why even the most pious amongst the clergy of the established church, are afraid to assert, the necessity of seeking only to the guidance and inspiration of the Holy Spirit; 'tis because the

Quakers,

Quakers, who have broken off from the church, have made this doctrine their corner stone.

If we loved truth as such; if we sought it for its own sake; if we loved our neighbour as ourselves: if we desired nothing by our religion but to be acceptable to God; if we equally desired the salvation of all men; then nothing of this spirit could have any place in us.

* There is therefore a *Catholic* spirit, a *communion of saints* in the love of God and all goodness, which no one can learn from that which is called orthodoxy in particular churches. It is only to be had by a total dying to all worldly views, by a pure love of God, and by such an unction from above, as delivers the mind from all selfishness, and makes it love truth and goodness with an equality of affection in every man, whether he be *Christian, Jew,* or *Gentile.* He that would obtain this divine spirit in this disordered state of things, and live in a divided part of the church, without partaking of its division, must have these three truths deeply fixed in his mind: *first,* that universal love, which gives the whole strength of the heart to God, and makes us love every man as we love ourselves, is the noblest, the most God-like state of the soul, and the utmost perfection to which the most perfect religion can raise us; and that no religion does any man any good, but so far as it brings this love into him. This will shew us, that true orthodoxy can no where be found, but in a pure disinterested love of God and our neighbour. *Secondly*, That in the present divided state of the church, truth itself is torn and divided asunder; and that therefore he is the only true Catholic, who has more of truth, and less of error, than is hedged in by any divided part. This truth will enable us to live in a divided part, *unhurt* by its division, and keep us in a true liberty and fitness to be assisted by all the good that we hear or see in any other part of the church. And thus uniting in heart and spirit with all that is holy and good in all churches, we enter into the true *communion of saints*, and become real members of the holy Catholic church, tho' we use the outward worship of only one part of it. It is thus, that the angels, as ministring spirits, assist, unite and co-operate with every thing that is holy and good, in every division of mankind. *Thirdly*, he must always have in mind this great truth, that it is the glory of the divine justice to have no respect of parties or persons, but to stand equally disposed to that which is right and wrong, in *Jew* and *Gentile*. He therefore that would like as God likes, and condemn as God condemns, must have neither the eyes of the Papist nor the Protestant; he must like no truth the less because *Ignatius Loyola* or *John Bunyan* were very zealous for it; nor have the less aversion to any error, because Dr. *Trap* or *George Fox* had brought it forth. Now if this impartial justice, is the spirit which will judge the world at the last day, how can this

Spirit

spirit be too soon or too much in us? Or what can do us more hurt than that which is an hindrance of it? When I was a young scholar of the university, I heard a great religionist say, that if he could believe the late *king of France* was in heaven, he could not wish to go thither himself. This was exceeding shocking: yet something of this temper must be more or less in those, who have, as a point of orthodoxy, worked themselves up into a hearty contempt and hatred of those that are divided from them. He that has been all his life long used to look with great abhorrence upon those whom he called *superstitious bigots, dreaming visionaries, false saints, canting enthusiasts,* must naturally expect they will be treated by God as they have been by him; and if he had the keys of the kingdom of heaven, such people would find it hard to get a place in it. But it stands us greatly in hand to get rid of this temper before we die: since nothing but universal love can enter into the kingdom of God.

We often hear of people of great zeal and orthodoxy, declaring on their death-beds their strict attachment to the church of *England,* and making solemn protestations against all other churches: but how much better would it be, if such a person was to say, " In this divided state of Christendom, I must conform to some divided part of it, and therefore I live and die in communion with the church of *England*; fully believing,

believing, that if I worship God in *spirit and in truth* in this divided part of the church, I shall be as acceptable to him, as if I had been a faithful member of the one whole church, before it was broken into separate parts. But as I am now going out of this disordered division, into a more universal state of things, as I am now falling into the hands of the great Creator and lover of all souls; as I am going to the God of all churches, to a kingdom of universal love, which must have its inhabitants from all people, nations, and languages of the earth; so in this spirit of universal love, I desire to perform my last act of communion in this divided church, uniting in heart with all that is holy, good, and acceptable to God in all other churches; praying, from the bottom of my soul, that every church may have its saints; that God's kingdom may come, his will be done in every division of Christians and men, and that *every thing that hath breath may praise the Lord.*"

We have often seen learned Protestants very zealous in pulling to pieces the lives of the saints of the *Romish* church, and casting all the reproach and ridicule they can, upon their wondrous spirit; tho' the lives of the saints of the primitive church may be exposed in the same manner. Now, whence does this proceed? Why, from a secret touch of that spirit which could not bear to have the late king of *France* in heaven; it proceeds from a partial, selfish orthodoxy, which

cannot

cannot bear to hear, or own, that the spirit and blessing of God are so visible in a church from which it is divided. But if a person be of this spirit, what does it signify where he has his outward church? If a *Romish priest* in the north of *England* could not bear the splendor of a life so devoted to God, so fruitful in all good works, as was that of the lady *Elizabeth Hastings*, if he should want to sully the brightness of her Christian graces, and prove her to have been no saint, lest it should appear, that the Spirit of God was not confined to the *Romish* church, would not such a zeal shew a worse spirit, than that of superstition, a greater depravity of heart, than the saying now and then an *Ave Mary?*

* The more we know of the corruptions and hindrances of piety in the church of *Rome*, the more we should rejoice, that in every age so many eminent saints, have appeared in it, whom we should thankfully behold as so many great lights hung out by God, to shew the true way to heaven, as so many joyful proofs that Christ is still present, even in that church, and that the gates of hell have not quite prevailed against it. Who that has the least spark of heaven in his soul, can help rejoicing in this manner at the appearance of St. *Bernard*, a *Teresa*, a *Francis* de *Sales*, in that church? Who can help praising God, that her invented devotions, superstitious use of images, and invocation of saints, have not so suppressed the graces of an evangelical life, but that amongst *cardinals, jesuits, priests, friars, monks* and *nuns,* some have been found, who seemed to live for no other end, but to give glory to God and edification to men, and whose writings have every thing in them, that can guide the soul out of the corruption of this life into union with God? And he who through a partial orthodoxy is diverted from feeding in these green pastures of life, whose abhorrence of jesuitical craft, keeps him from reading the works of an *Alvares du Pas,* a *Rodrigues,* a *Pere Surin,* and such like jesuits, has a greater loss than he can easily imagine: and if any clergyman can read the life of *Bartholomeus* a *Martyribus* a *Spanish* archbishop, who sat with great influence at the very council of *Trent,* without being edified by it, and desiring to read it again and again, I know not why he should like the lives of the apostolical fathers: and if any Protestant bishop should read the *Stimulus Pastorum* wrote by this Popish prelate, he must confess it to be a book, that would have done honour to the best archbishop, that the reformation has to boast of. O my God, how shall I unlock this mystery? In the land of darkness, over-run with superstition, where divine worship seems to be all shew and ceremony, thou hast those, who are fired with the pure love of thee, who renounce every thing for thee, who are devoted wholly to thee, who think of nothing, write of nothing, desire nothing but the honour, and praise, and adoration

that

that is due to thee, and who call all the world to the maxims of the gofpel, the perfection of the life of Chrift. But in the regions where light is fprung up, whence fuperftition is fled, where all that is outward in religion feems to be pruned, dreffed, and put in its true order; there a cleanfed fhell, a whited fepulchre, feems too generally to cover a dead Chriftianity.

The error of all errors, and that which makes the blackeft charge againft the *Romifh* church, is perfecution, a religious fword drawn againft the liberty of ferving God according to our beft light. Now, tho' this is the frightful monfter of that church, yet, even here, who, except it be the church of *England*, can throw the firft ftone at her? Where muft we look for a church that has fo renounced this perfecuting beaft, as they have renounced the ufe of incenfe, the fprinklings of holy water, or extreme unction? What part of the reformation abroad has not practifed and defended perfecution? What fect of diffenters at home have not, in their day of power dreadfully condemned toleration?

When it fhall pleafe God to difpofe the hearts of all Chriftian princes, entirely to deftroy this anti-chriftian beaft, and leave all their fubjects in that religious freedom which they have from God; then the light of the gofpel, the power of its minifters, the ufefulnefs of its rites, the benediction of its facraments will have proper time and place to fhew themfelves; and that religion which has the most of a divine power in it, whose offices and services do most good to the heart, whose ministers are most devoted to God, and have the most proof of the presence of Christ with them, will become, as it ought, the most universal. All that I have said on this matter, has been occasioned by the Doctor's appeal to vulgar prejudice; and is only to intimate, that the greatest evil which the division of the church brings forth, is a sectarian, selfish spirit, which with the orthodoxy of the *old Jews*, would have God to be only their God, and themselves only, his chosen people. If therefore we would be true Christians of the Catholic church, we must put off this partiality of the carnal *Jew*; we must enter into a Catholic affection for all men, love the spirit of the gospel wherever we see it; not work ourselves up into an abhorrence of a *George Fox*, or an *Ignatius Loyola*; but be equally glad of the light of the gospel wherever it shines, or from whatever quarter it comes; and give the same praise to God for an eminent example of piety, wherever it appears, either in Papist or Protestant.

To return. Dr. *Trap* supposing the world running into a charity that would ruin wife and family, asks his charitable *half-thinker*, " Did you never hear that *charity begins* at home? Did you never read that of St. *Paul*, If any provide not for his own, and especially those of his own house, he hath denied the faith, and is worse than

than an Infidel?" The Doctor's proverb I meddled not with, but the text of St. *Paul* I rescued from his grofs mifapplication. That text has no more relation to an exceffive charity, than to an exceffive fafting. The apoftle neither thought of this fin in this place, nor in any other part of his writings; nor does he ever give the fmalleft hint of the danger of falling into it. The only queftion was, whether poor widows, who had near relations, that could fupply their wants, fhould be maintained by the church? The apoftle determines the matter thus; tha if fuch perfons, who were thus able, did not thus provide for, that is, fupply the wants of their poor kindred, they were fo far from having the faith of Chriftians, that they wanted a goodnefs that was to be found amongft Infidels: this is the whole of the apoftle's doctrine in this text. He fpeaks of providing for thofe of our own houfe or family, in no other fenfe, than as it fignifies our charity to them, when they fall into diftrefs; but the Doctor, trufting to the found of the *Englifh* word *provide*, grafts all thefe errors upon this plain text. When it is faid, a perfon has provided well for his family, every one fuppofes that he has *laid up well in ftore*, or got an *eftate* to be divided amongft them for their future fubfiftance. From this ufe of the *Englifh* word, *provide*; the Doctor would have it believed, that the apoftle teaches every head of a

family

family to be carefully and continually laying up in store for his kindred. But the apostle is as infinitely distant from this thought, as from teaching them to get their cellars filled with strong liquors: when he here says, *provide*, he says only this, shut not your eyes to the wants of your poor kindred, but provide them with what they have need of, and don't let them fall to the charge of the church. The Doctor's second error is this; according to this text, a Christian ought not to hinder himself from thus laying up in store for his family, or leave them to live by their labour and industry, thro' an excess of charity to his poor neighbours. But the apostle has not one single syllable about this; and is as far from saying any thing like it, as from saying, that a Christian, when he makes a feast, should only invite his rich kindred and acquaintance. The one has as much of the apostle and the gospel for it, as the other. The Doctor's third error is this; that, according to this text, he, who by a daily, continual charity, has incapacitated himself to lay up in store, a fixed provision for the future maintenance of his family, is condemned by the apostle as *denying the faith*, and *worse than an Infidel:* tho' the apostle speaks no more here against such a person, than he speaks in the praise of *Ananias* and *Sapphira*.

The person here condemned, is not he who thro' a continual charity, is hindered from laying

ing up in store; not he, who, thro' a Christian love of relieving the distressed members of Christ, is content with helping his own family to food and raiment; but it is that Christian, who being able, is yet unwilling to support his near relations, that are fallen into poverty, and leaves them to be maintained by the church: this is the only Christian the apostle here condemns, as having put off the piety of the gospel, and wanting even the virtue of good-natured Infidels.

I said further, Had the apostle known a parent in his days, who, thro' his great charity for others, had reduced his own family to want of relief, he would have been so far from rebuking him as an half-thinking fool, or exposing him to others, as guilty of madness, that he would have told them, such a one had consecrated himself and family to the church, as the proper objects of their care. To which the Doctor gives this answer, " This he affirms, and this I deny; and as he produces no other proof, so I give no other answer," p. 69. What I said, has its proof from the common voice of Christianity in the apostles days; as may sufficiently appear from the following passage of St. *Clement*, fellow-labourer of the apostle, and bishop of no less a church than that of *Rome*. "We have known many amongst us, who have delivered themselves into bonds and slavery, that they might restore

restore others to their liberty; many who have hired out themselves servants unto others, that by their wages they might feed and sustain them that wanted." †

Will the Doctor now say, that this is no proof of that which I affirmed of the apostle, that he would have had a love for those who were become sufferers by their own charity to others? Does not this apostolical bishop make it his boast, and the glory of Christianity; not that they had some, but many such among them?

It was not only in the first church at *Jerusalem*, that the Christians had all things common. For St. *Barnabas* writing to some converted *Jews*, teaches them to call nothing their own in this world, because they were called to the common enjoyment of the things of eternity. *Communicabis in omnibus rebus proximo tuo; nihil dices quicquam tibi proprium; si enim communicatis invicem, in bonis, incorruptibilibus, quanto magis in corruptibilibus.* ‡

* An age after this, *Justin Martyr* thus glories of the power of the gospel-faith; "We, says he, who before we became Christians, loved our wealth and possession above all things, now give up all property in them, that they may be in common for all that want them. *Qui pecuniarum & possessionum fructus ac proventus præ rebus*

---

† 1 Epist. ad Cor.   ‡ Epist. Bar. No. 10.

rebus omnibus adamabamus, nunc etiam quæ habemus in commune conferimus, & cum indigentibus quibuscunque communicamus."§ What a lean, heathenish figure muſt the Doctor's proverb of charity *beginning at home*, have made in the days of St. *Barnabas*, *Clement*, or *Juſtin Martyr?* Or who durſt then have made ſuch an uſe of the text of St. *Paul*, as the Doctor has done, or coupled it with ſuch a proverb? Were any of theſe firſt ſaints to judge of this matter, the Doctor might, for ought I know, have a worſe reprimand from them for ſo doing, than if he had only coupled Cardinals with Pluraliſts.

In order to ſhew the Doctor that he was very unſeaſonably preaching againſt the ſin and folly of an exceſſive charity, when yet every part of the church wanted to be ſhewn how they were fallen from the goſpel degree of it, I ſet before him an imaginary Biſhop of *Wincheſter*, yet drawn according to the model of the holy Biſhops of the firſt ages. I ſuppoſed this Biſhop ſo filled with the Spirit of Chriſt, that he looked upon all the revenues of his ſee, with no other eyes, than as our Saviour looked at that bag that was carried along with him by his diſciples, as ſo much for his own neceſſities and the neceſſities of others. I ſuppoſed that in this ſpirit, he ſo expended his yearly income, that

§ 2 Apol.

that he chose to bring up his children strangers to all worldly figure, and in as low a state of labour as that to which our Lord and his apostles had been used. I supposed, that by a piety of life and conversation, equal to this exalted charity, he had instilled such an heavenly spirit into his wife and children, as made them highly thankful for their condition, and full of praise to God for the blessing of such a relation. Dr. *Trap*, tho' an antient divine, seems to start back with fright, at the sight of this apostolical bishop, and supposes, that if such a monster of a man was now to get into a bishoprick, he must needs make his children extraordinary wicked, fill them with abhorrence of his memory, and spread infidelity in the world, by making Christianity a jest to Infidels, p. 71.

I say, says the Doctor, *very clearly and plainly*, that *such a bishop must be a mad man*, p. 70. Now, if the Doctor will prove from the scriptures this bishop to be a mad man, it must be for the following reasons: *First*, because he had so mean a spirit, as to suffer the son of a bishop to work under a carpenter, as the Redeemer of mankind had done. *Secondly*, because he taught himself and his family to believe that which St. *Paul* believed, that *having food and raiment, we ought to be therewith content*. *Thirdly*, because he came up to the very letter of the great commandment, of *loving our neighbour as ourselves*.

Fourthly,

Fourthly, becaufe he imitated the fpirit of the firft Chriftians at *Jerufalem*, who accounted nothing to be their own that they poffeffed. *Fifthly*, becaufe he had turned himfelf and family from all the vanity of this world, the luft of the flefh, the luft of the eyes, and the pride of life. *Sixthly*, becaufe he feemed to have this of the apoftle fixed in his mind, " He that faith, he abideth in Chrift, ought fo to walk, as he walked." *Seventhly*, becaufe his life was fafhioned according to this doctrine of the Holy Jefus, " Learn of me, for I am meek, and lowly of heart: I am among you, as he that ferveth: whofoever will be great among you, let him be your minifter; even as the Son of man came not to be miniftred unto, but to minifter." For it may be faid with the greateft certainty, that if the Doctor will have any proof from the fcripture of the madnefs of this bifhop, it muft be as abfurd as the reafons here alledged.

Come we now to confider this bifhop according to the fpirit, practice and laws of the church in all ages. Any one verfed ever fo little in the hiftory of the church, muft fee at the firft fight, that this fuppofed bifhop is a true copy of the firft apoftolical fathers. And if this bifhop was to be accounted a madman, becaufe of the manner of his life, we muft come down feveral ages after *Conftantine*, to the *mitre* and triple crown, before we could find a bifhop in his fenfes. The *Clements*, the *Polycarps*, the *Ignatius's*, the *Irenæus's*, *us's,* the *Cyprian's,* the *Basils,* the *Ambrose's,* and a number that have long graced our calenders, as saints, must take their place among bedlamites: for they were all of them to a tittle, the very man I have supposed at *Winchester.* They considered every penny that was brought in by the gospel, as a provision for the poor, and themselves as only entitled to their common share out of it. They durst no more raise any of their relations to a splendor of life, or give them any figure from the revenues of the church, than commit sacrilege. They gloried as much in their own strict poverty and want of worldly figure, as in their having totally renounced idols.

But we have much more than primitive example for our bishop of *Winchester:* the doctrine and laws of the church have unanimously from age to age, to the very council of *Trent,* required every bishop to be of the same spirit of which we have supposed him. The church, both by the doctrine of fathers, and the canons of councils, constantly maintains; *First,* that the clergy are not proprietors, but barely stewards of the benefices they enjoy: having them for no other end, but for their own necessary, frugal subsistence, and the relief of the poor. ^a *Secondly,* that a clergyman using his benefice for his *own indulgence,* or the enriching his *own family,* is guilty of sacrilege, and is a robber and murderer of the poor. ^b *Thirdly,* that if a clergyman has

---

^a Nihil ecclefia nisi Fidem possidet.——Possessio ecclesiæ est Egenorum sumptus, *Ant. Ep.* 31.   ^b Si Pauperum Compan-

has a reasonable subsistence of his own, and is not in the state of the poor, then let his benefice be what it will, he has no right to use any part of it for himself, nor for his kindred, unless they be fit to be considered among those poor that are to be relieved by the church. ᶜ *Fourthly*, that every bishop and clergyman is to live in an humble, frugal, outward state of life, seeking for no honour or dignity in the world, but that which arises from the distinction and lustre of his virtues. ᵈ *Fifthly*, that a beneficed clergyman using the goods of the church for his own indulgence, or raising fortunes for his children, or their expensive education, is sacrilegious, and a robber of the poor. ᵉ *Sixthly*, that every clergyman is to die out of the church as poor as he entered into it. ᶠ *Seventhly*, that a clergyman dying, cannot leave or bequeath any thing to his children

---

peres sumus, & *nostra* sunt, & *illorum*. Si autem privatim quæ nobis sufficiunt, possidemus, non sunt illa *nostrum*, sed Pauperum *Procurationem* gerimus, non Proprietatem nobis Usurpatione damnabili vindicamus, *Auguf. Ep.* 50 *ad Bonif.* ᶜ Quoniam quicquid habent Clerici, Pauperum est——Qui bonis Parentum & opibus sustentari possent, si quod Pauperum est, accipiunt, *Sacrilegium profecto* committunt, & per Abusionem Talium, Judicium sibi manducant, & bibunt, *Hieron. Ep. ad Dammas.* ᵈ Episcopus vilem *Suppellectilem*, & *Mensam*, ac *Victum Pauperem*, habeat, & Dignitatis, sua Authoritatum Fide & Vitæ meritis quærat, *Concil. Carthag.* 4. ᵉ Memento quod *Pauperem Vitam* Sacerdos gerere debet, & ideo si superbiam habet, si magno gaudet Beneficio, præter victum & vestitum *quod speres*, Pauperibus dare non differat, quia omnia *pauperum* sunt. *Aug. Serm.* 37. *ad Fratres.* ᶠ Hujus tu e vicino sectare Vestigia, & cæterorum, qui Virtutum illius similes sunt, quos Sacerdotium & *humiliores* facit & *pauperes*.

dren or friends, but barely that which he had independently of the church. ᵍ

* May it not therefore well be wondered what could provoke Dr. *Trap* to censure our bishop as a madman, whose whole form of life, and use of his bishoprick, is not only after the model of the first and greatest saints that ever were bishops, but also such as the whole church from the beginning, both in council and out of council, from age to age, hath absolutely required of every beneficed clergyman, who would not be condemned

Hieron. Ep. 4. *ad Rustic.* ᵍ Præcipimus ut in potestate sua Episcopus Ecclesiæ Res habeat — ex iis autem quibus indiget, (si tamen indiget) ad suas necessitates percipiat. *Canon. Apof.* 40.——cas veluti Deo contemplante dispenset; nec ei liceat ex iis aliquid contingere, aut Parentibus propriis (quæ dei sunt) condonare. Quod si Pauperes sunt, tanquam Pauperibus subministret, ne eorum occasione Ecclesiæ Res depredantur, *Can. Apof.* 39. Manifesta sint quæ pertinere videntur ad Ecclesiam cum Notitia Presbiterorum & Diaconorum, ut si contigerit Episcopo migare de Seculo, nec *Res Ecclesiæ* depercant, nec quæ *propria* probantur Episcopi, sub occasione Rerum Ecclesiæ pervadantur: justum enim est ut sua Episcopus quibus voluerit, derelinquat, & quæ Ecclesiæ sunt, eidem conservantur Ecclesiæ. *Concil. Antioch*, chap. 24. Quicunque Clerici, qui nihil habentes ordinantur, & *tempore Episcopatus*, vel *Clericatus sui*, agros, vel quæcunque prædia nomine suo comparant, tanquam Rerum dominicarum *Invasionis Crimini* teneantur obnoxii, nisi admoniti, Ecclesia eadem ipsa contulerint. (*N. B.*) Si autem ipsis proprie aliquid *liberalitate* alicujus, vel *Successione* Cognationis obvenerit, faciant, inde quod ipsorum Proposito congruit. Sacerdotes ipsis quoque Filiis suis, quibus paterna debetur Hæreditas, nihil debent derelinquere, nisi quod sibi a Parentibus derelictum est: *Ergo* qui *ditior est* Sacerdos, quam venit ad Sacerdotium, quicquid plus habuerit, *non filiis debet dare*, sed Pauperibus, & Sanctis fratribus, ut reddat ea quæ Domini sunt, Domino suo. *Hieron. in Ezech.* chap. 46.

condemned by her, as sacrilegious, and a robber of the poor? They who would see the whole matter set in a clear light, may read an excellent treatise of the learned *Dupin*, wrote near the end of his life, where this truth is by him asserted and incontestably proved, *viz.* That whatever changes have been made in the nature and tenure of the goods and revenues of the church, or however they have been variously divided amongst ecclesiasticks, yet this has remained *always unchangeable and undeniable,* That a clergyman was no proprietor of his benefice; that he could only take so much of it to his own use, as was necessary to his subsistance, and then the remainder, be it what it would, belonged to the poor. This, says he, is strictly maintained by the canons of councils, both before and after the division of ecclesiastical revenues.

* But if this be the case, if this be an incontestable doctrine, supported by every authority that can be brought for any one doctrine of the gospel, have we not here an utter condemnation of pluralities? Is it not an affront to the gospel, to the plainest maxims of right and wrong, the whole authority of the church, to offer one single word in defence of them? Logical, scholastic distinctions and definitions of the nature of parishes and residence, can signify no more here, where the whole nature of the thing is to be avoided, than the same art of words, when used by *Jesuitical Casuists*, can justify the violation of moral

moral duties. And if Dr. *Trap* was only to look at this one doctrine, he would have no reason to think it so sad a thing, to see *Pluralists* coupled with *Cardinals*. " *See*, says the learned *Dupin*, rules which will appear hard to many of the beneficed clergy, but yet, they are true, conformable to natural equity, the laws, custom, and tradition of the church, and the practice of the most holy bishops; and woe be to those that observe them not! *Malheur a Ceux qui ne les suivent pas.*" † And therefore he concludes thus, " There may be many amongst the beneficed clergy who err in this matter, thro' an ignorance of that which is required of them; therefore what I have said ought to be taken in good part, as proceeding from charity, and a sincere love of truth."

† Ibid. p. 442.

SHORT but SUFFICIENT
CONFUTATION

Of Bp. WARBURTON's projected defence *(as he calls it)* of Christianity, in his *divine legation of* Moses, in a letter to the Right Reverend the Lord Bishop of London.

My LORD,

THE reason of my presuming to write to your lordship on the following subject is, because it is a matter on which your lordship has employed your excellent pen, greatly to the benefit of the world.

And the reason of my writing at all, is owing to a book newly published † in defence of bishop *Warburton*, in which your lordship, is charged with a multitude of contradictions, and inconsistencies relating to this point.

It is not my design to enter here as an assistant to your lordship. For this is quite needless.

My intention is, as mentioned in the title page. And because bishop *Warburton* has owned

---

† Free and candid examination of the bishop of London's sermons, &c.

ed this writer, as a most able defender of his scheme. I have taken occasion to shew, that it is a scheme so contrary to scripture, and the truth of things, as no art of words, or stretch of genius, however powerful in paradox, can ever be able to support.

The author of this book, as bishop *Warburton* assures us, † is too modest to make his name known to the world; a quality, which from the reading of his book, one would not suspect to be so predominate in him.—But though modesty has forced him to conceal his name, yet he has given us some information of his character. He begins; "I, who am a bare looker-on, and absolutely disengaged from all that bias of affection, which is so wont to warp the followers of an old system, or the inventers of a new, have done my best to examine this question with all impartiality."‡

Had one of the antient writers of *Greece* said this of himself, how positive, might a modern critic have been, from the decisive words, a *bare looker-on*, that he had never wrote upon the same subject before? And that therefore, any book of that kind ascribed to him, must infallibly be false and spurious. And yet, to the confusion of criticism, this author, who unasked, and of his own free motion, declares, that he begins this work as a bare looker-on, has for more than ten years

---

† Preface to critical enquiry, &c. ‡ Examination p. 2.

years before he made this declaration, been fweating in the thickeſt duſt, and heat of Doctor *Warburton*'s moſt ardent contention for novelties †

I have the Doctor's own words for this, both for the novelties, and this gentleman's wonderful zeal, and ſkill ſhewn in the defence of them, ſo many years ago.

" Notwithſtanding, ſays the Doctor, all that can be ſaid, much clamour will ever attend novelties, though never ſo ſtrongly proved.—But truth ſeldom thrives the worſe, for unreaſonable oppoſition; and it would ſeem (N. B.) *not to be far from its eſtabliſhment*, when ſuch writers, as the following, appear in its defence.—He hath eſtabliſhed what he undertook to defend, with ſuch extent of learning, and force of good argument, that I dare become reſponſible for all he ſays; and am willing, that thoſe of my opinions here debated, may ſtand, or fall, by the ſtrength, or the invalidity of this defence."‡

This compliment, ſo very hearty, as well as elegant, puts me in mind of another, which the learned Doctor made ſome time ſince, to the whole clergy of this nation; " a body of men, ſays he, the moſt learned, virtuous, and truly Chriſtian, that ever adorned a church, or ſtate." §

Theſe

† Critical enquiry, &c. publiſhed 1746.   ‡ Preface to the critical enquiry, p. 10.   § D. L. Vol. 1. Pref. p. 6.

Thefe two compliments are of fo very high a ftrain, that were it not for the gravity of the Doctor's character, and the ferioufnefs of the fubject, the reader might have thought himfelf obliged to underftand them both ironically. But if the Doctor meant no more by this, than to buy a peace with the clergy, it muft however be faid, that he gave more for the purchafe of it, than a man of a fcrupulous confcience would have given.

However the compliment paid to this modeft gentleman (who to be fure will, now never be able to let the world know his name) feems to have been comfortably received in fecret, by the ample return he has made the Doctor for it, in his new book. Where, fpeaking of a part of the Doctor's performance, he fays, " For this anfwer, I muft refer the reader to the *D. L.* where he will find the fubject handled with that force, folidity, and precifion of argument, which fo eminently diftinguifh the author from all his cotemporaries."

I fhall now only juft obferve, that the compliment made by the bifhop to the clergy, has here very much abatement made to it, by his great ally. For as matters now ftand, if this very clergy, good, learned, and Chriftian, beyond any thing ever heard of in the world before, fhould one and all unite in oppofing the bifhop, all that they could poffibly get by their pains,

pains, would be only to shew, how eminently he stands distinguished by force, solidity, and precision of argument from all his cotemporaries.

But no more of this. Bishop *Warburton* grounds his scheme, upon the doctrine of the Old and the New Testament. But seeing he affirms that to be of the greatest weight, which is taken from the New Testament, and this author also begins there, I shall do so likewise.

First, I shall clearly evince, that there is not in all the New Testament, one single text, which either in the letter, or the spirit proves, or has the least tendency, or design to prove, that the *immortality* of the soul, or its perpetual duration after the death of the body, was not an *universal, commonly* received opinion in, and thro' every age of the world from *Adam* to Christ. *Secondly*, That this doctrine or belief of a future state, was not *designedly secreted*, or *industriously hidden* from the eyes of the people of God by *Moses*, neither by the types and figures of the law, nor by any other part of his writings. From whence I shall occasionally shew, that the true *ground* and *method* of Christian redemption to eternal life, preached by the apostles, began with *Adam*, was the religion of *Adam*, and all his descendants. And also, that the writings of *Moses*, and the patriarchal faith, give the very same full proof of the immortality of the soul, or a future state, as the gospel doth.

Need

Need I not observe, that the whole merits of the debate, betwixt Bishop *Warburton* on the one side, and the whole Christian church of all ages, on the other side, lie wholly in these particulars, which, if they can be made good, the whole costly fabric of the Doctor's *projected defence of Christianity*, (as he calls it) built at the expence of such immense treasures of learning, fetched from all quarters of the antient and modern world, must have the fate which always happens to castles built in the air.

This learned writer, to shew, that the immortality of the soul, or its perpetual duration in a future state, was entirely unknown in all the former dispensations of God, until the coming of Christ, begins with this passage of St. *Paul*. "God hath saved us according to his own purpose, and his grace which was given us in Christ Jesus, before the world began. But is now made manifest by the appearing of our Saviour Jesus Christ, who hath abolished death, and hath brought life and immortality to light, thro' the gospel."

On which words he thus proceeds: "We are told, that God, before the world began, had decreed to restore mankind to that lost inheritance of eternal life, which they should forfeit by the disobedience of our first parents. It is added, that this secret purpose, was now at last made manifest by the appearing of Christ, who hath abolished death, and brought life, and immortality

mortality to light by the gospel. The apostle mentions two periods, one, when it was originally formed in the secret counsels of God, the other, when it was published and revealed. The opposition between these two states, seems necessarily to imply, that during the interval, it remained a secret. If the apostle may be allowed to be his own interpreter, it will be easy to establish this exposition by a parallel passage in the epistle to *Titus*. *In hope of eternal life*, which God, that cannot lie, promised *before the world began, but hath in due time manifested his word through preaching.* Agreeably to this, the author of the epistle to the *Hebrews*, assures us, that the *great salvation of the gospel*, that is, the *promise of eternal life, first began to be spoken by the Lord.* But how could he be the first who taught this doctrine, if *Moses* and the prophets had taught it long before? Or how did he begin to speak of that, which so many others had been commissioned to teach before? Sometimes we are told, that life and immortality are brought to light, sometimes that it was made manifest, sometimes that it first began to be spoken by Jesus Christ. The bringing to light, and making manifest, are equivalent to the beginning first to teach. And if so, the publication ascribed to Jesus Christ, must have been the first and original publication, and not merely the illustrating or giving new splendor to a doctrine, by the addition of one, or more circumstances unknown before. However, an eminent writer (meaning your Lordship) assures us, that Jesus Christ did not give the first notice of this doctrine. All that I need remark upon it, is, that this assurance seems directly to contradict the word of inspiration.

Your Lordship has also said, that the antient revelations *afforded a good proof of a future state.* This writer makes great shew of triumph over this most true assertion, and is continually bringing it forth as a proof of your inconsistency, both with yourself and the apostles.

But to follow him farther: " St. *Paul*, saith he, observes that Jesus Christ was sent to shew light to the people, that is, to the *Jews* and to the *Gentiles.* It is plain from hence, that he was a light to the first, in the same sense, in which he was a light to the last; and therefore as he was a light to the Gentiles, by revealing the myf- tery of redemption, in a restoration to life and immortality, to them *absolutely unknown*, it seems to follow, that he also enlightened the *Jews*, by the manifestation of a truth *equally unknown*. Agreeably to this account of things, *Zacharias*, in his prophecy upon the birth of *John* Bap- tist, says, *The day-spring from on high hath visited us, to give light to them that sit in darkness, and in the shadow of death, to guide our feet into the way of peace.* A description, which will by no means permit us to suppose, that they were enlightened with a good proof of a future state. If they had been enlightened with such a proof, they would have been

been in the region of life and immortality, and not in the verge and shadow of death. They would not have been sitting in darkness, but walking in the light, if they actually saw the grand object in question: how consistent it is, to assign a good view of an object, to a people sitting in darkness, must be left to the judgment of others. However, this seems to be the necessary consequence of affirming, that the *Jews* had a good proof of a future life."

This is the glaring contradiction, which he is continually charging upon your Lordship throughout his whole book. Again, he attacks your Lordship thus, from your own words: " St. *Peter*, says his Lordship, tells all Christians, that they are called out of darkness into a marvellous light. Ask the evangelists, they will tell you, *The day spring from on high hath visited us, to give light to them that sit in darkness, and in the shadow of death.* Ask any, or all the apostles, and they will tell you, their commission is, to open the eyes of the people, *and turn them from darkness unto light*. But how could the *Jewish* people have a *good view and prospect* of life, and immortality, if their eyes were not opened? How could they be called out of darkness, if their situation presented them with a good view of an object, which they were now first invited to behold? And how could they sit in the shadow of death, if they had been favoured with a good proof of a future state?

" It

"It would be ridiculous to say, that they sat in darkness, or that they had not their eyes, merely, because they did not see the object in its full proportion, or extent, or had not an exact view of every minute part, and the opportunity of surveying it quite round. The sitting in darkness and the shadow of death, evidently implies a total want of light, by which the people thus circumstanced, were to be enlightened; it being impossible to express the most entire ignorance in more emphatic terms."†

I have made these large quotations from this author, containing all his chief texts of scripture, and his comments upon them, in his own words, that there might be no complaint of my robbing his arguments of any of their force, for all that he farther says on this subject, is but mere repetition.

I shall now shew, that all his reasoning upon these texts is false in itself, and nothing at all to the purpose, as not touching the one great point in question, which is the doctrine or belief of a future state, or the immortality of the soul in a life after this.—And this I shall do, by making it plain, that not one of these texts, nor any other in all the New Testament, proves, or has the least tendency to prove, that the doctrine or belief of the soul's immortality, and a future state, was not known in and thro' every age of the world, before the coming of Christ in the flesh.

This

---

† Pages 4, 5, 6, &c.

This will be sufficiently done, by shewing, that the doctrine of the immortality of the soul, or its future existence in some kind of happiness or misery in another life, is a matter about which these texts say not a syllable, but leave it as untouched as the doctrine of the pre-existence of souls.

If it be asked then, What is the great discovery, new light and knowledge, declared in these texts, as newly made known to the world by the gospel? It is answered, that the one thing meant both by the letter and spirit of all these, and every other the like passages of scripture, speaking of that mystery, new light, or knowledge made known by the gospel, and unknown before, is absolutely nothing else, points at nothing else, and has nothing else implied in it, but the one whole process of Christ in his personality, his birth, his life, his sufferings, his death, his resurrection and ascension into heaven. This, and this alone; namely, The whole process of Christ, in all these important particulars, is the great salvation, the great mystery, the hidden wisdom of God, kept secret from the foundation of the world, and not manifested, nor possible to be manifested, but by Christ himself entering into, and going thro' all the parts of this process.—Of this process alone it is, that the apostles speak, when they declare the mystery opened in the gospel, to have been a mystery kept secret since the world began: and the reason why it was so is plain, becaufe it muſt be a fecret, and continue ſuch, till what was contained in it came into actual exiſtence, and thereby manifeſted itſelf.

Of this procefs alone, and its wonderful effects, it is that the apoſtles ſpeak, when they glory of the aboliſhment of death, and of life and immortality brought to light through the goſpel: becauſe it is the goſpel alone, that manifeſts the actual exiſtence of this procefs of Chriſt in all its parts. Nor do they ever ſpeak of any light, life, or knowledge, as formerly the hidden wiſdom of God, and now made manifeſt to the world, but ſolely that light, that life, and knowledge, which ariſes from ſome one or other, or all the parts of our Saviour's procefs, as the one only poſſible and actual Redeemer of the world.

That this is, the plain full truth of the matter, that the only thing, diſcovered to the world by the light of the goſpel, is the one whole procefs of Chriſt, muſt be acknowledged by every conſiderate man, even from the nature of the thing.—For what can the myſtery of the goſpel be, but the myſtery of Chriſt, as a Saviour, made known to the world? And what can the myſtery of Chriſt, as a Saviour made known be, but the manifeſtation of *what* he is in himſelf, in the power of his perſonality, in the efficacy of his birth, in the bleſſed conſequences of his life, his ſufferings, his death, reſurrection, and aſcenſion into heaven, as our *ſecond Adam*, or father

of

of a new, divine nature, derived into us by his wonderful procefs in all its parts.

Now as all thefe particulars make up the *whole manifeſtation* of the myſtery opened in the gofpel, fo there is not in any of thefe, the moſt diſtant *hint* given, that the doctrine of a *future ſtate*, was not as foon, as univerfally, and conſtantly known as the fall of man was. Nor do they any more imply, *fuch ignorance*, than they imply, the fall of man not known till Chriſt came in the flefh.—Now that which is not taught in, and by the procefs of Chriſt, cannot be taught by the manifeſtation of the gofpel myſtery. But in all our Saviour's procefs, there is no poſſibility of making any part of it prove, that the *immortality* of the foul, or its *deſtination* to a future life, was not the common belief, of every age from *Adam* to Chriſt.

For this wonderful procefs of Chriſt, which is the whole myſtery opened in the gofpel, is about quite *another kind* of life in the foul, than that which confiſts in its *bare immortality*. For immortality, confidered in itfelf, may as well be a curfe as a bleſſing. But this is not the life and immortality that the gofpel boaſts of. It leaves fuch natural immortality, which belongs as well to devils as men, as wholly untouched, as it does the original of the alphabet. And for this reafon, becaufe the *one knowledge* which the former world wanted, and the Chriſtian world got, is by all the evangeliſts and apoſtles confined

fined to that, which Christ, as God and man, was, did, suffered, purchased, and obtained, in and through the efficacy and merits of his process, till as a second *Adam*, he was placed at the right hand of God.

It is the living knowledge, the real participation of all these parts of our Saviour's process, as a God incarnate, that contains all that life and immortality, all the glad tidings of salvation, and light out of darkness, made known to the world by Christ and his apostles. Nor do they ever call the attention of mankind to any other new light or knowledge, but that of seeing and knowing, how every part of Christ's process had its particular and joint efficacy, to destroy the works of the devil, and the power of hell in fallen man.

This was the good news of *life and immortality* brought to light by a glorious gospel, which shewed the whole counsel of God towards fallen men; how they were before the foundation of the world seen in Christ, *predestinated to be made conformable to his image*, who by all that he was, did and suffered, from his first coming down, to his ascension into heaven, was the one, only possible means of their partaking again of the divine nature.

Every step of our Saviour's process from first to last, was only so many necessary steps of our progress out of the eternal death of sin and misery, into a participation of an heavenly life in Christ Jesus. And in this process is contained all that
Christian

Christian theology, which makes up the whole doctrine of Christ and his apostles.

No power of reasoning, no art of criticism, can force one single text of the New Testament to speak, or so much as hint at any other life or immortality but this, *as first* made known to the world by the gospel.—The natural immortality of the soul, is no part of its redemption, but belongs to it as it belongs to all angels, whether in heaven or in hell, and is an immortality no more purchased by the incarnation of the Son of God, than the immortality which belongs to *Lucifer* and his angels.—Therefore this cannot be that immortality, which is the gift of God through Jesus Christ. And therefore nothing that is said of that immortality, which comes to fallen man only by Jesus Christ, can be the least proof, that the belief of the soul's perpetual existence in a future state came first, or only by him, and was not always held by every age, from the beginning of the world.

Natural immortality has its full nature in the fallen angels; but the one immortality that comes by Jesus Christ, is the glory of the Holy Trinity, dwelling and manifesting itself in the immortal nature of the soul.

For this is a certain truth, that all that is divine and God-like in any creature, dwells as a supernatural gift or operation of God in it; which may be lost, as it was in angels, and *Adam*; and can be kept by no other power but that of faith:

nor regained, when loft, but by the return of that same faith, and full refignation to God. So that the natural immortality of angels or men, is only their capacity to receive the never-ending, but always increafing manifeftation of divine glory in, and thro' all the natural powers. And this is the one immortality made known, and purchafed for us through the bleffed Jefus, being and doing what he was and did, in our poor immortal nature, that had loft its God.

But to confider now the texts of the New Teftament, on which this author has endeavoured to eftablifh Bifhop *Warburton*'s opinion. The firft and chief of thefe is that of St. *Paul*; " God hath faved us, according to his own purpofe, and his grace, which was given us in Chrift Jefus, before the world began : but is now made manifeft by the appearing of our Saviour Jefus Chrift, who hath abolifhed death, and brought life and immortality to light through the gofpel."

Now every word in this paffage excludes all regard to the natural immortality of the foul, and neceffarily leads and confines us to that one life and immortality, to a life and immortality of the heavenly nature brought forth in our fouls.— For the life and immortality here granted to us, is exprefsly affirmed to be effected by Chrift's abolifhment of death. Therefore as is the death here abolifhed, fuch muft be the life that is brought forth in the ftead of it.

The

The death here abolifhed is not the natural mortality of body or foul, but that death, whofe deftruction is declared in thefe words of the apoftle, *Chrift was manifefted to deftroy the works of the devil:* and from that deftruction comes forth the one true life and immortality, which is an eternal union of righteoufnefs in and with Chrift, as a principle of a divine life eternally dwelling in us.

To be carnally minded, faith the apoftle, is death, this is the one death that Chrift is here faid to abolifh; but to be fpiritually minded is life and peace; and this is the one life and immortality that Chrift fets up in the ftead of death, by making us fpiritually minded, or as St. *Peter* words it, " partakers of the divine nature, by which we are made children of God, and if children, then heirs of God, and joint heirs with Chrift."

Farther, St. *John* faith, *This is the record, that God hath given unto us eternal life*; furely this is the one immortality brought to light by the gofpel. But to fhew us what, and wherein this immortal, or eternal life confifts, the apoftle adds, " and this life is in his Son: he that hath the Son, hath life, and he that hath not the Son, hath not life."

* Therefore this immortality, or eternal life given unto us of God, not only has nothing in it concerning the natural immortality of fouls, but is neceffarily to be underftood of quite another matter.

* For they only can have this eternal life given to them of God, who have the Son: therefore it has no relation to the natural immortality of souls, and they can only have the Son, of whom it can be truly said, " that Christ is of God become wisdom and righteousness, and sanctification to them."

* As another full proof of all that has been said, it may be added, that the life and immortality brought to light by the gospel, is purely conditional and only offered to mankind, as a gift of God, upon certain terms. And therefore does not, cannot mean the immortality of the soul, or its perpetual natural duration in a future state.

Thus, " God gave his only begotten Son, that whosoever believed on him, should not perish, but have everlasting life. Ye will not come to me, that ye may have life." Therefore the immortality of life revealed by the gospel, is purely conditional, and adventitious to the soul, such as may be received, or not received, and consequently cannot possibly be, or mean a natural immortality, for such immortality, it has no power of freely receiving, or not receiving upon terms.

That blessing of a heavenly immortality, freely given by God, is nothing else but a celestial holiness, purity and perfection brought forth in the soul, by its having the eternal WORD and SPIRIT of God again restored to, and united with it: called immortality, not because of its

eternal

eternal duration, but becaufe eternally free from all that, which is death, or the deadly evil of fin in the foul; called alfo fo, in oppofition to that natural immortality of devils, and damned fouls, which tho' never ceafing, is only an eternal death. So that no argument, from what is faid of the life and immortality made known by the gofpel, can be drawn into a proof, that the belief of a future ftate, was not the general belief of the world before. Becaufe the immortality preached by the gofpel, is a thing quite different from the natural, perpetual duration of the foul, and means neither more, nor lefs, than the *glory and perfection of a divine life*, to which *Adam* died the very day that he did eat of the forbidden tree, and which is quickened again, in and by the whole procefs of Chrift in our nature.

I come now, to my fecond propofition, namely, to fhew, that the doctrine of a future ftate, or the immortality of the foul, was not defignedly fecreted, or induftrioufly hidden from the eyes of the people of God by the types and figures of the Mofaic difpenfation.—My reafons for it are as follow. *Firft*, becaufe it is highly unworthy of God, to fuppofe, that it was, the end of thofe types and figures, defignedly to *fecrete*, or *hide* from the people of God, the knowledge *of any truth*, much lefs the knowledge of a truth, abfolutely *neceffary*, to the very poffibility of any fpiritual relation, or religious communication

cation between God and man, as that of the immortality of the soul, must be.—For though the Mosaic state, may be justly called a *region of darkness*, when compared to that *light* which has arisen from the process of Christ; yet so far as it went, and with regard to the people under it, it was a degree of *light*, and a degree of *life:* it was *some progress* in victory over death, it was *some opening* of divine light, an help to such kind of knowledge, as could be had in such a state, as was only formed to support, and keep up a faith, and hope, and expectation of such a redemption to come, as had been promised from the beginning of the world, but could have no open manifestation, till its *own existence* manifested itself. —It is therefore a gross mistaking the *whole nature* of the law, to consider its types and figures as *designedly* hiding any thing from man.—Their design was quite the contrary, namely, to convey *new* light and *farther* information. And though they may be said to be a *shadowy*, and imperfect representation, yet its whole intent is, to give some knowledge of the substance; and by its signs to make the things to come more expected, than they would have been without such types and figures.

Bishop *Warburton*, speaking of typical representation, saith, *it necessarily implies the throwing a thing into shade, or secreting it from vulgar knowledge.*

Typical

Typical representation, in the *law*, is not, cannot be the *throwing a thing into shade*, or *secreting* it from *vulgar knowledge*. For this supposes the thing typified to have been already *in existence*, or it could not be *thrown* into shade. But this hath no place in the Mosaic types and figures; they are not the putting any thing *already existent*, under a cover, but are a *degree* of light cast upon such a matter, as had *never shewn* itself, and which could therefore only be typically pointed at, till it came into actual existence.

Again, that typical representation does not *necessarily imply*, *the throwing a thing into shade, and secreting it from vulgar knowledge*, is plain from hence.—Baptism, and bread and wine in the sacrament, are merely corporeal types and figures of spiritual things; but if it was *necessarily essential* to typical representation, *to throw things into shade, and secrete them from vulgar knowledge*, it would follow, that these two sacraments could have no other end, but to cast the spiritual things of the gospel into shade, and secrete them from vulgar knowledge. Type, figure, and human language, with regard to spiritual things, have the same kind of imperfection, though not in the same *degree*; but yet teaching and informing, is the design of both of them.

Of the Mosaic types therefore it may justly be affirmed, that they were so far from *designedly* hiding, or covering any truths from man, that their whole intent was, to *uncover*, and make *less hidden*

hidden such things as at that time, could not be seen, or known as they were in themselves.— Nothing could possibly manifest the nature, power, and efficacy of Christ's process (the one thing typified) but its own real nature, come into *actual existence in all its parts.*—Therefore through every age of the world, from the first promise made to *Adam,* of *a seed of the woman to bruise the head of the serpent,* to that time, all the religious goodness of mankind consisted in their *walking before God* in an *implicit faith* of a full redemption, made known to them under representation of a seed of the woman, overcoming the mischief that the serpent had done to them. And through this *faith alone* it was, that all the holy men of old had their righteousness, and peace, and union with God. And *God was not ashamed to be called their God, inasmuch as having received the promises, and seen them afar off, and embraced them, they confessed they were strangers and pilgrims on earth, desired a heavenly country, and through faith looked for a city whose builder and maker is God.*

Hence are the following great truths undeniably evident, (1.) That *faith in Christ,* has always been, and always must be, the *only* ground of salvation possible to man, in any age of the world. (2.) That *this faith* itself, and all its power and efficacy, has always, as fully proceeded from Christ alone, as the faith of those who believed in him, when come in the flesh. For as then

Christ

Chrift truly faid of himfelf, *without me ye can do nothing,* fo it was equally true of the firft promifed feed of the woman, *that without it,* nothing good could have been done by fallen man.

Therefore, (3) the covenant of God with all mankind through Chrift, is a living, operative covenant of life and immortality, not firft begun, or firft made known, when Chrift was on earth, and died for us, but a covenant as antient as our firft parents, as univerfal as their offspring. And what the apoftle faith, that *God was in Chrift Jefus reconciling the world unto himfelf,* tells us a truth and goodnefs of God, that extends itfelf to every nation, people, and language, that ever hath been, or ever fhall be upon the face of the earth.

* And as an implicit faith in a promifed redemption was all the religion of the old world; all that could be done by the infinite wifdom of God, was according to the fitnefs of times, feafons and occafions (only known to himfelf) to give forth fuch typical and prophetic intimations of this redemption, as fhould more and more confirm their faith, and prepare them to fee, that the whole procefs of Chrift, when finifhed, was that very redemption firft promifed to all the world, in the promife made to the common Father of mankind, through fucceeding ages kept conftantly in view, by a train of types and prophecies.

* And

* And as the history and ritual of *Moses*, could not possibly design to take away the knowledge of any divine truths from the people of God, so least of all could they designedly hide from them a belief of the natural immortality of the soul: a truth absolutely necessary and essential to any spiritual relation, or religious communion between God and man.

* And indeed, *Moses*, is as free from any such *design*, as the apostles themselves.

* For to say, that the types of the law have designedly hid, from the people of God, all sense of the immortality of the soul, is as false, as bold and extravagant, as to say the same thing of the gospel.

For in the New Testament, not a word is to be found, that expressly affirms the soul to be naturally immortal; in this respect the law and the gospel are equally silent; and yet neither of them secrete, or hide it from the people of God, but both fully prove, and with the same kind of proof, the absolute necessity of believing it.

For as in the gospel it is never expressly asserted, and yet is fully proved, because unavoidably supposed, and necessarily implied in and by the open, and plain doctrines of the gospel: so it is with the books of *Moses*; they never expressly affirm the natural immortality of the soul, and yet give one, and the same full proof of it, as the gospel doth. Because the express doctrines

trines of every difpenfation of God, from *Adam* to Chrift, openly teach doctrines, which not by inference, but in the plain nature of the thing, unavoidably require, and neceffarily imply, the immortality of the foul, and the common belief of it in all ages of the church before the coming of Chrift.

The obtaining an union with Chrift, is the one life and immortality brought to light by the gofpel; but this immortality unavoidably requires, and neceffarily implies the perpetual duration of the foul's natural life. For nothing but an ever-enduring creature, is capable of enjoying an everlafting gift.

Therefore the gofpel, tho' never once exprefsly afferting, yet continually demonftrates the natural immortality of the foul.

And this is the whole truth, with regard to the *Mofaic* hiftory and types; they hide it, in the fame manner as the gofpel hides it, that is, not at all; and they fully prove it in the fame manner as the gofpel proves it, by doctrines which neceffarily require, and abfolutely imply it, in the firft conception of them.

For the hiftory of the creation and the fall of man, contains an exprefs covenant of a redemption, promifed to *Adam* and his fallen pofterity, in which a feed of the woman fhould do away the evil which the ferpent had brought into the human nature, that is, fhould reftore the firft, loft, heavenly life to mankind.

But

But this covenant, and the immediate benefit of it, could neither be wanted nor received, but by immortal creatures, that believed themselves to have an immortality, which had lost that glory and perfection which belonged to it at the first. Nor could such immortal creatures have any power of entering into this covenant any other way, than by an implicit faith in God. For it was a covenant of redemption, or return of their first glory, without the least intimation of the time, or age, when, or the means, or manner how it was to be brought to pass. Therefore such a covenant, and such a faith, in the very first conception of them, without the least reasoning or deduction, absolutely imply, and necessarily require a full belief of a future state.

And how could God better keep up a full sense of it, or more fix it in the hearts of men, than by placing and fixing all their faith and comfort, in a redemption certainly to come upon all the world, which yet might not come, till half the world was dead?

Or how could mankind possibly give into this faith, had they had the least doubt of the certainty of a life to come? For their faith in such an expected redemption, could not be either more or less, than their faith in a future state.

Therefore God's requiring this faith of them, was in the highest degree his requiring them to
believe

believe the ever-enduring life of their souls. Consequently, in the first revelation of God to man, life and immortality, as it means an ever-enduring state of the soul, was as fully, and in the same degree brought to light, as in the revelation of the gospel.

In the gospel it is proved, because an immortality of a heavenly life is made known, purchased and given by Christ, which necessarily implies an immortal nature in man, or he could not partake of it.

In the first revelation, it is equally proved, because a *redemption to come*, that was to be obtained by an implicit faith, without any knowledge of the time when it was to appear, whether before or after many generations of men were dead and gone, necessarily implies a full belief of a state belonging to man, that is beyond time, and the death of the body.

This proof of the natural immortality of the soul, thus inseparable from the first revelation of God, is so strong, that nothing need, or hardly can be added to it. For how could God more fully assert the immortality of our nature, than by requiring our faith in such a redemption? Or how could man more strongly declare his full belief of, such immortality, than by his faith in a redemption that had nothing to do with time, or the life, or death of the body in this present world?

Again,

Again, The murder, or martyrdom of *Abel*, and the translation of *Enoch* into heaven, both recorded for the instruction of the people in this very point, are two examples, and first fruits of the redemption promised to *Adam*, and all mankind; two invincible proofs, that this first covenant was a covenant of life and immortality, confirmed to mankind by facts strong and convincing, like those of Christ's resurrection and ascension.

For immediately after a covenant of redemption was made, the first good man after it, in the very beginning of the world, and the beginning of his own life, after his first act of divine worship, and as soon as God had declared his good pleasure in it, was slaughtered like a beast.

Now can there be a fuller demonstration, that the covenant of redemption was for life and immortality in a future state? Otherwise the first good man in the world lost all the benefit of God's covenant, merely because he was good; merely thro' the devotion that he shewed towards God, and the favour which God shewed towards him.

Therefore either *Abel*'s blood cries aloud the absolute certainty of a future state, or *Abel* must be said to have been undone, ruined, and deprived of all good, purely because of a friendship discovered between God and him.

This

This fact therefore, recorded by the Spirit of God assures all the Mosaic generations, that another life belonged to *Abel* and to them, besides that which *Abel* lost by his death. Does it not as directly, declare this, as when Christ said, his *kingdom was not of this world?* Does it not say the same thing, as when Christ said to his disciples, *fear not them that can only kill the body?* The same thing, as the voice from heaven, which cried, *blessed are the dead which die in the Lord?*

Again, Another proof of the same force, is the translation of *Enoch*. God saith by *Moses*, *Enoch walked with God, and was not, for God took him.* Now, could any the most expressive form of words, have told the ancient world with more certainty than this fact does, that God's covenant with man, was for a kingdom of heaven?

Our blessed Lord, when departing out of this world, faith to his disciples, *I go to prepare a place for you, that where I am, there ye may be also.* And does not *Enoch's* translation say as much, as if he had been sent again by God to say, *God has taken me from this world into heaven, to make it manifest to you, that where I am gone, there are ye to come also.*

Behold here the adorable goodness of God to the first and succeeding ages of the world! These two great articles of faith, which are now the comfort of the Christian world, namely, victory

over

over death, and afcenfion into heaven, had even then the utmoft and moft convincing proof given to them by God.

The old world, from the firft man, were all in a covenant of redemption.—Life and immortality was both by doctrine and example, made known to them, and nothing remained as a myftery or wifdom hidden in God, to be revealed in the laft times, but that one thing which could not be manifefted, till by its own actual exiftence it manifefted itfelf, namely, the wonderful procefs of Chrift in our fallen nature. By which procefs alone it was that all the faith, as well before as after Chrift, had all its efficacy.

Hence it is, that the faith and religion of the firft world was in fubftance, the very Chriftian faith and Chriftian religion, one and the fame way, and power of falvation; which onenefs confifts in this, that *Chrift, the fame yefterday, to day and for ever*, was the fame mediator between God and man from the beginning of the world, one and the fame power of life and falvation to murdered *Abel*, as to martyred *Stephen*.

This faith from this original, was their peace with God thro' Jefus Chrift, the very fame faith of which Chrift faith, *He that believeth in me fhall never die*. The fame faith of which he again faith, *If any man thirft, let him come unto me and drink;*

drink; he that believeth in me, out of his belly shall flow rivers of living water.

That this was the catholic, faving faith, common to all the patriarchial ages, we are affured by the Spirit of God in the epiftles to the *Corinthians* and *Hebrews*, telling in exprefs words, "They did all eat the fame fpiritual meat, did all drink the fame fpiritual drink, for they drank of that fpiritual rock that followed them, and that rock was Chrift."

Are we not told, that very fame thing of the patriarchal generations, which Chrift faid to thofe that believed in him, that by eating his flefh, and drinking his blood, they have eternal life?

In the eleventh chapter of the epiftle to the *Hebrews*, the fame fpirit, fpeaking of the patriarchal ages, faith, "All thefe died in faith, not having received the promifes, but having feen them afar off, and were perfwaded of them, and embraced them, and confefled they were ftrangers and pilgrims on earth,—who defired a better country, that is, an heavenly."

Bifhop *Warburton* is fo out of humour with this whole chapter, thus full of patriarchal light and glory, that he gives it the heathenifh name of the *Palladium of the caufe*, which he had undertaken to demolifh. And he accordingly attacks it with a number of critical inventions, that may as truly be called heathenifh; for they are in direct oppofition to all Chriftian theology.

He will have it, that the faith set forth in this whole chapter, is concerning a faith in the abstract, and not a specific faith in the Messiah. An invention as little grounded in the gospel, as goodness in the abstract, in opposition to specific goodness. Goodness in the abstract, if it hath any meaning, is all goodness, and therefore must have every species of goodness in it; so faith in the abstract, if it hath any meaning, is all faith, and therefore must have every species of faith in it.

His first reason, why this whole chapter is concerning a faith in the abstract, and not a faith in the Messiah, is taken from that definition of faith; " The substance of things hoped for, the evidence of things not seen."

And yet this very definition, if it had been intended to give the most distinct idea of the nature of faith in the Messiah, could not have been better expressed, for there is every thing in it that can fully set forth that very faith. For if faith in a Messiah to come, must be a faith in things hoped for, and a reliance upon the certainty of things not seen; if this, and nothing but this, can be a true faith in a Messiah to come, how could it be more directly pointed at, than by making it to be *the substance of things hoped for, the evidence of things not seen?*

For in this definition, not only the true object, but the true efficacy of faith in the Messiah is set forth, in that it is made to be such a real foretaste,

foretaste, and participation of things hoped for, and not seen, as is justly called, the very substance and evidence of them.

Again, the Doctor appeals to the following words, as proof, that the faith described in this chapter, is not a faith in the Messiah, " He that cometh to God, must believe that he is, and that he is a rewarder of all those that diligently seek him." Which words contain neither more nor less, than if it had been said, " He that cometh to God, must believe that he is a fulfiller of his promises to all those that truly believe in him, and them: for God cannot be considered as a rewarder of mankind, in any other sense, than as he is a fulfiller of his promises made to mankind in the covenant of a Messiah. For God could not give, nor man receive any rewards or blessings, but in and through the one Mediator. Therefore to believe in God, as a rewarder, and blesser, is the very truth, and reality of a right faith in the Messiah.

The Doctor has another proof, which he says, puts the matter out of all doubt. In this chapter it is said, By faith *Rahab* the harlot escaped, by faith the *Israelites* passed through the red sea, by faith the walls of *Jericho* fell down. " But was any of this, a faith in Jesus the Messiah?"

Now not to rob this argumentation of any of its strength, it must be allowed to proceed thus.

Joshua's faith could not be in the Messiah, or the promises of God made to his forefathers.

But why so? Because by his faith the walls of *Jericho* fell down.

Just as theologically argued, as if it had been said, *Abel*'s faith could not be a faith in the seed of the woman, promised to his parents; because by his faith " he offered unto God a more acceptable sacrifice than *Cain*."

Enoch's faith could not be in a Messiah to come, because by his faith he was taken up to God.

Abraham's faith could not be in the Messiah, because by his faith, " He sojourned in a strange country, chose to dwell in tents, and looked for a city that hath foundations, whose builder and maker is God." His faith could not be in a Messiah to come, because by his *faith he offered up* Isaac, *his only begotten son*.

Having set the Doctor's argument in its best light, no more need be said about the worth of it.

At last comes his invincible argument, which if it was as strong, as he gives out, all that went before might have been spared.

" To evince it impossible, says the Doctor, that faith in the Messiah, should be meant by the faith in this chapter, the apostle expresly saith, that all those, to whom he assigns this faith, had not received the promises; therefore they could not have faith in that, which was never proposed to their faith. For how should they

they believe on him, of whom they had not heard?"

Now if this argument has any good logic in it, it muſt follow, that no one, whether patriarch or prophet, before, or after the law, ever had, or could have faith in the Meſſiah, for all who died before the birth of Chriſt, muſt have died without receiving the promiſes, which were then firſt received, when good old *Simeon* could ſing, " Lord, now letteſt thou thy ſervant depart in peace, for mine eyes have ſeen thy ſalvation."

But St. *Paul*, ſpeaking to the *Jews*, faith, " Behold, we declare unto you glad tidings, how that the promiſe, which was made unto the fathers, God hath fulfilled the ſame to us their children."

Here, by the Spirit of God himſelf, is made known to us, the true difference between receiving, and not receiving the promiſes. The fathers, who could only ſee them afar off, are thoſe who died without receiving the promiſes, that is, without receiving the things promiſed. And their children who lived to ſee the promiſes fulfilled, are they that received the promiſes, that is, the things promiſed.

Farther, the Spirit of God ſaith, " all theſe died in the faith, not having received the promiſes."

But how could they die in this faith? It was for this only reaſon, becauſe they had not received the promiſes, that is, the things promiſed. For if they had, they could not have died in faith, but in the enjoyment of things promised.

The Doctor therefore has unluckily pitched upon that, as an argument against the possibility of their faith in the Messiah, which is the very reason, why they did die in the faith of him. For the holy Spirit saith, they all died in the faith; and then the reason is added, why they did, namely, because not having received the promises; therefore their not having received the promises, is the reason why they died in the faith of them. And their faith had this foundation, because they had seen the things promised, as afar off, that is, long after their own deaths, and therefore to be fulfilled, or made good in a future life. Consequently, their faith was in a redemption to come in a life after this; which surely may be affirmed to be a true faith in the promised Messiah, or in all that, which had been promised, from the first joyful notice, which God gave of him, *in a seed of the woman to bruise the head of the serpent.* Which in gospel language is called, *destroying the works of the devil*, and bringing all that to life again, which died in *Adam's* transgression.

It is added of these holy men dying in the faith of promises *seen afar off*, that they *were perswaded of them, and embraced them, and confessed they were strangers and pilgrims on the earth ; now they that say such things, plainly declare, that they seek a better country, that is, an heavenly.*

What

What an extravagance is it therefore in the learned Doctor, to say, *How should they believe in him of whom they have not heard*; as in the least degree applicable to those saints of the old world? For their faith was in promises made to them, but not fulfilled before their deaths, which they beholding as afar off, died in the fullest faith and expectation of a blessed life and heavenly country in virtue of them. Therefore they believed in that, of which they had heard, they knew what it was that they believed, *namely*, a redemption from all the evil of their pilgrimage on earth, to a life in heaven.

Our blessed Lord said to the *Jews*, *Your father* Abraham *rejoiced to see my day, and he saw it, and was glad*. Surely then *Abraham* had faith in the Messiah, and yet he is numbered by the apostle amongst those, who died not having received the promises.

But now, though *Abraham*'s rejoicing at the sight of that day, was a sufficient proof, that his faith was in the Messiah, yet the *implicit* faith of the more antient, patriarchal world in *that*, which they had not seen, as *Abraham* had, was as *right* a faith in the Messiah, as *Abraham*'s was. This point is determined, in the following words of Christ. *Thomas, because thou hast seen me, thou hast believed: blessed are they, which have not seen, and yet have believed.*

This, and this alone, is the only real difference between the religion of the faithful before, and after

after Chrift. *Before Chrift*, the living faith, was in a Meffiah to come in fome wonderful, but unknown way. By this faith, they ftood under the blefled power of the *feed of the woman*, and from generation to generation were kept in the one true covenant of life, and union with God.

After Chrift, the fame living faith, rejoiced in a Meffiah made known by a miraculous birth, in the fallen human nature, redeeming it out of every evil of life, of death, of fin and hell, till it was placed, as God and man in one perfon, at the right hand of God in heaven.

Now when in procefs of time, the covenant of life between God and man, had loft much of its effect, and the people of God had greatly fallen away from the faith and piety of the firft patriarchs, (perhaps not more remarkably than the Chriftian world is fallen from the truth and faith of the apoftolic ages) it pleafed God by *Mofes*, to introduce the defcendents of the patriarchs into a new *covenant of care, and protection over them*.

Which covenant was not a *new progreffive ftate* of that firft one true religion, that alone unites God and fallen man, nor given for its own fake, or becaufe of any intrinfic goodnefs in its wafhings and purifications, but granted to the *hardnefs of their hearts*, as a *temporal means* of keeping a fallen people from falling farther under the blindnefs and vanity of their earthly minds.

The

The firſt covenant was ſo perfect that nothing could be added to it, but the manifeſtations of that which was promiſed in it. It was a promiſe of life and redemption to mankind, to be fulfilled in and by the ſeed of the woman. Now the promiſe, and the fulfilling of it, are not (as in human matters) two *diſtant, ſeparate* things, that begin at different times, nor can the one ever be without the other. They both began together, and muſt exiſt together. The end, that is, the fulfilling, grows out of the beginning, goes along with it, and has all its efficacy from it; and the beginning, that is, the promiſe, is only ſo much of the end.

That which Chriſt did, ſuffered, and obtained in our fleſh, calling all to turn to God, to deny themſelves, to enter into the ſtricteſt union with him, giving all divine graces, and yet only *according to their faith in him*; that very ſame, the ſeed of the woman from the beginning was always doing, yet ſolely *according to their faith in it.*

* The loſs of *this faith* in the firſt ages of mankind, gave birth to that which is called the *heathen,* or *rational* world; for they both began together, and brought forth a race of people, full of blindneſs, wickedneſs, and idolatry. For ſo far as they departed from faith, ſo far they fell from God, under the dominion and government of their reaſon, paſſions, and appetites. And thence began the kingdom of this world, and the wiſdom,

wisdom of this world, which ever must have full power over every man, as soon as he ceases to live by faith.

* *Reasoning* instead of faith, brought about the first dreadful change in human nature, no less than a real death to God. And nothing but faith instead of reasoning, can give any one fallen man power to become again a son of God. Now to the end of the world, this will be the unalterable difference between faith in God, and reasoning about the things of God: they can never change their place, or effects; that which they did to the first man, that they will do to the last.

* It *matters* not, how much the *revelations* and precepts of God are increased, since the first single command given to *Adam*; for no more is offered to our reasoning faculty by the whole bible, than by that single precept. And the benefit of the whole bible is lost to us, as soon as we reason about the nature and necessity of its commands, just as the benefit of that first precept was lost in the same way.

Hath God indeed said, ye shall not eat of every tree in the garden? This was the first essay, or beginning of reasoning with God. What it was, and did then, that it will always be, and do. Its nature, and fruits will never be any other, to the end of the world. And though in these last ages, it hath passed through all schools of quibbling, and is arrived at its utmost height of art, and precision of argument, yet as to divine matters, it

stands

stands juft where it ftood, when it firft learnt that logic from the ferpent, which improved the underftanding of *Eve.* And at this day, it can fee no deeper into the things of God; give no better judgment about them, than *that* conclufion it at firft made, that *death* could not be in the tree which was *fo good for food, fo pleafant to behold, and to be defired for knowledge.*

In fhort, thefe two, faith and reafoning, have, and always will divide all mankind, from the beginning to the end of the world, into two forts of men.

The faithful, thro' every age, are of the feed of the woman, the children of God, and heirs of redemption.

The reafoners are of the feed of the ferpent, they are the Heathens thro' every age, and heirs of that confufion, which happened to the firft builders of the tower of *Babel.*

* To live by faith, is to be in covenant with God; to live by reafoning, is to be in compact with ourfelves, with our own vanity, and blindnefs.

* To live by faith, is to live with God in the fpirit and power of prayer, in felf-denial, in contempt of the world, in divine love, in foretaftes of the world to come, in humility, in patience, long-fuffering, obedience, refignation, abfolute dependence upon God, with all that is temporal and earthly under our feet.

* To live by reasoning, is to be a prey of the old serpent, eating dust with him, groveling in the mire of all earthly passions, devoured with pride, imbittered with envy, tools and dupes to ourselves, tossed up with false hopes, cast down with vain fears, slaves to all the good and evil things of this world, to-day elated with learned praise, to-morrow dejected at the loss of it; yet jogging on year after year, defining words and ideas, dissecting doctrines and opinions, setting all arguments and all objections upon their best legs, sifting and refining all notions, conjectures, and criticisms, till death puts the same full end to *all the wonders* of the ideal fabric, that the cleansing broom does to the wonders of the spider's web, so artfully spun at the expence of its own vitals.

* This is the unalterable difference between a life of *faith*, and a life of *reasoning* in the things of God; the former is from God, works with God, and therefore all things are possible to it; the latter is from the serpent, and therefore vain opinions, false judgments, errors and delusions are inseparable from it.

Every scholar, every disputer of this world, nay every man, has been where *Eve* was, and has done what she did, when she sought for *wisdom* that did *not come* from God. All libraries are a full proof of the remaining power of the first sinful thirst after it: they are full of a knowledge

knowledge that comes not from God, but from the first foundation of subtlety that opened her eyes. For as there cannot be any goodness in man, but so far as the divine goodness works in him, so there cannot be any divine truth, or knowledge in man, but so far as God's truth and knowledge works in him?

Indeed nothing but the one Spirit of Christ, living and working in man, from the beginning to the end of the world, can possibly be the source of any goodness, holiness, or redemption of man.

The scriptures abound with proof of this. What can be more decisive than the following words? *If any man hath not the Spirit of Christ, he is none of his. If Christ be not in you, ye are reprobates.* And must not this be equally true of every man in the world? As true of all men in the patriarchal as in the gospel ages? *If any man,* says the apostle; therefore no regard is had to time or place, but where there is *any man,* there this truth is affirmed of him by the apostle, that unless he hath the Spirit of Christ he is none of his, but is a reprobate. But if none can be Christ's, but because they have his Spirit living in them, and none can be God's, but because they are Christ's, it follows that if Christ was not the Spirit and power of *that* first, universal covenant made by God with fallen *Adam,* if he was not that which was meant by the *seed of the woman,* if his Spirit was not from that time the real bruifer of the ferpent's head, both *Adam*, and all his pofterity, for much more than three thoufand years lived and died mere reprobates, and that, by an unavoidable neceffity, becaufe they had not the Spirit of Chrift living in them.

And now, my Lord, I think I have fufficiently proved not only my two propofitions, but alfo that the firft covenant with *Adam*, by the feed of the woman, was the one Chriftian means of falvation, fo wonderfully manifefted by the whole procefs of Chrift revealed in the gofpel. Therefore it is a truth of the utmoft certainty, that from the beginning of the world to the end of it, there never was, nor ever will be any more, or any other, but one and the fame true religion of the gofpel, which began with *Adam* and *Eve* thro' Jefus Chrift, the one mediator and reconciler of God to man, who was as certainly the life, ftrength, and falvation of the faithful in the old world, as he was in after-times, when the Son of the Virgin *Mary*, *the way, the truth, and the life,* to all that have faith in him.

And indeed a plurality of religions, or means of falvation, is as grofs an imagination as a plurality of gods, and can fubfift upon no other foundation.

A better religion neceffarily fuppofes a better God, and a change in religion a change in that God that makes it. A partial God, with-holding

ing the *one true power* of salvation, till the last ages of the world, is as atheistical as *Epicurus*'s god.

In sundry times, and in divers manners, it may please the wisdom of God, to vary that which is only an outward help to the truth of religion; but the inward spirit and truth of salvation, is as unvariable as God himself.

The law therefore of *Moses*, as consisting of carnal ordinances, not only *makes nothing perfect*, but brings nothing new into the one covenant of redemption, but was only a temporary, provisional help, *added because of transgressions, till the promised seed should come*; that is, till the whole process of Christ, should in its last and highest degree of evidence manifest itself in all its parts.

* *This law* then no more belonged to the *true religion* of the Old Testament, than of the New, neither did it ever stand *between* these two dispensations, as in their stead. No: it was merely on the *outside* of both, had only a temporary relation to the true religion, either before or after Christ, but was no more a *part*, or *instead* of them *for a time*, than the hand that stands by the road, directing the traveller, is itself a part of the road, or instead of it.

Now, tho' the reason of man ought not to pretend to fathom all the depths of divine wisdom, in the whole of this *additional covenant*, yet two ends of it are apparent.

First,

First, To bring this corrupted people of *Israel* into a new state of such observances, as might preserve them from the gross superstitions and idolatries to which they were too much inclined. And this, by a *ritual* of such condescensions to their carnal minds, as might nevertheless be a school of restraints and discipline, full of such purifications, types, and figures, as gave much spiritual light and instruction, both backwards and forwards. Backwards, as truly significative of their fallen state, daily memorials of their lost purity and perfection: *forwards*, as variously pointing at *that promised* victory over the serpent, which had been the constant faith and hope of their forefathers.

Secondly, That by a theocracy added to this ritual, which shewed itself in a covenant of continual *care and protection*, openly blessing their obedience, and punishing their rebellion, and working all kinds of miracles in the overthrow of their enemies, not only they themselves, but all the rest of the world, might be forced to see and know, that there was no God, that had all power in heaven and on earth, but the one God of *Israel*.

As to the *Israelites* themselves, this temporal covenant was a great instance of God's goodness towards them. For they were thus called out of idolatry, separated from the rest of the world, built into an holy church of God, put under a most amazing theocracy, indulged for a time with a ritual of carnal inſtitutions, becauſe of the hardneſs of their hearts, which ritual was full of every inſtruction by doctrines, types, figures and miracles, all ſhewing in the ſtrongeſt manner, that they were to be heirs of the heavenly promiſes made to their forefathers.

And as to the reſt of the world, no particular meſſage or meſſenger, tho' new riſen from the dead, proclaims to them in ſo powerful a manner, the vanity of their idols, the knowledge of the one true God of all the world, as this remarkable body of people ſet up in the midſt of the world did. So that the law, tho' nothing but a temporal covenant of *outward care and protection*, was not only moſt divinely contrived to preſerve the faith of the firſt holy patriarchs, and guide them to the time and manner of receiving the promiſes made to their fathers, but it was all mercy to the reſt of the world, being no leſs than one continual, daily, miraculous call to them to receive bleſſing and protection, life and ſalvation in the knowledge and worſhip of the one true God of heaven and earth.

Now when the children of the patriarchs, were to be entered into this new covenant, the utmoſt care was taken by the Spirit of God, that to eyes that could ſee and ears that could hear, enough ſhould be ſhewn and ſaid, to prevent all *carnal atheiſm* to temporal and outward things, and bring forth a ſpiritual *Iſrael*, full of that faith and piety, in which their holy anceſtors, as pilgrims on earth,

earth, had lived and died devoted to God, in hope of everlasting redemption.

To this end *Moses*, tho' bringing them under a ritual of bodily washings and purifications, yet that they might use them only as outward confessions and memorials of an inward spiritual pollution, and as types and figures of their being to be delivered from it; is led by the inspiration of God, not only to insert in the books of the law, the most sublime doctrines and heavenly precepts of patriarchal holiness, but to lay before them, for their daily instruction, a history of the most deep and affecting truths: truths that had every thing in them fitted to awaken and keep up that strong hope of an eternal redemption, under the power of which, the holy patriarchs had overlooked every thing in time for the sake of eternity.

I mean, the most wonderful history of the creation and curse of this world, of the high origin of man and his dreadful fall from it, his redemption and covenant of life restored in a seed of the woman, the lives and deaths of the holy patriarchs, their patience under all sufferings, their contempt of worldly advantages, their heavenly visions, revelations and speeches from the invisible God, keeping them thereby in an holy intercourse with the *invisible world*, full of faith and hope of the good things of eternity.

To mention one or two of those great doctrines of

of *Moses*, which set forth the original perfection and heavenly nature of man.

God said, *Let us make man in our own image and likeness*. Is not this as high a doctrine of *immortality*, does it not give the same instruction, raise the same hope, and call for all the same elevation of the heart to God, as when St. *John* saith, *Beloved, it does not yet appear what we shall be; but we know that when he shall appear, we shall be* LIKE *him?* Just the same truth, and fitted to have the same effects, as when *Moses* said, God made man in his own LIKENESS.

St. *Paul* says, *God was in Christ, reconciling the world unto himself*. A comfortable doctrine indeed, and full of hope of immortality; yet only the same comfort and hope of immortality which had been openly preached by *Moses*.

When *Moses* bringeth in the Deity, as saying, *The seed of the woman shall bruise the head of the serpent*; he preaches *that* very same gospel, and in the same manner which the apostle did. For his words plainly teach, *that God was in the seed of the woman reconciling the world unto himself*; as when St. *Paul* says, *that God was in Christ reconciling the world to himself*; the difference is nothing else, but in two different names given to our Redeemer.

* Now tho' *Moses* was the first *recorder* of the gospel salvation in a written book, yet was he not the first *preacher* of it. For it was proclaimed in *Adam*'s day, from heaven, as the birth of
Christ

Chrift in the flefh, in the days of
when God faid, *The feed of the wom*
the head of the ferpent, the fame g
falvation was *proclaimed from he*
himfelf, as when the angel faid to
Unto you is born this day in the city
Saviour, which is Chrift the Lord.

* But how can we know this? O
own teaching. For nothing can be t
God by the creature, but that whic
known of himfelf.—So far as G
the creature, and manifefts himfelf
truly knows, and *is taught of God*
knowledge of God, however lear
deep it may pretend to be, is as va
ous as *that goodnefs* which procee
thing elfe, than God's good Spirit li

* Genius, parts and literature,
forth with wit and rhetoric, have n
divine knowledge; they can no
than the luft of the eyes and the pri
generate humility and purity of
accomplifhments live and act in a f
own, and have no more power
themfelves any living knowledge
the art of painting to the life, can g
of *creating* life.

* The blindnefs, and follies whic
run both the antient and modern wo
of religion, are a full proof of th
trine of divine revelation, *namel*

(now the defaced image of God) is so miserably changed and fallen from his first created state, that nothing less than a new birth, can bring him again into the region of divine *truth*.

And hence it is, that tho' religion has its deepest ground in the nature of man, tho' God be *essentially*, present in the souls of all men, yet from the fall of *Adam* to the end of the world, it will be an immutable truth, that *strait is the gate and narrow is the way that leadeth* unto divine knowledge; and none but the simple of heart, *the poor in spirit*, or the real followers of Christ can find it.

* But it is time to have done. I shall only trouble your Lordship with the few following remarks.—Dr. *Warburton* says, " He has proved that the doctrine of a future state of rewards and punishments is not to be *found in*, nor did make a *part* of the Mosaic dispensation."† The Mosaic dispensation means nothing else, but a *temporary* ritual, and a *temporary* theocracy of worldly blessings and curses to support it. These are its fixed bounds within which it is confined.—Therefore, to prove that a state *beyond* this world, was not to be *found in*, nor did make a *part* of a state, that is confined to this world, is as easily and as vainly done, as to prove that the *Garden of Eden* is not to be *found in*, nor makes a *part* of a map that is confined to *England*. And to infer *that* the *Israelites* therefore had no notion of

† D. L. Vol. II. page 474.

of an immortality, becauſe it was not a *part* of their ritual, is no better than to infer, that the people of *England* can have no notion of the garden of *Eden*, becauſe nothing of it is to be ſeen in the map of this iſland.—But tho' not in the *ritual*, yet *Moſes* in other parts of his books written for the inſtruction of thoſe to whom he gave the ritual, has given them the fulleſt notice and higheſt proof of that *godlike* and *immortal* nature they received at their creation, ſhewing them to be the children of the *patriarchal covenant*, heirs of all the promiſes of eternal redemption made to their fathers from the beginning of the world. Nay, the moſt heavenly doctrines and precepts given by the apoſtles to the redeemed of Chriſt, as *heirs of immortality*, are to be found in the books of *Moſes*.

Dr. *Warburton* takes much pains to get rid of the only true ſenſe of the following texts of *Moſes*. Thus, *Let us make man in our own image and likeneſs*. From theſe words, he ſays, *it is inferred, that the ſoul is immaterial*. But he thinks *Moſes intimated quite another matter*. And ſo do I; for to intimate the *immateriality* of the ſoul, by ſaying, that man was made in the *image and likeneſs* of God, is quite ſhort of the ſenſe of the words: to ſay, that the ſoul is *immaterial*, is ſaying no more, than that it is not a *circle* or a piece of *clay*, it is ſaying nothing at all of it but only of ſomething that it is not. Therefore *Moſes* cannot be ſuppoſed to intimate ſuch a nothing

thing as this, by the image and likeness of God. But he asserts a much higher matter, namely, that being created in the image of God, he was made a partaker of the divine nature, and therefore had not only immortality, but the riches and perfections of the Deity grounded and growing up. And this is the true ground of our eternal happiness, that is, of that *eternal increase* of union, perfection and glory, which the redeemed soul will find in God; it is because the image of God, being as a seed sown into it at its *creation*, it will to all eternity, after his admission into heaven, open more and more its divine nature, and spring forth in new and farther fruits of *glory, beatitude* and *union* with God.

Every thing that is endless, numberless in the depth of eternity, is endless and numberless in the essence of the soul; what *seeing* is, what *hearing, feeling, &c.* are in their boundless variety, and ever increasing newness of delights in eternity, these, with all their wonders, are the innate birthright and sure inheritance of every immortal godly soul. And on the other hand, the same boundless, numberless depth and growth of every tormenting, painful, frightful sensation, will open itself in every soul, *that* has lost its God, and is left to its own immortal life within itself.

Vain therefore, is that principle published to the world, by a celebrated philosopher of the last century, that the soul in its *first created state*,

is

is a mere *rasa tabula*, or *blank paper*. A fiction, that is contradicted by all that we know of every created thing in nature.

For every creature of this world, animate or inanimate, is in its degree, a *microcosm* of all the powers, that are in the great world, of which it is a part. And nothing through all this universe, has in its essence, only the nature of a *rasa tabula*, or blank paper, but is in its kind, full of the riches, and powers of all outward nature.

In like manner must it be with the eternal world; every thing which comes from it, must be in its degree, a *microcosm* of all the powers and glories of eternity.

Let it be said, that the *matter of this world*, was in its first created state, free from all extension, solidity and parts, and this would be as grave a saying, and as much founded in nature, as the *rasa tabula* of the soul: say again, that by degrees it got a materiality of length, breadth and parts, from *without*, and this would be no greater a wonder, than that a soul, created inwardly destitute of any principle of knowledge, should from outward causes grow up into a profound philosopher. *Again*, say that the soul was at first, but a *blank paper*, till the organs of the body began to act upon it; and may not the enemies of religion, as justly say, that it must be the same blank paper again at the last, when the body shall be broken off from it?

If

If therefore the *Essay upon human understanding* (which the Doctor calls the most original book that ever was published) has produced a metaphysicks, in many points dangerous to religion, and greatly serviceable to false, and superficial reasoning, it is not to be wondered at, since so eminent an error, is the fundamental principle on which it proceeds.

But to return to the Doctor: he says, "The divine image and likeness must consist in something that is peculiar to man,—that the two things *peculiar* to man, are his shape, and his reason; that it cannot be in his shape, therefore it must be in his reason."†

The divine image and likeness cannot consist in something that is peculiar to man. It might as well consist in his shape, as in his faculty of making *syllogisms*; but on the contrary, it must consist in that, and only that, which is, peculiar to God. Nor could man possibly be created in the image and likeness of God, unless something peculiar to God, had been the divine glory and perfection of his creaturely life. For the creaturely life, and all that is peculiar to it, is at the utmost distance from God, and can only have a likeness to that, which is to be found in creatures. —God dwelling in a supernatural way in the creature, is the only possible image of God that can be in it. The fallen angels have every thing that was creaturely *left* in them, but they are horrible

† Page 534.

rible devils, becaufe they have loft their fupernatural image of God, which dwelt in them at their creation. They have ftill reafon, craft and fubtlety; but becaufe they have nothing, but what is peculiar to the creature, they are all rage, torment and mifery.

The Doctor therefore, inftead of appealing to two things in man, his fhape and his reafon, as his true diftinction from beafts, fhould have faid, by the authority of *Mofes*, that only one thing was peculiar to man, as his glorious diftinction both from fallen angels, and terreftrial animals, and *that* one thing is, his being created in the image and likenefs of God. As to his outward fhape, confidered only as different from other animals, there is but little diftinction in it; becaufe they are as different in fhape from one another, as man is from them all. And if man at his creation had had no higher a gueft within him, than his reafon, his fhape would have been little better, than that of a fox, or a ferpent. For reafon, when not under the government of a higher principle, is that fame craft, and cunning, *that* is vifible in variety of beafts; and is for the moft part, as earthly an inftrument of mifchievous paffions, and lufts in man, as it is in beafts. And what is more, it muft be fo, till it comes under the government of *that*, which was the *image and likenefs* of God, in the firft creation of man.

* What is the difference between reafon in St. Paul, a *Spinofa*, a *Hobbes*, or a *Bolingbroke?*
None

None at all, or no other than in their outward shape. Therefore if reason be the divine image and likeness of God in man, a *Hobbes* and a *Bolingbroke*, had as much of it as St. *Paul*. And a man that is all his life long reasoning himself into atheism, and the wisdom of living according to his own lusts, must be allowed to give daily proof of his having the image and likeness of God, very powerfully manifested in him.

The Doctor's great proof, that reason is the image and likeness of God, is because *Moses* immediately adds, *Let them rule over the fish of the sea, and over the fowls of heaven, and over the beasts of the earth.* " For what, says he could invest man with this dominion *de facto*, as well as *de jure*, but his reason?"†

Our blessed Lord, at leaving the world, saith, " These signs shall follow them that believe; in my name, they shall cast out devils, they shall speak with new tongues, they shall take up serpents, and if they drink any deadly thing, it shall not hurt them." Now let it be asked, *what could invest the believers in Christ with this dominion* de facto, *as well as* de jure, *but their reason?* Both this question, and the solution of it, is just as found, and theological as the Doctor's.

For it was not any thing of their own, but solely the name, that is, power of Christ dwelling, and operating in them, that invested them with the dominion over devils, serpents, diseases, and

* D. L page 554.

and all outward deadly, or hurtful things. Now *that* which gave this power, to the believers in Chrift, was *that very fame*, which gave to the firft perfect man, a *power of ruling* over all the creatures of this world, and of living in full fuperiority and dominion over all that was, or could be hurtful, and deadly, in fire, or water, heat or cold, or any elementary things. So *that Adam* whilft ftanding in his firft ftate of glory, and power, had the fame reafon to fay of all *that* he was, and did, that which St. *Paul* faid, yet *not I, but Chrift that liveth in me.*

And how the Doctor came to think of any other power, as the *ability* of man to *rule* over the creatures, is very ftrange, fince the gofpel has fo plainly told him, *that they only are the children of God, who are led by the Spirit of God*. If therefore the firft man, created in the image and likenefs of God, may be fuppofed by his creation, to have been a child of God, then fure is it, that he had the *Spirit of God*, living and working in him. And that furely may be allowed to have been his *true* and his only qualification, to have and exercife a dominion over the reft of the creation.

The Doctor, in order to find out *that* image, and likenefs of God in man, of which *Mofes* writes, looks into the conftitution of that *two-legged* animal, who is *the difputer of the world*. As likely to fucceed, as if in order to find out *that paradife,* of which *Moses* writes, he should search for it in the *hundreds* of *Essex*, or in the *wilds* of *Kent*.

For *Moses*, to prevent the folly of looking for the divine image in any thing, that is *natural* to the *present* state of man, has given us assurance, that *this first* man, created in the image of God, died the very day that he did eat of the forbidden tree. And that nothing of this divine man remained but terrors within, and such a figure of himself, as filled him with shame and confusion.

And a greater than *Moses* has told us, *that* man, in his present *natural state*, is so dead to that first divine glory, that he has no possibility of entering into the kingdom of God till he is born again from above. This sufficiently shews *that* he who will find out in what the image of God in man consisted, must as the apostle saith, *walk by faith and not by sight.*

The next text of *Moses*, which the Doctor miserably injures, is thus quoted by him, " The Lord God formed man of the dust of the ground, and breathed into him the breath of life, and man became a living soul; that is, say the objectors, had an immortal soul."

Who the objectors are, I know not; but the truth of the text requires us to say, that therefore man had a divine and godlike soul, a true offspring of the divine nature. Because the breath or Spirit of the holy triune God, was that breath by which he was made a living soul.

—And therefore the riches of this firſt life in man, were the riches of the divine nature maniſeſting itſelf in the ſoul.

But the Doctor will have it, that only an unlearned *Engliſh* reader, can collect any thing to be divine in the ſoul, from the words of *Moſes*, as not knowing that what is tranſlated a living ſoul, ſignifies, in the original, only a living animal. But this, every *Engliſh* reader may know to be a vain criticiſm; for no ſtreſs is laid upon the expreſſion, a living ſoul, no more than if it had been ſaid, a living animal. But the full proof of the divine greatneſs of the human ſoul, lies ſolely in this, that the breath or ſpirit of the holy Trinity was breathed into it, and was that which made it to be a living ſoul, and therefore the life that aroſe in it, was the life of God in the ſoul.

The Doctor thus comments upon the words of the text. "God, the great plaſtic artiſt, is here repreſented, as making and ſhaping out a figure of earth and clay, which he afterwards animates or inſpires with life. He breathed into this ſtatue the breath of life, and the lump of clay became a living creature."

Had this elegant and moſt graphical deſcription been only found in ſome minor poet, or ſchool declamation, it might have been overlooked; but in a proſe treatiſe of divinity, it ought not to paſs uncenſured. I know of nothing that can equal it, unleſs it be ſuppoſed that ſome ingenious

nious anthropomorphite, reading thefe words, *and the Lord God did unto Adam and Eve make coats of skins, and cloathed them*; fhould thus defcribe the matter, " Here, God, the great artift, is reprefented, as having the fkins of beafts before him, and with his divine hands, cutting, fhaping and joining them together in forms of garments, fitted to the fize and diftinction of the firft man and his wife."

I may defy any one to fhew, that this comment does not pay as great a regard to the *letter*, and do as much honour to the fenfe of this fcripture, as the Doctor's doth to the other text.

The facred text, *God formed man* of the duft of *the ground, and breathed into him the breath of life*, is a fhort and full declaration of a moft important truth, namely, that man was brought into being, *in a twofold nature*, having the nature of this outward world, and the nature of heaven; the former fignified by his being formed of the duft of the ground, the *latter*, by the breath of God breathed into him. To be formed out of the duft of the ground, is the fame thing, as if it had been faid, that he was formed out of all the *riches*, *powers*, and *virtues* that are in this whole vifible world. For every property of nature is hidden in the earth. And man, fo far as he was defigned to be a creature of this outward world, is therefore faid to be formed out of the earth, becaufe the earth is not only the treafure-houfe of all that is in outward nature, but is the *mother* of all the three other elements. And as all things of this world, whether animate or inanimate, are from the earth as their mother, so in the earth is there every power and blessing of life, to sustain every thing *that* has its body from it; as appears by that fruitful power, which is continually giving forth itself in all kinds of vegetable food, *fitted* to the wants of every living creature.

* What therefore can it be called, but a most deplorable blindness in learned reason, to consider man as making his first entrance into paradise in no *better a state than that of dust and clay*, formed into a dead lumpish figure of a man, for this reason, because he was said to be formed out of the dust of the ground? Blindness indeed! when it is so evident, *that* even now, after the curse is in the earth, yet every thing, even the poorest *weed* that comes out of the dust of the ground, is in a much higher state, and enters into this world with a degree of life from its mother *the* earth.—Had the Doctor never seen, or heard of any other things formed out of the earth, but such as our potters, and dealers in clay can make out of it, there might have been some sort of excuse for his *Adam* of dead clay formed out of the earth. But when every day of his life has shewn him that almost infinite variety, powers, virtues and wonders in the kingdom of vegetables, all coming out of the earth, and nourished by it; when the scripture has told him

that

that the beasts and cattle of all kinds were formed out of the earth, and their flesh and blood from it, and their daily sustenance from its fruitful womb: it is strange to a degree of astonishment, that he should hold, *that* out of this *rich* earth, when in its paradisical state; when man, the glory of the creation, was formed out of it, and God the former, nothing would come forth, but a dead lump of clay in the figure of a man.

Again, What a total disregard has the Doctor here shewn to the very letter of scripture? The text saith, *God formed man out of the dust of the ground*, nothing else is ascribed to God, as his work in this matter; but the Doctor adds quite another matter as the work of God, namely, shaping and forming lumpish clay into a dead figure of a man.

And then follows another fiction equally against the letter of scripture. For he says, that AFTERWARDS, God, breathed life into it. But in the scripture account, there is not a syllable of any first, or afterwards.—Two things are spoken of the birth of man, and as they cannot be spoken both at once, so one must come after the other in the relation of them. The scripture mentions them as two distinct things; and the reason of mentioning them thus distinctly, is not to teach us, they were done at two different times, the one first, and the other afterwards, but to give us the assurance, that man came into the world in a twofold nature, the one from the heavenly breath of God, and the other from this visible world.

But the union of these two natures in the formation of man, was owing to one, and the same operation of God.—There is no sooner, or later, in the beginning of the soul, and of the body: the beginning of one, is the beginning of the other.

To suppose that man was made a dead image, and afterwards had life breathed into it, is no better philosophy, than to suppose, that God first created the vegetable creature, and afterwards added a vegetable life to it; that he first created the globe of the sun, and afterwards added heat and light to it.

God said, Let the earth bring forth the living creature. What a folly to suppose, that the creature, and its life, are two separate things, that the one came first, and the other afterwards? No better, than supposing, that a circle and its roundness, are two separate things, that first comes forth the figure, and afterwards its roundness.

But the general design of the *D. L.* is to establish this most horrible doctrine, that *Moses* designedly and industriously secreted from God's chosen people, all thought of any eternal relation that they had with God; which is the same as saying, that he designedly suppressed the one only possible foundation of true religion. For the

the immortality of the human nature, is the only ground of homage and regard to an invisible and eternal God. And unless man was by nature essentially related to God, and the eternal world, it would have been as unreasonable for the God of the eternal world to call man to an heavenly adoration of him, as to bid earthly flesh and blood *be*, and *do* that which angels are, and do in heaven. Therefore the first notice from an eternal God, given to man of a religious homage due to him, and the bare capacity of man to embrace such notice, is the greatest proofs that man has something of the eternal God in him. For as nothing can hunger, but that which by nature both wants and has a capacity to eat; so nothing can receive a religion relating to the eternal God, but that which has within itself, both a want and capacity to partake of the eternal world. And had not man an eternal spirit in him, as an offspring of the eternal God, he could no more want to have any intercourse with the eternal world, than a fish can want to be out of the water. Nor could any taught adoration of the one eternal God enter any further into his heart, or be of more use to him, than so much religion taught to a parrot. For man being, or believing himself to be, as merely a creature of this world, as the parrot is, could no more regard any thing, but what his earthly nature has a fondness for, than the parrot doth. *Let us eat and drink for*
to-morrow

to-morrow we die, would be the highest and truest philosophy, if there is no more of a divine life, or heavenly nature in man, than in the chattering sparrow. In this case, worldly craft, whether in a fox or a man, is the highest use of its natural powers. For if the earthly life is equally *the all* of both, earthly wisdom must be *equally* the perfection of them both. For it can no more be the duty of an earthly creature to be heavenly minded, than of a celestial creature to be carnally minded.

If therefore the *Israelites* under *Moses*, were by him directed to consider themselves merely as creatures of this world, having nothing to enjoy, or hope for, but the good things of this life, it must be said he did all that well could be done, to make them an *earthly, covetous, rapacious, stiff-necked* and *brutal* people. And all the complaints which the prophets have brought against them, on that account, ought to have been made only against *Moses* himself, and the religion that was set up by him. For a religion only offering, and wholly confining people to earthly enjoyments, may surely be said, not only to make, but even require them to be wholly sensual and earthly minded. And every hearty believer of such a religion, is by his very faith called upon, to make the most that he can, of the *lust of the flesh, the lust of the eyes, and the pride of life.*

* *Moses*

"*Moses* faith, "Hear, O *Israel*, the Lord our God is one Lord; and thou shalt love the Lord thy God with all thy heart, and with all thy soul, and with all thy strength." Now these *Israelites* looking backwards to God's covenant of redemption, made with their forefathers, of which they were the undoubted heirs; and forwards to this new covenant of a new theocracy, added, as God's peculiar mercy to them in this life, to keep them to himself, to support them under their afflictions, and to arm them with patience in waiting for that eternal redemption, in the faith of which, their ancestors had died so full of joy and comfort: in this double view of their state under God, which *Moses* had so fully set before *them*, and with the strongest injunctions to be daily teaching them to their children, they had the highest reason to rejoice in God, and to love him with all their heart and soul and strength.

But to suppose that *Moses*, designedly secreting from them, the knowledge of that eternal relation they had to God, on which the hopes of their forefathers were founded, and on which he himself was made able to chuse the afflictions of Christ, has something very shocking in it. For if *Moses* was so good a man, because he had faith in the eternal redemption promised from the beginning, can there be more cruelty, than in supposing him, designing by his religious system, wholly to obliterate all thought and remembrance

brance of God's unchangeable covenant of life, and extinguish all sense and hope of a redemption to come? To what purpose is it to say to such a people, shut up in earthly hopes, "Thou shalt love the one God of heaven with all thy heart?" For if he had succeeded in his design, fixed them in the belief, that they had no treasure but in this world, we have Christ's word for it, that the affections of their hearts could go no where else, saying, as an eternal truth, *that where our treasure is, there must be the heart also.* So that in this case, no love of God, and therefore no other divine virtue, could have any place in those who conformed to the design of *Moses.*

The Doctor, with some indignation, tries to evade this unavoidable consequence. " The true foundation of morality is the will of God. But is not the distinction between right and wrong, perpetually enforced by the law of *Moses* on this principle? This then is the spring of all virtue, and to give it the greatest efficacy, the love and fear of God is there incessantly inculcated. But how does a long or short existence, a life here, or elsewhere, affect at all the practice of virtue so founded?" †

All this is quite beside the point, and leaves the *Jews* under the same incapacity of every divine virtue, as has been above asserted. For a short or long existence, is here never thought of, as

† *D. L.* page 587.

as a reason, why we should, or should not be morally good. For duration, considered in itself, whether short or long, is only a natural consequence of *that kind* of life, which the creature hath. For, such as is its *internal* nature, such is the good, and evil *that* belongs to it, without any regard to its longer or shorter duration.

Now it is the internal nature of man, not considered as short, but as wholly earthly, and created for only *earthly goods*, *that* is the reason, why such a kind of life is incapable of any divine virtue, and cannot possibly have any other love, affections or tempers, but such as are confined to this world: and also, why every kind of envy, greediness, craft, and contrivance how to get the most of every earthly thing, must govern every man, that has only the earthly nature in him, as unavoidably, as they govern birds, and beasts. And to tell such a people of a goodness, to which their earthly nature does not lead them, as it leads every other animal to *that* which it likes, is as vain, as to preach to the sparks, not to fly upwards. Nor can a nature, wholly earthly, any more sin by coveting only earthly things, than the *lion* sins, by having all his heart set upon his prey.

But the Doctor has a maxim, by which he proves, that the *Jews*, though wholly confined to earthly hopes, and enjoyments, yet might and ought to have been heavenly minded, *namely*, because *the true foundation of morality, is the will*

of

of God. And yet this very maxim is itself a sufficient proof, than an earthly people, created only for earthly goods, are by the very will of God, directed to be earthly minded. For the will of God, in every creature, is manifested by *that kind* of nature, which it hath only from God. Therefore earthly creatures, by being earthly minded, pay as full obedience to the will of God, as pure heavenly spirits by their being heavenly minded. Therefore if man is only an animal of this world, by the will of God, distinguished only from other creatures, by superior skill, subtlety, and contrivances, (as they are from one another) he neither is, nor can be, under any other law, relating to his good and evil, but that which is the law of all other animals, that have all their good and evil from this world. And as it is as good in the wolf, to be ravening, as in the lamb to be harmless, because they both follow their created nature; so if man is as merely a creature of this world, as they are, when he, by his superior subtlety, in order to make the most of his worldly life, either feigns the innocence of the lamb, or puts on the ravening wolf, he follows his nature, as they do theirs, and is just as good and as bad as they are. And to tell such a man of the beauty of holiness, or call him to the denial of his own will, for this reason, because the true foundation of virtue, is the will of God, would be to as much purpose, as if you was only to require him never to sleep any more, because holy angels never sleep in heaven. For what can a creature that can have no good, all its life, but that which is like the

good

good of milk and honey, have to do with any divine virtue?—If therefore *Moses* designedly, fixed the *Israelites* in a belief, that they had no good to hope for, but that which flesh and blood could find in earthly things, they were by him taken out of the sphere of every virtue, that can be called godly or divine, and could have no fear of God, but like that, which they might have towards him, or the giants, nor any love of God, but that which they had to their bellies.

Farther, that the Doctor has not entered into any right conception of the subject, he is upon, is plain from his asking, " But how does a short or long existence, a life here, or elsewhere, at all affect the practice of virtue so founded?"—It just so much affects it, as place, or space affects the existence of bodies. They are not brought forth by place or space, but they could have no existence but in place or space. And thus it is, that duration affects the practice of all divine virtue, it could have no possibility of existence, but in a nature incapable of dying. —Corruptibility, and divine goodness, are as impossible to be united, as life and death.— Death may as well exert the functions of life, as a mortal creature breathe heavenly tempers and affections. For though the duration of the creature is not the ground, or reason of any divine virtue, yet no creature can be capable of it, but that, which by the divinity of its birth, is born immortal.

What

What an inconsistency, to say of a creature of a short existence, or whose life is vanishing away, that its true father is in heaven, and that it ought therefore " to be perfect as its heavenly Father is perfect?" Can that which is daily tending to non-existence, be daily growing up in the perfection of God, or that which is always approaching towards death, be a child of the ever-living God? As well might it be said of the mushroom, that it has the angels in heaven for its brethren, as of man, beginning to exist to-day, and ending his existence to-morrow, that he is a child of his everlasting Father in heaven,

There are some other egregious errors which I intended to have remarked, but I am already got beyond the proper bounds of a letter.—But holy *David*'s case, I cannot but mention, as sufficient to have deterred the Doctor from an hypothesis, which has obliged him to place this sweet singer of *Israel* amongst those, who had not the least thought of any eternal relation to God. This holy *David*, the type of Christ, " who knew that God had sworn with an oath, that out of the fruit of his loins, he would raise up Christ to sit on his throne:" this great prophet, who foretold the resurrection of Christ, *that his soul was not left in hell, neither did his flesh see corruption*; this *David*, thus deep in the counsels of God, and acquainted with the great article of the resurrection, this spiritual, typical, prophesying *David*, is, for the sake of the Doctor's project,

ject, crowded amongst those, who were not allowed to have any other relation to God, or any thing else to hope from him, or thank him for, but the blessings of a temporal life, till death had put the same end, to all of *David*, as it did to those few sheep, that he once kept. And what is still worse, the same *David* is made the most zealous preacher of the folly of fearing, or hoping for any thing after death: and is appealed to by the Doctor, and his assistant, as giving the most full evidence against all happiness; but that of this life, and represented in his divine transports, as setting forth the wisdom of believing that the life of man ends like that of rotten sheep, in a death *that* brings him into the dark land of forgetfulness; singing gloriously, "the dead praise not the Lord, neither any that go down into silence. In death there is no remembrance of thee: in the grave, who shall give thee thanks?"

Thus it is, that *David*, by these gentlemen is made a preacher against a future state; not considering that such infidelity would have been worse in *David* than it possibly can be in any modern infidel. But the truth is, the holy prophet in all passages of this kind, is only calling upon God for the continuance and full manifestation of the blessings of *that* temporal theocracy, which could only be given by God, or received by man whilst he was on this side death. And the *darkness*, *silence*, or *insensibility* affirmed of death, has no relation to a *total end* of life and sensibility,

sensibility, but solely to an end of all *enjoyments* of the blessings promised by the divine theocracy. *David*, as *son* of *Abraham*, *Isaac* and *Jacob*, had their faith and piety, and such his psalms are full of heavenly devotion, and flaming with divine love. But *David*, as a *son* of the covenant made with *Moses*, was also an heir of the temporal blessings of the theocracy; and in this capacity, had a right to say, *Why do the wicked prosper? Wilt thou shew thy wonders in the grave?* That is, canst thou give thy promised temporal blessings, when death has taken away all possibility of receiving them?

But if it could be supposed, that *David* by the foregoing expressions, meant to give up the promises of eternal redemption made to all his forefathers, and called the world to look for no more but what they could get in this vale of misery; what excuse can be made for the Christian church, which from first to last, has made such heathenish songs a part of the gospel service? For in this case, these psalms may be justly esteemed prophane, as having a more direct tendency to beget and fix infidelity in the hearts of men, than the hymns of the Heathen poets.

I must yet add a word, upon the Doctor's most theological account of man's first ability to speak articulate words.

" In judging, says he, only from the *nature of things*, one should be apt to embrace the opinion

nion of *Diodorus Siculus,* that first the men lived for some time in woods and caves; after the manner of beasts, uttering only *confused sounds.*† And yet it is hardly possible for a man to make a judgment more contrary to the nature of things. For does not the nature of almost all animals, beasts and birds shew us, that they have a natural untaught language, not consisting of *confused sounds,* but distinct by an articulate difference and intelligible to every one of the same species? If therefore the nature of things will allow us to suppose, that man was created as perfect in his kind as the animals were in theirs, then it will oblige us to affirm, that the first of mankind had from nature, an untaught language, as suitable to the ends of their creation, as distinct and intelligible to themselves, as that of birds or beasts is to them in their several kinds. Now it must not be said that the Doctor has adopted the whole opinion of *Diodorus,* tho' so highly (as he thinks) conformable to the nature of things; for he has given up that of man's living *in woods and caves,* and has only chosen to stand by that which is much the worst part of it, namely, his natural inability to utter any thing *but confused sounds.*—However, to make amends for all this poverty of speech, in which man was brought forth by God; the Doctor has a conjecture, how it soon came to be better with him. In scripture, says he, " we find that
God

† D. L. Vol. II. page 81.

God taught the first man religion, and can we think he would not at the same time teach him language? Again, when God created man he made woman for his companion, but the only means of enjoying that benefit was the use of speech. Can we believe that he would leave them to get out of the *forlorn condition of brutality* as they could?"†—Shocking and even blasphemous words! For little short can it be of that, to say, that man, created in the image and likeness of God, was created in a *forlorn condition of brutality?* Can any infidel more despise and ridicule all that is said both in the Old and New Testament, concerning man's creation, his high birth and destination, his fall and redemption, than is here done?"

In the scripture we are told, that man in the first, perfect state of his creation, came forth a living image and likeness of the all-perfect God; that he came forth in this exalted state of perfection, above all other animals of this world, in order to be a lord and ruler over them. Can there be a more open ridicule made of all this, than to hold, that this first glorious image of God came forth in a *forlorn brutal condition*, unable to utter any thing, but *confused sounds?* Or what can be more unbecoming a Christian Doctor, than to espouse such a paltry notion from the authority of a pagan *Greek*, in full contradiction to all that *Moses*, Christ and his apostles

† D. L. ibid.

apoſtles have ſaid of the firſt heavenly nature, divine birth and glorious prerogative of man? What a mockery is here made of the whole Chriſtian ſyſtem, which ſuppoſes man to have fallen from ſuch a high degree of heavenly union with God, that nothing leſs than the birth of the Son of God in fallen man, could reſtore him to that perfection which he had at firſt? What a folly to talk of the fall of man, if he came out of the hands of God in a forlorn condition of brutality?

But the Doctor comes now to his full proof, that man had at firſt no articulate ſpeech, and that he was actually taught it afterwards by God; "God brought every beaſt of the field, and every fowl of the air unto *Adam*, to ſee what he would call them."

And yet, ſo unlucky is the Doctor, that no words can give a higher proof, that *Adam* had not only an articulate ſpeech, but in ſuch a degree of perfection, as none of his natural ſons, not the whole tribe of linguiſts, critics, and grammarians, ever had, or can poſſibly have. For if it could be ſuppoſed, that any man was a hundred times more knowing than the Doctor is, in what he calls his *enigmatic, curiologic, hierogliphic, emblematic, ſymbolic* profundities, yet if all the beaſts of the field, and all the fowls of the air, were to be brought before him to be diſtinguiſhed from one another, by articulate ſounds of his voice, even ſuch a man would be as unequal to the

the tafk, as a *Tom Thumb*. And of all the abfurdities, *that* ever were heard of, furely none can equal that, of fuppofing, that *Adam* had not articulate fpeech, but had it to learn at a time, when he was called to the exercife of the higheft perfection of language, namely, to diftinguifh fuch an infinite number of creatures, by different articulate founds of his voice. It is like fuppofing, that a man whofe eyes had no natural power of diftinguifhing one thing from another, fhould on that account, have all the creatures in the world, brought before him, that he might defcribe every difference in form, and figure, that belonged to them.

The Doctor has by ftrength of genius, and great induftry, amaffed together no fmall heap of learned decifions of points, doctrines, as well Heathenifh, as Chriftian, much the greateft part of which, the Chriftian reader will find himfelf obliged to drive out of his thoughts, as foon as he can in good earneft fay, *What muft I do to be faved?*—This collection of decifions, he calls his *projected defence of Chriftianity*, which if it was fuch, Chriftianity muft have been but poorly provided for its fupport by the four gofpels. I fhall make no doubt of his intending, what he fays by them. But a project in defence of Chriftianity, is not more promifing, than a trap to catch humility. The nature of things allows no more of the one, than of the other. To be a defender of Chriftianity, is to

be

be a defender of Chrift, but none can defend him in any other degree, than fo far as he is his follower. To be with Chrift, is *to walk as he walked,* and he *that* is not fo with him, is *againft him.*

There are two ways of embracing Chriftianity, the one is as a *finner,* the other as a *fcholar;* the former is the way taught by Chrift and his apoftles, the latter is the invention of men, fallen from the Chriftian life under the power of natural reafon, and verbal learning.—Now thefe two ways are not to be confidered, as only the one better than the other, but in fuch a difference, as right and wrong, true and falfe, bear to one another. For there is no poffibility of taking one ftep in Chriftianity, but as a finner, for it has no errand but to the finner, has no relief but for fin, and nothing can receive it, but the heart wounded, and wearied with the burden of its own fin. All the gofpel is but a foreign tale, a dead letter to the moft logically learned man in the world, who does not feel in the depth of his foul, that all the reafonablenefs, and excellency of gofpel truth, lies in that fund of fin, impurity, and corrupt tempers, which are infeparable from him, till he is born again. And if the Doctor, in his application to the Deifts, had preffed home this affecting truth, which ftands at the door of every man's heart, and is the only ground of Chriftian redemption, he had fhewn a better care and concern for their

Vol. VI.   P   fouls,

souls, and had done more to awaken them out of their infidelity, than by all that wit and satyr in his dedication of his book to them. For like begets like; love and seriousness in the speaker, beget love and seriousness in the hearer; and he that has no earnestness towards unbelievers, but that of perswading them not to lose their share of the love and mercy of God in Christ Jesus, towards helpless fallen men, can only do it, in the spirit and language of that love and goodness, in whose arms, he longs to see them embraced.

But as no man ever came to Christ, but because he was weary, and heavy laden with the burden of his own natural disorder, and wanted rest to his soul, so nothing can help men to find the necessity of coming to Christ, but that which helps him to find and feel a misery of sin and corruption, which in some, the care and pleasures of this life, and in others the happiness of finding themselves wits, and polite scholars, never suffered them to feel before.

Our Lord's parable of the *prodigal* son, contains the whole matter between God and fallen man. It relates nothing particular to this, or that person, but sets forth the strict truth of every man's state, with regard to his heavenly Father. For every son of *Adam* has every thing in him, that is said of that prodigal; he has lost his first state, is wandered as far from his heavenly Father and country, has abused and wasted

his

his Father's bleſſings, and is that very poor ſwine-herd, craving huſks in a land of famine, inſtead of living in the glory of his Father's family; and of every reader of that parable, it may be juſtly ſaid, *Thou art the man.* And no ſon of *Adam*, do what he will, can poſſibly come out of the poverty, ſhame, and miſery of his fallen ſtate, till he finds and feels, and confeſſes from the bottom of his heart, all that which the penitent prodigal found, felt and confeſſed.

I ſhould have had much uneaſineſs, my Lord, in expoſing ſo many groſs errors both in the matter, and manner of the Doctor's books, did not my heart bear me witneſs, that no want of good-will, or due reſpect towards him, but ſolely a regard to that which ought only to be regarded, has directed my pen.

The End of the SIXTH VOLUME.

THE CONTENTS

Of the Sixth Volume.

An Extract from Mr. Law's *Serious Call* to a *Holy Life*.

CHAP. XVIII. Page

Recommending devotion at three o'clock, called in scripture the ninth hour *of the day. The subject of prayer at this hour may be* resignation *to the divine pleasure. The nature and duty of conformity to the will of God in all our actions and designs.* — — 3

CHAP. XIX.

Of the excellency and greatness of a devout spirit. — — 19

CONTENTS.

An Extract from Mr. LAW's Later Works.

           Page

An extract from the case of reason, or natural religion, fairly and fully stated. In answer to a book, entitled *Christianity as Old as the Creation.*

The introduction, *shewing the state of the controversy.* —   —   —   30

CHAP. I.

Enquiring, whether there be any thing in the nature and condition of man, to oblige him to think, that he is not to admit of any doctrines or institutions, as revealed from God, but such as his own reason can prove to be necessary from the nature of things. —   32

CHAP. II.

Shewing from the relation between God and man, that human reason cannot be a competent judge of the fitness and reasonableness of God's proceedings with mankind, either as to the time, or matter, or manner of an external revelation. —   —   82

CHAP.

CHAP. III.

Shewing how far human reason is able to judge of the reasonableness, truth, and certainty of divine revelation. — 93

CHAP. IV.

Of the state and nature of reason, as it is in man; and how its perfection in matters of religion is to be known. — 107

CHAP. V.

Shewing that all the mutability *of our tempers, the* disorders *of our passions, the* corruption *of our hearts, all the* reveries *of the imagination, all the* contradictions *and* absurdities *that are to be found in human life, and human opinions, are in effect the mutability, disorders, corruption, and absurdities of* human reason. — 129

An extract from Mr. LAW's Serious Answer to Dr. Trap's four sermons, on the sin, folly, and danger of being Righteous overmuch. — — 138

Some animadversions upon Dr. Trap's late reply. — — 206

CONTENTS.

                            Page

A short but sufficient confutation of Bishop Warburton's projected defence (as he calls it) of Christianity, in his divine legation of Moses in a letter to the Right Reverend the Lord Bishop of London. — 250

www.ingramcontent.com/pod-product-compliance
Lightning Source LLC
Chambersburg PA
CBHW031850220426
43663CB00006B/566